TAX
FACTORS
IN
BUSINESS
DECISIONS

TAX
FACTORS
IN
BUSINESS
DECISIONS

Dan Throop Smith

Professor of Finance
Harvard University

Prentice-Hall, Inc., Englewood Cliffs, N.J.

Printed in The United States of America
Library of Congress Catalogue Card No.: 68–9274

Current Printing (last digit):
10 9 8 7 6 5 4 3 2 1

PRENTICE-HALL INTERNATIONAL, INC., *London*
PRENTICE-HALL OF AUSTRALIA, PTY. LTD., *Sydney*
PRENTICE-HALL OF CANADA, LTD., *Toronto*
PRENTICE-HALL OF INDIA PRIVATE LTD., *New Delhi*
PRENTICE-HALL OF JAPAN, INC., *Tokyo*

Preface

The purpose of this book is to give students, and others who may be interested, a better understanding of the reasons for and the significance of the provisions of the federal income, estate and gift tax laws which are especially relevant to business decisions. The emphasis here is on the "Why" and "So What" of the laws.

In the typical tax course, the exposition is largely descriptive, with little explanation of why the various provisions have been adopted or of the logical relations between them. In descriptive courses, there is even less attention to the ways in which the tax laws influence business decisions. This book describes the bearing of tax factors on decisions in various areas of business and, equally important, sets the tax factors in some perspective along with other considerations which may be much more important. Even a tax specialist should recognize that if one had to choose between ignorance of tax laws or an obsession with minimizing taxes, the latter would probably more often lead to bad business decisions.

The material here has been developed over the past twenty years for a course in taxation at the graduate level. It has all been rewritten to be usable also at the undergraduate level. Though it is intended to be self-contained, references are made to specific paragraphs in the Prentice-Hall *Federal Tax Handbook* for detailed descriptions of various provisions of the law. Thus, this book may be used to supplement a course based on the *Handbook* or the Prentice-Hall *Federal Tax Course*. Alternatively, it may be used, as it has been by the author, as the basic text, with the *Handbook* or the *Course* as supplemental material. All *paragraph* references are to the Prentice-Hall *Federal Tax Handbook; section* references are to the Internal Revenue Code.

Since the provisions relevant to an area business decision are scattered throughout the law, the chapters here do not in most instances follow the sequence in the usual tax course. The tax factors relevant to compensation policies, for example, include laws concerning ordinary individual taxable income, capital gains, tax-exempt trusts, deductions for business expense, and accounting methods. Whether the reader is a student receiving his first introduction to the tax laws or a businessman wishing to get a general survey of tax factors, this organization by areas of decision seems more useful.

Many provisions of the present law are more comprehensible if one understands the earlier provisions and the problems which developed under them. Where it has seemed appropriate, therefore, some history of the law is given. The historical material may also help to induce an appreciation of the law's constant evolution and of the pressures which influence the changes.

The varying degrees of thoroughness on different subjects inevitably reflect the interests of the author; hopefully this corresponds to either the importance or the complexity of the law. In a few chapters, including those on partnerships, tax-free corporate reorganizations, and taxable purchases and sales of corporations, certain noted sections give rather detailed descriptions. These sections may be omitted without loss of general comprehension.

In any case, no apology is offered for these differences in treatment. Many years ago, a book on bank management appeared in which a chapter of identical length was devoted to each functional group of employees and officers in the chronological sequence in which they came to work in a business day. The only point remembered is that some janitors prefer to sweep from the center of a room and then collect the dust around the walls, while others prefer to sweep from the walls into a single pile in the center. Unfortunately, some of the published descriptions of the tax law are equally undiscriminating, with as much as two-thirds of a page devoted to a special relief provision of the law which could not be relevant to a dozen taxpayers. The varying length in this book reflects a revulsion against such a failure to be selective.

The sequence of topics is inevitably a matter of individual choice. The chapter on estate and gift taxes, for example, is placed toward the front of the book because the author has found a familiarity with these taxes relevant to various considerations regarding closely controlled companies. Others will prefer to postpone discussion of them to the end of the course. The chapter on business expenses is pulled forward in deference to the opinions of others, though the author prefers to finish a discussion of taxation as it affects individuals before starting the treatment of business tax.

The author uses the material in this book in conjunction with *The Federal Tax System: Facts and Problems*, published by the Joint Economic Committee, an invaluable source of concise statements on public policy issues and tax statistics. More fundamentally, this material, supplemented by the Prentice-Hall *Handbook*, is used as background for a series of business cases requiring decisions to be made in the light of all relevant tax and nontax considerations. This use of decision cases has been found desirable for those students who want only a general familiarity with tax laws and are likely to be repelled by a mass of detail. It also seems to be a useful introduction for those who expect to become tax specialists, though some may feel that a prospective specialist should master the details of the law before going on to appraise its logic, or lack of logic, and its significance.

The author has strong convictions about many parts of the tax law. These are forthrightly stated in *Federal Tax Reform: The Issues and a Program*. In the present book, an attempt has been made to keep out subjective value judgments, but where beliefs are especially strong, the attempt has not always been successful.

The author would like to express his appreciation for the helpful comments and suggestions of the following reviewers on behalf of the publisher: Harold Bierman, Jr., Professor of Accounting and Managerial Economics at Cornell University; Mortimer Caplin, partner, Caplin and Drysdale (formerly U. S. Commissioner of Internal Revenue); Herman Clurman, Associate Professor of Taxation, New York University School of Commerce; Robert E. Schlosser, Director of Professional Development, American Institute of Certified Public Accountants; and Ray M. Sommerfeld, Professor of Accounting at the University of Texas at Austin.

To my successive research assistants over many years, David A. Stuntz, I. Robert Rozen, Gerald F. Lahey, Edward B. du Pont, and Mark R. G. Johnson, one or another of whom wrote earlier versions of much of the material in this book, I give my renewed thanks, with recollections of pleasant personal and professional associations. And to a generation of students, ever critical and ever appreciative, I am glad to express a professor's gratitude for those class reactions which make an academic life so stimulating and satisfying.

DAN THROOP SMITH

Contents

ix

I

Tax Factors

in Compensation Policies

The Tax Concept of Compensation

The high level of individual income tax rates constitutes a strong inducement to receive any type of income, including compensation, in a form which is tax-exempt. To the extent that this is not possible, the high degree of progression in the tax rates gives an inducement to shift the receipt of income from years when one is subject to high rates to years when one expects to be subject to lower rates or to convert ordinary income into capital gains, which, at all times, are subject to a lower tax rate.

This chapter will deal with the all-inclusive nature of the tax concept of compensation. Various attempts have been made to secure compensation indirectly in forms which might be considered as not constituting income or not subject to tax in the absence of special provisions in the law. Alleged gifts to employees or their survivors and the vast array of fringe benefits are familiar examples. The next chapter will discuss the tax treatment of compensation which is shifted into later years or received in a form subject to the capital gains tax rate, that is, with pension plans, deferred compensation contracts, and stock options. Since it is the high degree of progression in the individual income tax rates and the existence of top rates far above 50 per cent which make special forms of compensation so attractive from the standpoint of taxation, a brief description of the origin of the rate structure itself will provide some background for an understanding of this aspect of our tax problems. A class discussion of the issues will almost inevitably uncover strong advocates of most of the conflicting opinions found in the Congress.[1]

[1] The full range of opinion was stated by three children in a one-room Montana school where the author was given the challenge by his daughter, the teacher, of

1

PROGRESSION IN INDIVIDUAL INCOME TAX RATES

The individual income tax has been progressive from the moment of its adoption in 1913. At that time, the normal rate was 1 per cent, with a surtax at rates rising from 1 to 6 per cent on larger incomes. The top rate reached 77 per cent during the First World War and dropped back to 25 per cent during the latter part of the 1920's. It was drastically increased to 63 per cent in 1932 and has never since been below that level.

During World War II, the top rate reached 94 per cent. It fell back to 82 per cent by 1948, but was pushed up again to 91 per cent at the time of the war in Korea in 1950 and stayed at that level until 1964 when it was reduced in two stages to 70 per cent, effective in 1965. The bottom rate applicable to taxable income above the exemption has ranged from the original figure of 1 per cent to a high of 23 per cent in 1944. It was 20 per cent after 1954 when the top rate was 91 per cent and became 14 per cent in 1965.

A tax may be regressive, proportional, or progressive. A regressive tax is one in which the burden is proportionately greater on those with smaller resources; a flat tax on articles of general consumption with inelastic demand is regressive in its effect. The tax on cigarettes is a typical modern example. Since the consumption of cigarettes does not vary widely with income, the tax burden is proportionately greater on a person with a small income. A tax on salt, imposed in some Asian countries in earlier times, is the extreme example of a regressive tax. A proportional tax is, as the name indicates, one which is in proportion to the tax base; a proportional income tax would apply the same rate to all taxable income. A progressive tax, one in which the rate of tax increases as the tax base increases, is usually justified on the grounds of "ability to pay." There is an almost instinctive feeling that as income increases each extra thousand dollars becomes less important to the recipient so that, if a family with an income of $5,000 pays $200 in income tax on an extra $1,000 of income, a family with a $50,000 income can fairly be taxed

---

discussing tax policy with her pupils. Before any mention was made of specific taxes or their use in providing funds for government expenditures, the question was put as to how much tax on $500 of additional income a family with $5,000 should pay, if a family with $2,000 paid $40 on an extra $200. The first child said "$100, because it is the same percentage." A second child disagreed, saying that "they should pay more because money is not so important to them." A third child immediately agreed, but with the caution, "not too much more, or they won't work so hard." Never has the whole subject been so neatly summarized.

for something more than $200 on an extra $1,000 of income. But the question is, how much more? Though there is widespread acceptance of the concept of progressive tax rates, there is no agreement on the appropriate degree of progression.

Opinions on fairness are based on an individual's feeling about the relative importance of a dollar of income to him compared to a dollar of income to someone in an altogether different economic position which he can perhaps only vaguely imagine. Quite apart from what may be considered as fair, one's attitude on income tax progression is influenced by his opinion as to the degree of inequality which is felt to be "good" or acceptable in society.

In addition to the issues of equity and social policy are the economic problems of rates which may be so high that they unduly discourage or distort effort and investment. Each individual will make his own appraisal of the relative importance of pecuniary and nonpecuniary incentives for productive activity and investment. The nonpecuniary satisfactions in business and professional activities seem to be quite important for most people, and it is manifestly false to believe that high tax rates bring activity to a halt. But it also seems true that high rates can distort the form of activity and divert attention into socially unproductive efforts to minimize taxes instead of getting on with the world's work by truly productive activity which increases both an individual's and society's income. Whenever an income tax rate exceeds 50 per cent, it becomes more important to save a dollar of taxes than to earn a dollar of income, a fact which cannot be expected to go unnoticed by those affected.

Though the idea of progression is generally accepted, it does not follow that each tax should be progressive. Burden is measured by the composite effect of a tax system, no one part of which is capable of providing all required revenues. The federal income tax and the estate and gift taxes are the principal progressive taxes in our system of federal, state, and local taxes. A belief that the income tax is too progressive must be tempered by recognition of the proportional and regressive character of other taxes, just as objections to certain taxes as regressive should be tempered by the fact that income tax rates are very progressive and reach high levels.

It is important to keep in mind both marginal and average tax rates. The marginal rate is the top bracket rate applicable to an increment of income; it is the rate which influences decisions on an increment of activity or investment. With a progressive tax, the marginal rate by definition must exceed the average rate and may be very much higher. The average rate is significant statistically in determining the fraction of total income taken by taxes, or the difference between personal income before taxes and disposable income. But too frequently, reference is made to average rates in ways which belittle or even ignore the existence of much higher marginal rates.

As an extreme hypothetical example, one might compare the effects of two rate structures one of which has a rate of 10 per cent on the first $10,000 of income and 70 per cent on the second $10,000, the other, a flat rate of 40 per cent on all income. For a person with an income of $20,000, in each case the average rate is 40 per cent and the total tax is $8,000. But the effects of the two tax systems on incentives and decisions almost certainly would be quite different, with the after-tax remainder from an additional dollar of income equal to 60 cents in one case and 30 cents in the other. To repeat for emphasis, one must always be on guard against being misled by any statements which brush aside marginal tax rates by noting that average rates are lower, as they must be in any progressive tax.

The foregoing considerations, though necessarily dependent on subjective evaluations, are at least subject to rational consideration. The rate structure in the law, however, is the result of a political process in which maneuvers to secure a political advantage or create a political image are likely to prevent the development of any consensus of rational, though honestly differing, opinions. When applied to a change in an existing rate structure, the concept of progression is itself subject to different interpretations, with protagonists of different forms of change seizing on the approach which supports their respective programs.

Consider, for example, the tax increase in 1932 which pushed the top rate from 25 to 63 per cent. At that time, the bottom rate was being raised from 1½ to 4 per cent, or by 167 per cent. This was the significant increase from a revenue standpoint; then, as now, it was the bottom rates applicable to all taxable income which determined the yield of the income tax system. But given the acceptance of the idea of progression in the income tax system, the question arose as to the fair change in the top rate.

One possibility was to increase the top rate by about the same proportion and this in fact was what was done, the increase from 25 to 63 per cent amounting to an increase in the rate of 150 per cent. It might be argued that this was not even a progressive tax increase on the larger incomes. But note the difference when one looks at the effects of the change in tax rates on the net income after tax. At the bottom, net income was reduced from the previous 98½ cents to 96 cents on the dollar of pre-tax income, or by a little over 2½ per cent, while at the top it was reduced from 75 to 37 cents, or by more than half. Thus, even a proportionate increase in tax rates, when the rate structure is already progressive, is very progressive in its impact on net income after tax.

Even an increase of the same number of percentage points on each existing rate is progressive in its effect on net income. An increase from 14 per cent to 15 per cent would reduce net income from 86 cents to 85 cents, or by about 1.15 per cent, while the same one percentage point added to a 70 per cent rate would reduce net income from 30 cents to 29 cents, or by 3.33 per cent.

When tax rates are reduced, the effects are reversed. A reduction from a 90 per cent tax to 80 per cent doubles the net income after tax, a result which cannot be achieved by any reduction in a bottom tax rate of 20 per cent. Even complete elimination of a 20 per cent tax would increase income only from 80 cents to one dollar, or by 25 per cent. Once very high tax rates have been adopted, this method of describing the effects of a tax reduction in terms of the increase in net income stands in the way of a reform of tax rates to secure what might be generally accepted as a more sensible and healthy structure. The advocates of reform are subject to criticism about who gets the greater benefits.

If frequent changes in individual income taxes come to play an active role in fiscal policy, the alternative methods of raising and lowering taxes will become significant. Hopefully, they will receive dispassionate consideration before the pattern is set. One must keep in mind and distinguish changes in tax rates, in tax liabilities, and in net incomes, as well as changes in proportions and in absolute amounts.

The most frequent proposal is for proportionate changes in tax liabilities at all income levels. The use of the word "proportionate" obscures the fact that the impact of such an increase is highly progressive in terms of reduction in net income. With a range from 14 to 70 per cent, a 10 per cent increase in tax liability across the board reduces net income at the bottom from 86 cents to 84.6 cents but from 30 to 23 cents at the top. Alternatively, one might change each rate by an equal number of percentage points, which would still make an increase progressive in its impact on net income. A third alternative would be to apply an incremental tax to the existing net income after tax. Each of these methods of change is subject to various interpretations and can be described in various ways, depending on individual preconceptions and prejudices.

Ideally, it would seem desirable to get the individual tax rate structure established with whatever degree of progression is deemed appropriate on social, political, and economic grounds and then develop a scheme for changes in tax liabilities for short-term fiscal purposes—if there are to be such changes—which will not drastically modify the progressivity of the system. A change of an equal number of percentage points in each bracket would be much better from this standpoint than an equal proportionate change in tax liabilities.

THE BROAD CONCEPT OF TAXABLE COMPENSATION

The remainder of this chapter will cover various forms of compensation or fringe benefits which have at one time or another become controversial and on which rather detailed tax rules have developed over the years. The purpose of discussing these topics, and the other subjects in this book, is to give some understanding of the policy issues involved and to suggest the alternatives which may be adopted in the law in the future. The descriptions here are not complete or detailed. They are intended to provide a setting which will make the details of the law more understandable and, hopefully, even interesting. Even trivial provisions of the law often represent a political response to a problem on which there are conflicting opinions and objectives. In brief, the approach here is that the tax law should be understood rather than learned mechanically.

The statute itself is very broad in defining taxable income, merely including "compensation for services, including fees, commissions, and similar items" among the itemized forms of gross income (par. 1301, sec. 61(a)). The regulations amplify this simple statement with numerous examples and the important statement that "If services are paid for other than in money, the fair market value of the property or services taken in payment must be included in income" (reg. 1.61–2(d)(1)).

In general, the courts have upheld the Internal Revenue Service in its efforts to apply a broad concept of compensation. Two lines of demarcation have developed in litigation, however, and specific statutory provisions have been added to give more precise rules on some difficult areas. The first of the two lines of demarcation involves a decision as to whether certain payments are gifts or compensation. Is a payment to the widow of the deceased president of a company a nontaxable gift or is it indirect compensation for the prior services of her husband? The second line of demarcation involves a decision as to whether certain payments are primarily for the benefit of the employer or the employee. Is the provision of free room and board for a resident faculty member in the undergraduate living quarters of a university given primarily to improve the educational environment or is it indirect compensation? These and innumerable similar questions are difficult to answer and opinions inevitably differ. The subtle distinctions in the extensive litigation on the subjects attest to the difficulties encountered by jurists in interpreting the law. A listing of cases on the distinction between compensation and gift, with brief digests of some of them, covers sixteen pages in a loose-leaf service (Prentice-Hall, *Federal Taxes*, pars. 7046–55). A class discussion on the equities involved will demonstrate the range of opinion among laymen.

The courts have adopted a rule which is applied frequently in tax cases that the decision depends on all the facts and circumstances. The intent of the payor is particularly relevant; thus, even if the resident faculty member preferred his quarters in undergraduate housing above any form of housing which he might buy or rent, the fact that it was provided because his presence was expected to extend the educational atmosphere beyond the classroom would—if this were accepted as a fact—be controlling. And the fact that a painting received as a gift from a company to which gratuitous suggestions have been made was enjoyed by the recipient even more than it would have been if received as payment for contractual services would be unimportant, so long as it was established that the primary intent of the payor was to make a gift.

Gifts or Compensation

Neither the treatment of a payment on the payor's own books nor the stated purpose is necessarily controlling in determining the tax status to the recipient. The point of view taken by the courts is well summarized in the introductory paragraphs to a review of the leading cases in Prentice-Hall, *Federal Taxes*:

> The Supreme Court has laid down principles applicable to gift v. income questions in general: A voluntary transfer without compensation is not necessarily a gift for tax purposes. A transfer is not a gift if there is a legal or moral obligation for it, or if the "donor" expects a benefit from the transfer. But the absence of a legal or moral obligation will not make it a gift. A transfer is a gift if made from "detached disinterested generosity." What counts most in deciding the question is the donor's "dominant reason [for] making the transfer." *Comm. v. Duberstein*, par. 7051(10).

> With respect to payments where a formal employment relationship exists, the decisions are as varied as the circumstances under which the payments arose. The Supreme Court has stated that a gift is none the less a gift because inspired by gratitude for past faithful services of the recipient. *Bogardus v. Comm.*, par. 7048(5). However, later decisions have tended to limit the application of the case. (par. 7046)

In the *Duberstein* case referred to above, the Supreme Court over-ruled a circuit court decision which had treated as a gift an automobile received by an individual from a corporation for which he had secured business. This opinion of the Supreme Court established the proposition that the absence of a legal or moral obligation does not make a payment a gift, which in turn was described as made from "detached or disinterested generosity." This statement substantially restricted the concept of a gift. (*Comm. v. Duberstein* [1960], 363 U.S. 278, 805. S.Ct. 1190.)

It is apparently still possible for payments to be treated inconsistently for tax purposes by the payor and the recipient. It is quite understandable that an employer might claim that a payment was a gift, thereby fore-going a deduction, in order to reinforce the recipient's contention that the amount involved is nontaxable. But enforcement of the law reasonably requires the taxability to the recipient to be determined independently. However, it seems somewhat surprising that payment taken as a de-ductible expense by the payor can be treated as a gift by the recipient.

In the absence of a statutory provision requiring consistency of treatment, the courts have had to develop rules based on individual situations. One cannot safely generalize from a single case that the same type of payment will be treated similarly in other cases; if any of the surrounding circumstances differ, the decision might go the other way. Thus, there are decisions both ways regarding payments to widows of former employees and to retired employees (par. 1303). Even payments by congregations to retired ministers have their own set of decided cases (P.-H., *Federal Taxes*, par. 7050(50)).

In 1962, a new provision of the law concerning travel and enter-tainment expense included a $25 annual limitation per donee for deductible gifts (sec. 274(b)). Prior to that time, gifts to individuals of larger amounts might be deductible to the extent that they constituted ordinary and necessary business expenses, though, as indicated above, employers might forego the deduction to reinforce the claim to nontaxability by the recipient. With the limitation on gifts, if an employer does want to secure significant deductions for direct payments to individuals, they must come under section 404(a)(5), dealing with plans other than qualified pension, annuity, profit-sharing or stock purchase plans in which em-ployees' rights are nonforfeitable, or section 404(b), dealing with methods of contribution or compensation having the effect of a plan (par. 1820(e)(f)). But deductions under these two sections are limited to amounts which constitute reasonable compensation in an aggregate sense. Thus, since 1962, if an employer claims a deduction, the action is more likely to give the payment the character of compensation, but it will not necessarily do so.

Sick Pay

The development of a reasonable tax treatment of amounts received in continuation of wages or salary while an employee is away from work sick presents some troublesome problems. There is no controversy over the deductibility of payments by an employer to an insurance company or an independent fund handling an accident or health plan. Nor has there ever been any serious thought, so long as the plan is a general one, of having the employer's payments allocated among the employees and taxed to them currently as imputed income (par. 1217(b)). The controversy has developed over the tax treatment of benefit payments when received by employees. For a person who receives his regular pay while absent from work because of sickness, there seems no reason for tax exemption; indeed favorable tax treatment would be an inducement to malingering. However, for a low-bracket employee who may receive only half or less of his regular pay, taxation of the proceeds seems harsh. But where should the line be drawn between these extremes?

The present provisions of the law can best be understood if one understands how they evolved (par. 1217(d), sec. 105(d)). Prior to 1954, amounts received under insured plans were wholly tax-free; all other amounts were taxable in full. This treatment had developed at a time when most plans for wage earners were insured and gave benefits which fell far short of full pay, while executives when sick commonly continued to receive their normal salaries directly from their employers. Two major changes occurred with the passage of time. Many large companies preferred to handle their own sick pay plans and had medical staffs to check on the bona fide character of sickness. Thus, companies choosing self-insurance found their employees penalized by the taxation of benefits which were no larger than those of insured plans. Also, some insurance companies offered full salary plans for executives on a cost plus basis in order to make the benefits tax-exempt. The insurance company on such a policy had no reason to check on the validity of a claim for sick pay, and a management group could tell one of its members to "go take a rest until you feel better," thereby giving him tax exemption on his regular salary.

The changes which seemed to be called for by 1954 included the removal of the discrimination against self-insured plans and some ceiling on the benefits. Benefits from all plans were made tax-exempt, but with a $100 weekly tax-free maximum. (In 1957 the Supreme Court ruled that pre-1954 noninsured plans could be exempt—a not unusual anomaly of timing in the development of the tax law.) An attempt was made to work out a formula by which no one would be better off by receiving tax-exempt sick pay, but this was not found to be feasible. It was feared at that time that the selection of any single percentage of pay as the dividing line between taxable and tax-exempt benefits would be taken as a government-approved figure for such plans, and that this would involve unintended intervention in what was commonly part of a package negotiation in collective bargaining agreements. To reduce the number of claims for tax exemption and the associated administrative work from Monday morning absences, minimum waiting periods were also established. The waiting periods depended on whether the case involved hospitalization on the presumption that hospitals would admit only real medical cases. Tax exemption of no more than $100 a week did not appear to give sufficient inducement for pretended sickness or sufficient inequity for real sickness with full pay.

The law was further tightened, refined, and complicated in 1964 by adding new waiting periods and providing that if the sick pay exceeds 75 per cent of regular pay nothing will be tax exempt for the first 30 days. An additional ceiling of $75 a week for the first 30 days is established for those whose benefits are 75 per cent or less of regular pay, but tax exemption during the first seven days of the 30 days applies only if the employee is hospitalized for at least one day during this period. The requirement for hospitalization is intended to assure the genuine character of the claim for sickness. After 30 days, the $100 ceiling applies, without the 75 per cent rule. Hopefully, the tax advantages of tax exemption are not sufficiently great to induce further pressure for admission to our overburdened hospitals.

The determination of what is meant by absence from work has presented some interesting questions for administrative determination. A teacher becoming sick during a summer vacation when no specific activities are required is not deemed to be absent from work and hence does not get tax exemption. One of the first inquiries put to the Internal Revenue Service for an opinion after the 1954 Act involved a member of Congress during a period when Congress was not in session. Was he presumed to have a full-year job such that absence from his normal activities in his district because of sickness constituted absence from work? He was, and it did.

Insurance Premiums Paid by Employers

Though the payment of the premiums on an individual insurance policy is treated as income to the employee involved (unless the company is itself the beneficiary), just as would the payment of a grocery bill, the premiums on group life insurance and group medical insurance are generally not treated as income to the employees covered (par. 1306). This exclusion probably arises from a combination of public policy considerations, such as the desire to encourage private provision for emergencies and survivors and the difficulty of finding any fair way to allocate the costs of group insurance among a number of people with dissimilar medical backgrounds and varying desires to be insured.

In 1964, section 79 was added to the Code. This taxes to the individual concerned the cost of any group life insurance with a face value in excess of $50,000 paid for by an employer. Under the general rule, with group life insurance ordinarily ranging from one to two-and-a-half times annual compensation, insurance up to and in excess of a million dollars was provided for some executives. Though the amounts were always proportionate to compensation, the larger absolute amounts were claimed to be outrageous by those who started a campaign for limitations. It was amusing, though not surprising, that the amount which was deemed to be outrageous was usually a bit above the amount available to the critics. Those made subject to the limitation understandably feel that they are discriminated against and that so long as the benefits of a plan are proportional to compensation, the payments of premiums by the employer should be either taxable or tax-free to all concerned.

Split-dollar insurance constitutes an involved arrangement on the borderline of indirect compensation. Prior to 1964, an employer could pay the premium up to the annual increase in the cash surrender value of the life insurance policy, with an employee paying the rest of the premium, and with no presumption of indirect compensation to the employee. The employer thus was always in a position to recoup his outlay, but without interest. The employee had a declining net insurance for his part of the premium, which also decreased over the years. Since the interest on the funds accumulating with the insurance company was taken into account in setting the premiums, and since this interest was not taken into account in fixing the employer's share of the premium, the net premium left to be paid by the employee was less than he would have had to pay for insurance purchased by himself directly. In effect, the employer was making an interest-free loan indirectly, through the insurance company, to the employee of the funds which were accumulating against the policy. After several years of discussion on the subject, the law was changed in 1964 to tax the employee on the cost of one-year term insurance of whatever amount he would receive from a policy for the year in question, less the premium paid by him that year (par. 1306). The tax advantage of this form of insurance is thus removed, and another form of indirect compensation, perhaps as devious a one as has yet been developed, has been brought within the definition of taxable income.

Board and Lodging

In numerous instances, it is essential that employees be constantly available at their place of employment or at least living nearby. Prison guards are a classic example, as are resident hotel managers. To tax such individuals on the value of board and lodging, the acceptance of which they may find very irksome, seems harsh. But what of the owners of a resort hotel who designate themselves as co-equal resident managers and hire an assistant manager to do all the work? Or what credence should be given to the claim of a corporate executive that his choice would be to live in his home in a remote spot in the country and that he and family stay in a city apartment provided by his company only because of the insistence of the employer that he be available every day?

The tax law has had to find an acceptable position between these extreme positions. The statutory provision is brief and states simply that the value of meals and lodging shall be excluded from the income of an employee if they are furnished for the convenience of the employer, but only if meals are furnished on the business premises of the employer and only if the employee is required to accept the lodging as a condition of employment (par. 1307, sec. 119). And the regulations covering twelve lines of text in the Code run to less than three double-column pages. It is somewhat surprising that none of the six examples of meals furnished for the convenience of the employer covers the business advantages of providing executive dining rooms to bring together people who may not see each other frequently under circumstances where they have opportunity to discuss, perhaps with outside guests, longer-range business problems. A faculty member who has taught in places with and without a faculty club can testify to the value to an academic employer of bringing together, through provision of luncheon facilities, people from various fields of intellectual interest who might seldom meet otherwise. Presumably the same advantages exist in other trades and businesses.

A special provision giving clergymen exclusion of the rental value of parsonages is based entirely on social policy with no pretense that is consistent with the general rule of convenience to employers. The extension of the exclusion to rental allowances in lieu of a parsonage was added to remove discrimination between clergymen who received parsonages and those who received cash allowances. This selective relief provision has not led to pressure for similar treatment of other professional groups with low incomes, probably simply because the custom of giving living quarters has not developed in other activities.

Travel Expense

The opportunity for harassment of taxpayers is conspicuously apparent in tax audits regarding travel and entertainment, if they are required to support with a receipt and justify every use of a taxi instead of a subway and every other trivial expense in travel. But the opportunity for abuse is also conspicuously apparent if an executive can be told to go abroad and look over the market potential or the prospects for a branch plant, and to take his wife along to be sure he gets a feminine point of view. In closely controlled companies where the executive might simply tell himself to take the trip, there is opportunity for flagrant abuse.

The statutory provision is straightforward with the simple statement that deductible trade or business expense includes "traveling expenses (including amounts expended for meals and lodging other than amounts which are lavish or extravagant under the circumstances) while away from home in the pursuit of a trade or business" (par. 1827, sec. 162(a)(2)). However, a new section (274) was added to the Code in 1962 under the general heading "Disallowance of Certain Entertainment, etc., Expenses," parts of which specifically referred to travel in pursuit of a trade or business and to substantiation of expenses. This section, which is notable in that its purpose is solely to disallow certain expenditures which would otherwise be allowable under other sections of the Code, and the regulations thereunder, must be read in conjunction with section 162(b). As amended in 1964, section 274 requires an allocation of travel expense for foreign travel on trips exceeding one week if the time spent other than for business purposes is 25 per cent or more of the total time. The purpose of this limitation is to prevent a tax deduction for foreign travel where a few hours or days of business were used to justify the deductible expense of getting to and from a vacation spot. The statute is categorical in requiring allocation for that fraction of "expenses which under regulations prescribed by the Secretary or his delegate, is not allocable to such trade or business or to such activity."

But regulations under section 274 mercifully leave open the opportunity to demonstrate that "he did not have a major consideration in determining to make the trip, of obtaining a personal vacation or holiday," and if the taxpayer is an employee, other than a managing executive, he is not presumed to have control over the travel merely because he does have control over the timing of the trip, and the travel expense is allowed in full (reg. 1.274–4(f)(5)). These relief provisions are conspicuous examples of administrative interpretation, consistent with the intent of Congress, to make the application of the law less onerous than the apparent letter of the law. The same requirement for allocation was originally imposed for domestic travel, but later removed after vigorous complaints by representatives from resort areas.

Those who have read the advertisements for cruises following conventions, with minimal professional conferences en route and at the destination, and with activities for wives ostensibly geared to the professional careers of their husbands, are likely to think that the rules might be tighter. Those who have been embarrassed to discover that their presence as speakers at a convention was apparently designed to give an extended schedule with more time for golf and pool-side activities than to provide substance to the deliberations are likely to be convinced that "expense account living" may still be sufficiently pervasive to weaken the morale of those taxpayers who cannot partake of it.

The requirement for substantiation abolished an old court-made rule under which the courts made a close approximation of the amount in instances where the evidence indicated that deductible travel and entertainment expenses had been incurred but the exact amount could not be determined. Under the new provision, a taxpayer must be prepared to substantiate the amounts.

The administrative provisions have gone through a succession of versions, not all of which have been associated with statutory changes. For many years, all reimbursed expenses theoretically had to be included in an employees' gross income and the expenses then deducted by him in computing his taxable income, but these wash items were almost universally ignored. At one time in the 1950's, the designers of the tax forms, unaware of practice in the field, added a special line to show the amount of reimbursed expenses. Since the form was not released until close to the end of the year and most employees had not even kept duplicate copies of their expense statements, the problem of reconstructing the necessary data would have been enormous. The Commissioner had to announce that for the year in question, the Service would ignore its own form. Since most employees in fact simply get actual reimbursement of expenses, the task of preparing annual totals, with first an addition and then a deduction for identical amounts, seemed pointless and not conducive to respect by taxpayers. The notorious line 6(a), which had brought the matter to general attention, was later quietly dropped.

The present regulations seem to be accepted as establishing a sensible procedure (par. 2408, reg. 1.162–17 and 1.274–5(e)). Employees who report to and substantiate their expense with employers, whether they receive advances or reimbursement or charge the employer by use of credit cards, generally need do no more than check a box on their return indicating that they follow this procedure. If the reimbursement exceeds the actual expense, which may occur if a lump-sum expense allowance is given, the excess must be reported as income. If the reimbursement falls short of the expenses and the employee wishes to claim a deduction for the excess of expenses, he must show total expenses by broad categories, the time away from home, and the amount of direct and indirect reimbursement.

The accounting to an employer may be by broad categories such as transportation, meals, lodging, and entertainment. Detailed records of incidental items are not required, and standard per diem allowances up to $25 or 125 per cent of the government allowance for its own employees and standard mileage charges for the use of automobiles are acceptable. In brief, for employees working for companies which exercise normal caution in handling travel advances and reimbursement, there is no tax complication whatsoever; they need only put a check mark in a box on their returns.

In closely controlled corporations, and for self-employed individuals, the enforcement problem is greater because there is no third party to which the Internal Revenue Service can look for an independent audit. Simultaneous audits of tax returns of corporations and their owner-manager are useful for this as well as for other purposes. Furthermore, the statement in the regulations that taxpayers will not ordinarily be required to substantiate expense account information when it has been reported to an employer is specifically not made applicable to situations where the taxpayer is related to his employer (including situations where the employer is a corporation more than half of the stock of which is owned by one family) or in other cases where it is determined that the procedures used by the employer for reporting and substantiating expenses are not adequate (reg. 1.162–17(d) and 1.274–5(3)(5)). Self-employed individuals must always be in a position to substantiate their expenses.

Travel expenses of wives produce endless controversy for both employees and self-employed individuals. There are numerous instances where the presence of wives is desirable in carrying out a business purpose. But there are also numerous instances when other taxpayers paying their own way resent the expense account travel of other couples in the same resort areas. The regulations provide that the expenses of a wife are deductible only if the wife's presence "has a bona fide business purpose" as distinct from her "performance of some incidental service" (reg. 1.162–2(c)). Litigated cases and published rulings indicate that the rule is applied rather strictly (P.-H., *Federal Taxes*, par. 11,356). It comes as an unpleasant surprise to many academic people to learn that a person giving lectures from time to time under most circumstances must include in income the reimbursed travel expenses of his wife. Travel expense reimbursement for husband and wife to and at a resort are a common form of compensation for a lecture; that part allocable to the non-lecturing wife is taxable to the husband (Rev. Rul. 64–9).

Entertainment Expense

The present fairly strict provision of the law regarding entertainment expense was adopted in 1962 as the major item of legislation in an attempt to eliminate "expense account living." The problem is universal. Our rules are probably somewhat more strict than those in other countries, although one finds very tight restrictions on one or another item in other countries. In England, a deduction for entertainment is allowed only for overseas buyers, and in Germany at one time anyone entertaining a business customer was supposed to include in his own income the two or three marks which represented the amount he was saving by not eating at home. Certainly our statute is now specific in its limitations and disallowances (par. 1828, sec. 274). Proposals for tightening the law have always met objections from the representatives of unions of employees in the entertainment facilities, who are often more vociferous in their objections than the industries themselves.

Section 274 starts with a broad disallowance of activities and facilities used in connection with activities generally considered to constitute entertainment, amusement, or recreation unless the activity was directly related to the active conduct of trade or business, or the facility was used primarily for the furtherance of the trade or business, and in no case shall the deduction exceed the portion of the expense directly related to the active conduct of the trade or business. There are specific exceptions to the disallowance covering such items as business meals, food for employees in company restaurants, recreational facilities for employees other than officers and owner-managers, and business meetings of employees, stockholders, or directors. Recognition is given to executive dining rooms as a specified exception to the disallowances of section 274, but this reference is not directly relevant to the tax treatment of those who eat in them (reg. 1–274–2(b)(2)(ii)).

The requirements for record keeping are substantial, and there are many areas for controversy as to whether an activity was directly or indirectly related to a business activity or whether a facility was used primarily to further a trade or business. Is a yacht, for example, the ideal place to demonstrate to customers the non-skid quality of tennis shoes? But in general the rules are not onerous or difficult under the standards followed by most large corporations as a matter of business policy. There was a time when negotiations for employment of top management in many instances gave as much attention to lump-sum expense and enter- tainment allowances as to salary, since the former were regarded as tax- free compensation, but this practice had been fairly well eliminated prior to the 1962 legislation. However, situations such as a claim for a deduction for the expenses of a daughter's wedding on the ground that the guests were customers or potential customers, and a willingness to litigate, un- successfully, the disallowance of the deduction indicated that the tax law was in danger of coming into more disrepute than those who at- tempted to flout it. The present rules on entertainment represent public reaction to past abuses expressed through the White House, the Treasury, and the Congress.

Since 1962, the tax forms have required employers to indicate whether they have claimed any deductions for expenses of maintaining a resort property or pleasure boat, expenses of leasing or owning a dwell- ing for employees or customers, traveling expenses for employees' fam- ilies at conventions, and vacations for employees and their families. These are perennial areas of suspected abuse, of concern to tax officials in all countries. This requirement prevents such expenses from being lost to sight when they are included in other accounts, as they may quite prop- erly be for accounting purposes. Tax authorities are now put on notice and can make such further inquiries as they may find appropriate.

Moving Expenses

For many years, the moving expenses of an existing employee could be paid by the employer without being taxable to the employee on the grounds that the outlay was for the benefit of the employer. But moving expenses of new employees were taxable to the employee, since it was held that the benefit was primarily to the employee to put him in a posi- tion, physically, to earn his prospective income. This distinction led to both subterfuge and uncertainty because some employers hired people at their existing locations and assigned them brief duties there. It was not clear for how long and how substantial the duties had to be to make a newly hired college graduate an established employee who would not be taxable on the cost of moving paid by the employer. Also, some com- panies refused to participate in such arrangements, and graduates were confronted with substantial differences in the after-tax value of similar job offers, as well as an early lesson in the varying concepts of tax ethics among individuals and business firms.

In 1964, the law was broadened to provide nontaxability for moving expenses of new, as well as old, employees, though a new employee must include the reimbursement in his gross income and take a deduction for the expenses (par. 1302(a)). The law now also allows deductions for moving expenses of all employees to the extent that they are not reimbursed by the employer (par. 1827). Moving expenses as defined in the Code and the regulations include the cost of moving household goods and personal effects and the traveling expenses of all members of the taxpayer's household. They do not, however, include living expenses incurred after disposing of an old residence or while waiting to get into a new one.

The deduction for moving expenses is limited to an employee. Self-employed individuals cannot deduct moving expenses. This apparent discrimination against the self-employed is presumably due to the difficulty of determining the bona fide character of employment of a self-employed person. A general deductibility of moving expenses would create a strong temptation to make all changes of residence tax-deductible by doing, or holding oneself available to do, a little work in one's profession at the new location. But a previously self-employed person can qualify by becoming an employee at the new location. The bona fide character of the status of employment is assured by the requirement that the deduction is allowed only if the taxpayer is a full-time employee for 39 weeks in the year subsequent to the move. The 39-week rule applies to the deduction by the employee for nonreimbursed moving expenses. The rule does not apply to expenses paid by the employer or to reimbursed expenses; employers in protecting their own interests are presumed to protect the revenue by paying moving expenses only in cases of genuine employment.

Prizes and Awards

Prizes and awards have been generally treated as income since 1954 when section 74 of the Internal Revenue Code was adopted (par. 1302(b)). Only prizes given without any action on the part of the recipient in entering a contest and with no requirement for substantial future services as a condition for receiving the prize qualify as tax-exempt. The intent of Congress was to give tax exemption only to such public awards as Pulitzer and Nobel prizes. Prior to 1954, the tax status of prizes was quite uncertain, with decisions turning on seemingly trivial distinctions as to the extent of services rendered by amateurs appearing on a radio program or the purpose of an employer in giving vacation trips to leading salesmen.

Special Problems of Compensation in Closely Controlled Corporations

Thus far, the principal issue regarding indirect compensation has been whether amounts would be taxable to employees. Deductibility by the employer has been presumed under the general rule allowing deductions of ordinary and necessary expenses (par. 1801). The only limitation noted was in connection with gifts, which makes it necessary to have payments to retired employees and their survivors come under the deduction for compensation if they are to be deductible.

But the deduction for compensation is limited to amounts which are reasonable (par. 1816–17). This could limit a payment to a retired employee, but it is vastly more significant in restricting payments to owner-managers of closely controlled corporations who are tempted to withdraw profits in the form of salaries and bonuses. The limitation of the deduction for compensation to reasonable amounts was adopted in the Revenue Act of 1918 to prevent siphoning off war profits as compensation instead of dividends. It has been continued in one form or another ever since (sec. 162(a)(1)).

The regulations state that reasonable compensation is "only such amount as would ordinarily be paid for like services by like enterprises under like circumstances" at the date when the contract for services was made (reg. 1.162–7(b)(3)). Payments on a contingent basis are not disallowed even if the payments under them turn out to be greater than the amounts which would ordinarily be paid for the services, but it is noted in the regulations that contingent compensation "invites scrutiny." The litigation has been extensive, both as to amounts paid to fully active employees and to relatives who were only active to a minor extent. It has been held that a deduction for compensation which is unreasonable may even lead to criminal penalties for willful evasion of income tax (P.-H., *Federal Taxes*, par. 11,612(15)).

The need for severe penalties to prevent tax abuse is apparent if one compares the impact of the various possible adjustments. The inclusion in income of the recipient is likely to be a more severe penalty than the disallowance of the deduction to the corporation, and disallowance is not always justified. So long as the salary plus indirect compensation does not exceed reasonable compensation for the work, the corporation would still be entitled to a deduction as indirect compensation. But in closely controlled companies, for example, even with a disallowance to the corporation, it will still be cheaper to provide company cars and vacations if the owner's marginal individual tax rate exceeds the corporate rate, as is likely to be the case in successful ventures. The significance of tax adjustments for high-bracket individuals thus increases from a disallowance of a company deduction on the grounds that an expense is not for a business purpose, to a second step which requires inclusion as individual income but with continued deductibility to the company.

The ultimate and probably only really effective penalty for abuse is a double-barreled adjustment: disallowance to the company on the grounds that the combined value of salary and indirect benefits exceeds reasonable compensation or that it is in the nature of a dividend, and inclusion as taxable individual income, either compensation or dividend, to the person involved.

The combined loss of a corporate tax saving worth 48 cents on the dollar plus a 70 per cent individual tax, especially if the cash to pay the individual tax must come from additional income which itself is taxed at 70 per cent, can make the cost of company cars for all members of the family rather substantial. An outlay of $1,000 if deductible and nontaxable to the individual would have a net cost of $520. If nondeductible to the corporation and taxable to the individual at 70 per cent, the cost would be $3,333, if the individual had to get the cash to pay his additional taxes from nondeductible income payments to him from his corporation. (The cost to the corporation would become the full $1,000 on which the individual would owe $700 in taxes, but this $700 would be the 30 per cent left after a 70 per cent tax and he would accordingly have to receive $2,333 from his corporation.[2])

Scholarships and Fellowships

Section 117 of the Internal Revenue Code, establishing the tax status of scholarships and fellowships, was adopted in 1954 and was developed in the Congress in conjunction with new sections on prizes and awards

---

[2] The size of the penalty is also the measure of the temptation. Perhaps the most striking "horror case" (a phrase used in the Congressional Committees and the Treasury to describe a flagrant abuse) was a divorce settlement which provided for the exclusive use of a company car for the divorced wife of the owner-manager until her remarriage. If this were an integral part of the settlement, and there was no fraud through concealment, a person not squeamish about his standing with tax authorities or concerned about the probable intensity of future audits might shrug off any combination of disallowance and inclusion in personal income as a "nice try, though unsuccessful."

(par. 1302(c)). But in contrast to the section on prizes, where the intent was to prescribe a tight rule, the intent with respect to scholarships was to be as liberal as possible without inviting abuse. Thus, scholarships for degree candidates are generally nontaxable. But if services are required to be rendered to the grantor, an amount up to the normal compensation for the services is taxable. This limitation is designed to remove the temptation for universities to give all graduate student instructors "scholarships" in lieu of compensation. But an exception to the limitation allows the tax exemption to apply where the services are required for the degree, as in practice teaching for a degree in education.

Because of the existence of postdoctoral fellowships in some professions, notably medicine, provision was also made for tax-free treatment of them. But here the opportunity for abuse was greater—any employer might have been tempted to give an employee a fellowship in lieu of salary for necessary research—and limitations were established both on the amounts ($300 a month for a maximum of thirty-six months) and on the source (the grantor had to be a tax-exempt organization or a government agency).

The temptation to maneuver oneself into a tax-exempt position, even by professional people who know that their action if successful would clearly violate the intent of the law, was nowhere more clearly shown than in the suggestion of a group of faculty members in a major university that terms of sabbatical leaves should be modified to permit the regular salaries which were paid during such leaves to qualify, to the extent of $300 a month, as postdoctoral fellowships. In the one case known to the author, the proposal was summarily rejected by the university administration.

To guard against this sort of maneuver, which was anticipated by those who had become somewhat cynical in drafting relief provisions in the law, at one stage in the development of section 117, the postdoctoral fellowships were to be made tax-exempt only if they fell far short of one's previous earned income, thereby removing any temptation to convert part of a regular salary into a tax-exempt form. The problem is similar to that of tax exemption for sick pay when it is equal to a regular salary. But it was convincingly argued by the medical profession that postdoctoral fellowships often went to those who had previously had only the minimal pay of interns and residents and hence the relief would be unavailable where it was most needed to give maximum effectiveness to the limited funds available for research grants.

2

Tax Factors
in Compensation Policies

Tax Factors in Deferred Compensation

At the start of the previous chapter, it was noted that the high individual income tax rates provided a strong inducement to try to receive compensation, or any other type of income, in a form which would not be subject to tax. It was further noted that as a second best alternative progressive rates on ordinary income encourage attempts to shift income from years when one is subject to high tax rates to years when one is subject to lower tax rates. If the shift is forward in time, there is a further advantage if the funds which would otherwise have been paid in taxes can be invested to produce income in the meantime. Such shifts usually involve pension plans, deferred compensation contracts, and stock options. This chapter covers their treatment under the tax law.

The tax law contains rather generous provisions for pension plans, so long as they are used for all or a general group of employees and not designed primarily for the benefit of officers or others subject to the higher tax brackets. The law is also quite liberal in allowing the receipt of compensation to be deferred, so long as a contract is made prior to the time when the income is earned. Such contracts can be made on an individual basis with no requirement for general use and are in fact usually made for only one or a very few people in a company.

Capital gains treatment is given to certain stock options which meet the precise requirements of the tax law. Income for personal services, or personal investments, may also be converted into corporate income through the use of closely controlled corporations with ultimate realization as individual capital gains. The taxation of personal holding companies is covered in a later chapter.

Advantages of Deferral of Income

A person in full-time employment typically will have steady and even increasing earnings, at least among salaried personnel, up until retirement. It is not possible, therefore, to gain much advantage by spreading income during periods of employment except insofar as unusually high bonus payments attributable to any one year may be paid out and taxed to the recipients over a period of succeeding years, a procedure which in fact is often followed. However, since the income of almost everyone is substantially less after retirement than before, any arrangement by which the receipt and taxation of income can be postponed until after retirement will ordinarily reduce appreciably the total tax payable on it.

If the dollar amounts involved are large, the tax savings may increase dramatically the net income after taxes. For example, if receipt of a segment of income could be postponed from a time when it would be subject to a 70 per cent tax to a later period when it would be subject to a 40 per cent tax, the net income derived from it would be doubled. Since the net income realized from any given amount of gross income varies inversely with the applicable tax rate, any projections of tax savings from a postponement of receipt of income for a particular person must take account of his present income and his prospective income after retirement, with assumptions as to future tax compared with present rates.

The tax calculations on the advantages of deferred receipt of income become somewhat more realistic, though more complicated, if it is assumed that an individual will attempt to provide his own retirement income out of current savings in the absence of some form of deferred income from his employer. Following this approach, one can determine at various income levels the net retirement income which can be provided from a specified increase in present salary which is assumed to be saved and invested, or the amount of salary increase required to provide a given amount of retirement income. When an individual builds up his own retirement fund out of current savings during his active years, allowance must be made for the current taxes on the investment income from the capital which he accumulates. Thus, a person subject to a 70 per cent tax rate who invests his savings at 4 per cent would have a net return of only 1.2 per cent after taxes to add to his fund of savings for retirement.

Calculations on personal arrangements for retirement income can be simplified if it is assumed that an individual uses his current savings to purchase an annuity. In this case, the earnings on the savings are, in effect, determined by the assumed interest rate in the annuity contract and are not subject to tax in the hands of the individual until he begins to draw his annuity. Insurance companies pay a tax on a special basis which substantially exempts from current tax the interest which is assumed in the actuarial calculations on their contracts. If an individual invests his savings in an annuity policy, the accumulated interest will be taxed only as the annuity payments are received after retirement.

The general tax rules applicable to annuities provide tax exemption for the recovery of the actual investment in the annuity spread over the life expectancy of the annuitant. The excess of each annuity payment over the amount which is treated as a return of capital is deemed to represent accumulated interest and is taxed currently as ordinary income when received. By contrast, when an individual makes his own investments and the accumulating income is taxed as earned, it is, of course, not taxable as it is withdrawn from capital and spent later during retirement years. The advantages of shifting the tax on the accumulating income to postretirement years can make annuities attractive investments for high-bracket people in spite of the low interest rates assumed by insurance companies.

Various forms of pension plans and deferred compensation arrangements have been developed by corporations for business reasons quite unrelated to tax advantages. However, the tax advantages for highly paid officers and employees may be so large as to become dominant in formulating compensation policies, though to qualify for favorable tax treatment the plans must not be limited to such people.

PENSION PLANS

The tax law contains several favorable provisions for pension plans financed in whole or in part by employers. Employers may take current deductions for their contributions to qualified pension funds on behalf of their employees (par. 1820). Employees are not currently taxed either for the employer's contribution or for the income accumulating in the pension fund. There is no tax imposed on the employee until payments are made to him after retirement, at which time the full amount received, consisting of both the employer's original contributions and the income earned on them during the intervening period, is taxed to the retired individual as ordinary income (par. 1303).[1] A trusteed qualified

---

[1] If employees have made contributions to the pension fund from their own after-tax income, their total contributions are treated as a capital investment in an annuity and part of each pension payment is regarded as a tax-free recovery of capital under the general rule applicable to annuities.

pension fund is itself exempt from tax under section 501(a); there is no income tax imposed either on the trust or on the potential beneficiaries with respect to investment income earned and accumulated (par. 3021(a)–(b)).

The provisions of the tax law relevant to pension plans are found in several places in the Internal Revenue Code. Section 401 gives the conditions for qualification. Section 402 gives the rules for the taxability of beneficiaries of both exempt and nonexempt employees' trusts, and section 403 states the basis for taxation of employee annuities provided under various trusts or by direct purchases by certain tax-exempt organizations. Section 404 states the conditions for deductions by employers for payments to employees' trusts and for deferred compensation. The tax exemption of employees' trusts is authorized in section 501. Prohibited transactions for tax-exempt entities including employees' trusts are described in section 503, and sections 511–14 impose a tax on any unrelated business income which they may have.

Though the discussion here is in terms of pension plans, the tax provisions apply generally to "qualified pension, profit-sharing, and stock bonus plans," which is in fact the heading of section 401 of the code. The regulations distinguish the three forms of plans by their purpose (reg. 1.401–1(a)(2)). A pension plan is established and maintained to provide for the livelihood of employees or their beneficiaries after retirement. A profit-sharing plan enables employees to participate in the profits of the employer on the basis of a definite formula for allocating contributions and distributing the funds accumulated. A stock bonus plan provides employees' benefits similar to those of profit-sharing plans except that the benefits are distributable in stock of the employer and the contributions by the employer do not necessarily depend on profits.

The necessary conditions for qualification of pension, profit-sharing and stock bonus plans for this favorable tax treatment are specified in section 401 (par. 3021(a)). The principal purpose of the restrictions is to prevent the use of tax-favored plans to give disproportionate benefits to stockholder-employees or key employees.

Historically, the tax law with respect to pension plans developed at least as much out of the difficulties of imposing current taxes on employees as it did from any conscious desire to give favored tax treatment. The critical fact which makes current taxation to employees almost impossible is the absence of current vesting in most retirement plans. Typically, pension plans provide for coverage of employees who have attained a certain age and/or have been employed for a specified number of years, as for example, 30 years of age and five years of employment. However, to receive actual pension benefits on retirement, a person must have been employed for a considerably longer period and have attained a much higher age. An employee thus may have no vested rights to a pension until he has been employed for 10, 15, or 20 years and/or until he has reached an age of 50, 55, or 60. Thus the annual contribution of the employer is not directly related to the costs of providing specific pensions for designated employees but is, rather, based on assumed rates of labor turnover in addition to the actuarial factors of age and life expectancies. An attempt to allocate to individual employees and tax them currently on their potential shares in the pensions which will in fact be realized only by some of them would meet with understandable objections by those who are in doubt about staying with a company long enough to qualify for a pension.

When the tax rules concerning pension plans were being formulated, their tax advantages were of negligible significance for most employees because of the relatively low rates of tax imposed on most incomes. Even now for people subject to a bottom rate of 14 per cent, the tax advantages of postponement of income are not sufficiently great to be of much importance in determining attitudes toward the existence of a pension plan. However, for employees in the higher income brackets, the tax advantages are likely to become of dominating importance. For this reason, the requirement that a pension plan qualifying for favorable tax treatment must not discriminate in favor of stockholders or key employees is important.

The business reasons for pension plans are numerous. They may be used to permit the retirement of older employees and the maintenance of corporate vigor without creating bad labor or community relations. Plans with delayed vesting may be used to retain employees. Many plans have been adopted as part of package settlements with unions. During the wartime freezes on wages and salaries, pension plans could be and were used in lieu of wage and salary increases. As plans have been adopted by some companies, others have had to establish them to maintain their competitive positions in hiring and holding ordinary employees and executives.

PROBLEMS IN DETERMINING CONDITIONS FOR QUALIFICATION OF PENSION PLANS: In establishing the conditions in the law for qualification of pension plans, continuing problems exist in making the standards strict enough to avoid abuse through plans set up primarily for high-bracket employees without at the same time making the conditions unduly complicated or requiring the inclusion of groups of employees who do not need or desire pension plans. The conditions for qualification which have been in the law since 1942 require either a coverage of a specified percentage of employees or the existence of a plan which in its coverage does not discriminate in favor of employees who are officers, shareholders, persons whose principal duties consist of supervising the work of other employees, or highly compensated employees (sec. 401(a)(3)(B)). Most plans qualify by ruling of the Internal Revenue Service under the second discretionary alternative. Nor may plans discriminate in their benefits in favor of the aforementioned employees (sec. 401(a)(4)).

The law specifically provides that a classification shall not be considered discriminatory merely because it excludes employees all of whose remuneration is subject to tax for social security old-age benefits or because benefits based on that part of remuneration not included in the social security tax base differ from the benefits based on the remuneration so included (sec. 401(a)(5)). The purpose of these two provisions in the law is, as noted in the regulations, "intended to permit the qualification of plans which supplement" the old-age and survivor benefits of the social security system (reg. 1.401–3(e)). But to avoid the discrimination in favor of highly paid employees, when a plan does apply only to earnings above the social security tax base or gives larger benefits for such earnings, the plan must typically be integrated with social security benefit payments; that is, pension payments to higher-paid employees must not be greater in proportion to earning than social security payments are to the first segment of earnings which are used as the social security base. If larger pension benefits are provided for larger incomes, then lower-paid employees must be given pensions sufficient to maintain the same proportion between combined social security and pension payments at all income levels.

Administratively, it has been determined that the combined old-age and survivors social security benefits paid for by employers' contributions are considered to be 150 per cent of the old-age insurance benefits alone and that 22 per cent of total benefits is attributable to employee contributions. As an example of integration for a plan applicable to earnings in excess of the social security tax base, the regulations authorize normal retirement benefits not in excess of $37\frac{1}{2}$ per cent of average annual compensation in excess of the social security tax base with no death benefits before retirement, normal retirement for men not lower than 65 and other conditions relating to optional benefits and benefits for early retirement or retirement before completion of fifteen years of service (reg. 1–401–3(e)(2)).

There have been indications that a lower percentage figure might be required for integration as the social security law has been amended with changes in benefits, financing and the level of income subject to social security taxes. A reduction in the percentage would create major problems for existing qualified plans. Benefits to lower-paid employees would have to be increased, with substantial increases in cost, or benefits to higher-paid employees would have to be reduced, with unacceptable effects on morale. For plans just meeting the requirements of integration with benefits applicable to income earned above the social security level, coverage would have to be extended to other employees if the benefit scale were continued. The extent of these problems is well recognized and at least has been partially responsible for extended delay through 1967 in issuing revised regulations after the amendments to the social security system in 1965.

The requirement for integration with social security benefits has been subject to a good deal of criticism on the ground that it makes qualification unreasonably difficult and feasible only on the basis of expert advice. The burden is spoken of as being especially great on small companies which find it so complicated to set up a pension plan for nonunionized employees, for example, that the attempt may be abandoned, resulting in a competitive disadvantage with larger companies.

It is quite common in ordinary business practice to want to set up separate pension plans for different categories of employees. Each union may have its own preferred form of negotiated plan. Salesmen on a commission basis may be thought to be better covered by a different plan than that used for engineers in the production department. Salaried employees quite frequently are subject to different rules as regards pensions than are employees paid at hourly wage rates. These business reasons often make it desirable for a company to set up several pension plans, which action in turn requires qualification under the general nondiscriminatory clause of the tax law including compliance with the administrative requirement of integration with social security benefits.

In the course of the tax legislation in 1954, an attempt was made to specify categories of employees for which pension plans would automatically receive qualification, without regard to integration with social security benefits. All salaried employees, or all employees in a particular department or plant, or all employees covered by a contract negotiated with a union, were among the categories tentatively considered for separate treatment, with separate pension plans for any of them automatically qualified without reference to comparative benefits for other groups. In large corporations, such groups could be treated separately with little possibility of abuse by high-bracket taxpayers, and it would appear to be sound tax policy to permit such separate treatment.

A problem arises in connection with small companies where in the ordinary course of events there may be only a very few salaried employees or employees in a particular department. And if this situation does not exist in the natural course of business arrangements, it may readily be created to secure the tax advantages that would go with it. Though there may be no reason why salaried members of a sales department should not get larger pensions in proportion to average earnings than members of some other department if that situation arises out of a reasonable business decision, a separate pension plan should not be permitted if it turns out that the only salaried members of the sales department are controlling stockholders, especially if the pensions for such employees are equal to the best five years of annual earnings, whereas for all other employees pensions do not exceed half of average annual earnings.

Because of the fear of such abuse in small companies, along with other reasons, the new conditions for qualification of pension plans provided in 1954 in the tax bill in the House, along lines recommended by the Treasury, were not adopted by the Senate Finance Committee or the Senate. This rejection was also in line with later recommendations of the Treasury. The need to develop simpler conditions for qualification continues.

LUMP-SUM WITHDRAWALS FROM PENSION PLANS: Lump-sum withdrawals, prior to or at the time of retirement, present a special problem in connection with qualified pension plans. If an individual leaves a company before retirement age, the plan may provide that he can withdraw in a lump sum the then value of his future benefits (par. 3021(d)). To impose an ordinary tax at such time on the full amount of the payment would produce a peculiarly heavy tax if the amount involved was sufficient to push the recipient into much higher tax brackets than those to which he is regularly subject. It is to prevent tax burdens of this sort that lump-sum withdrawals under certain prescribed conditions are treated as capital gains. This treatment, however, in many instances gives a much lower tax than would be due if the amounts were paid out over the years of retirement as is ordinarily contemplated.

Some people, for example, may substantially reduce their total tax by immediately taking the amount due them under a pension plan, paying a capital gains tax on it, and then purchasing an annuity with the net amount received. Since the cost of annuities thus purchased becomes their tax basis, owners can exclude from their annuity receipts, under the general rules applicable to annuities, an amount sufficient to recover their investments over their life expectancy. In effect, they pay an immediate capital gains tax on their entire accumulation in the fund for the privilege of having this same amount excluded from taxation as ordinary income over their life expectancies. The possible advantages of transactions of this sort will depend upon the incomes and the applicable tax rates of the individuals concerned and the life expectancy of the annuity.

Some sort of presumptive averaging would appear to be better than capital gains treatment of lump-sum withdrawals. This would make it possible to avoid an unfair application of very high tax rates which might otherwise be applied to a lump sum but at the same time prevent possible abuses and also prevent the lower rates of tax properly accorded to true capital gains from being misapplied to something which really represents earned income rather than capital appreciation.

Prohibited Transactions and Unrelated Business Income of Pension Trusts

Since 1954, pension trusts have been subject to the same restrictions regarding prohibited transactions as are applied to charitable and educational organizations which qualify for tax-deductible contributions (par. 3134(d)2). The prohibited transactions include loans without security and a reasonable rate of interest or other transactions on a preferential basis with the creator of the organization or related parties. The general purpose of this limitation is to prevent abuse by securing a tax deduction by transferring funds to a trust or charity when the funds are returned by it to the transferor on other than an arm's length basis.

The requirement that adequate security be given for loans created an anomalous situation for pension trusts, however, because the word "security" is interpreted in a strict legal sense and debentures would not qualify no matter how high their credit rating and marketability while mortgages would qualify no matter how specialized the pledged property or how unmarketable the mortgage obligation. The law was amended to remedy this defect and permit pension trusts to invest in part of an issue of debentures of the employer, the rest of which is held by others (sec. 503(h)).

Another provision of the law taxes most tax-exempt entities, including employees' trusts, on their unrelated business income (par. 3442). This had been found necessary to prevent tax-exempt organizations from misusing their favored tax position by carrying on an active business in unfair competition with ordinary taxpaying concerns. The concept of unrelated business income is extended to cover certain rental income when substantial debt is incurred to secure the rental property, that is, when the tax-exempt organization is in a sense "trading on its equity" and trying to extend the tax exemption given to the income from its own funds to income from borrowed funds. The unrelated business income provisions would not apply to the ordinary investment of a typical employees' pension trust. They are no more than reasonable restraints on anyone who might be tempted to depart from a normal type of portfolio investment in the use of tax-exempt trusteed funds.

Tax Treatment of Nonqualified Pension Plans

When provisions for pensions are made directly for individual employeès, or for groups which do not permit qualification for the special favorable tax treatment described previously, different tax rules apply (par. 1820(e) and 3021(d)).

If employees have nonforfeitable rights to the pension or other benefit, the amounts paid by the employer are treated as current income of the employee and the employer gets a current deduction for the same amount. This situation most commonly occurs when a company buys an annuity policy for one or a few employees. The effect of the tax rule is to give the same result as though the employee had received the money from the company and then purchased the annuity himself. In the absence of this rule, employers would be able to spread at will the compensation of favored employees.

If rights to future pensions are forfeitable, employees are not taxable until they receive the benefits or until the rights become nonforfeitable. This rule regarding employees is reasonable and necessary to avoid taxing a contingent future benefit. But in these cases employers do not get deductions for their payments at any time, either when payments are made to a fund or outside agency, if one is used, or when the employee receives his benefit payment and is taxable on it. This denial of deduction to employers has been criticized as being unduly harsh, and it has not always been upheld by the courts. It has been proposed to change the present law to provide for simultaneous deductibility by employers and taxability to employees.

Those who argue for the change in the present tax treatment of forfeitable pension rights urge it in fairness to employers and further state that the deferral of deduction to employers, in comparison with qualified pension plans, will prevent collusion between employers and employees in postponing the receipt of income for favored employees. In favor of the present treatment, it is argued that the proposed change would authorize funded deferred compensation contracts for one or more employees. An attempt was made to work out a solution of this problem in 1954, but it was abandoned under the existing time pressures. In view of subsequent developments concerning unfunded deferred compensation contracts, described below, the problem requires further attention.

The general conditions for qualification and operation of pension trusts can be described briefly, as has been done here. But the subject is vastly more complicated than it appears to be from these general statements. Indeed, the regulations on sections 401–04 alone cover sixty-six double-column pages. Much of the detail is designed to prevent abuses, but the limitations may trap an innocent though unwary employer. Specialists in the subject know their way among the intricacies and can construct a simple and straightforward program with assurance that it will qualify for favorable tax treatment. But for the management of a small business, a glance at the text of the law or the regulations will make the mere idea of a qualified pension plan seem formidable indeed, and the need to seek the advice of experts is another discouraging factor to those trying to operate small independent businesses.

Retirement Plans for Self-Employed and Owner Managers

In 1962, the tax law authorized self-employed individuals and owner-employees to establish retirement plans for themselves (par. 1821). Enactment of section 401(c)–(f) followed many years of complaint by groups of professional people that they were at a disadvantage in comparison with members of the same profession who worked as employees of corporations or other individuals. Extensive testimony was given on the relative advantages of employment and self-employment, including facts and desires regarding retirement, and on the difficulty of providing retirement income from savings out of after-tax income by self-employed people.

The benefits to self-employed people and owner-employees are quite limited. A maximum contribution of 10 per cent of earned income or $2,500, whichever is less, can be made to the plan, and only one-half of this was deductible in computing taxable income under the original allowance. For years beginning after 1967 a full deduction is allowed. An owner-employee cannot qualify a plan for himself unless he includes under it all of his employees with more than three years service. The restrictions in the law are extensive and precise, running to more than seven pages of the Internal Revenue Code itself. For many self-employed people, even for those in the highest tax brackets, the limited tax benefits have not seemed sufficient to justify the time and expense needed to set up and operate a plan or contribute to an existing standardized plan.

DEFERRED COMPENSATION CONTRACTS

The simplest way to spread income is through a long-term employment contract which provides specified amounts of income up to the normal retirement age, with smaller amounts in subsequent years. The later payments may be stated to be additional compensation for consulting or other services to be given in those years. The tax treatment of contracts of this sort is not specifically covered in the Internal Revenue Code or in the Regulations, and their status was somewhat uncertain because the Internal Revenue Service did not issue rulings on them for many years prior to 1960. Though income is typically taxed as received for cash basis taxpayers, there was a real possibility that, under the concept of constructive receipt, the income paid after retirement would be deemed to have been earned during the years prior to retirement, with the present value of the subsequent payment either taxed currently as the rights to receive it were built up, or taxed in full in the year of retirement (par. 2702(a)). This result could be catastrophic to the holder of such a contract because the total tax due might exceed the cash compensation currently received.

Provisions in individual employment contracts providing for services to be rendered or other conditions to be fulfilled after retirement were often used to make it less likely that a person holding a contract could be asserted to have any rights to receive his postretirement income until he met all the specified conditions. For employers, tax deductions are taken for deferred compensation as payments are made, and there is typically no attempt to fund currently the sums necessary to meet future obligations under deferred compensation contracts.

Deferred compensation contracts may be written for the business purposes which are often stated in them, that is, to prevent a key employee from joining a competitor after retirement or to secure the benefit of advice from an "elder statesman." However, in many cases the possibilities of joining a competitor may be remote, and the actual seeking of advice rather perfunctory. The great tax advantages of spreading income over the period until death, with survivors' benefits also provided in some cases, make it hard to dissociate business from tax objectives.

Before 1960, deferred compensation contracts were used only to a limited degree, and business attitudes toward them varied considerably between companies. In some instances, they were not even considered seriously because of possible resentment by executives who did not receive them or because of possible repercussions on stockholder or labor relations.

In other companies, such contracts were regarded as appropriate to balance the advantages which exist in closely controlled corporations where owner-managers are kept on the payrolls until death and in some professions where senior partners extend their earnings indefinitely.

In other special situations, a deferred compensation contract was used as the only possible means to compensate a highly paid executive for giving up his nonvested pension rights in a company from which he moved. Even a liberal pension plan in the company to which he moves is not likely to give a man coming under it for his last ten or fifteen years of active work a retirement income equal to what he would have had if he stayed on with a single company at a lower salary for his entire business life. Thus, deferred compensation contracts may offset the freezing effects of nonvested pension plans. Some of the seemingly very generous contracts for newly hired chief executives have in fact been calculated to do little more than offset the net loss in pensions arising from a transfer between companies.

In January 1960, the Treasury issued a ruling (Rev. Rul. 60–31) stating its interpretation of the existing law on five detailed deferred compensation arrangements. These were apparently selected or designed to give guidance on the full range of possible plans. The general ruling stated that advance rulings would not be given in specific cases, but the five examples were regarded as giving sufficient guidance to permit contracts to be made in the future with full confidence as to their tax consequences.

The ruling was regarded as quite liberal. The key factor in assuring postponement of taxability until actual receipt is the absence of any prior right to receive cash. So long as the contract is made before services are rendered, and so long as there are no funds specifically set aside to meet the future payments, there will apparently be no basis for applying the concept of constructive receipt. Cases given covered not only employees but also authors and athletes. A contract to spread royalties on a book over many years after they were earned was approved, so long as the contract was made before the book was published and any royalties were earned. The two examples involving athletes were held to give rise to current taxability; but, in one case, this was due to the fact that a sum was delivered to an escrow agent designated by a football player and, in the second case, it was held that a boxer had entered into a joint venture with a boxing club and hence his share of the gate receipts was attributable to him immediately.

The 1960 ruling clarified the situation for all taxpayers, and deferred compensation arrangements have since been used more frequently and openly (par. 2715(a)). There can be certainty as to their tax consequences.

Though some care is needed to come within the indicated conditions to give tax deferral, any taxpayers who may be in a position to defer the receipt of income should be able to get the benefits of deferred taxation without working out elaborate arrangements to do so.

From the standpoint of public policy, the general availability of tax deferral on unfunded deferred compensation gives a competitive advantage to well-established companies whose simple contractual obligation will be regarded as adequate in dealing with employees and others receiving compensation for services. Since any action that gives greater assurance than that arising from a simple contract may lead to immediate taxation on grounds of constructive receipt, a small publishing company will be at a disadvantage in dealing with authors of prospective best sellers, as will small employers generally. Also, a brain surgeon could have complete confidence in a deferred compensation contract to work in the medical department of a utility company, but would be skeptical about performing operations on individual patients with the fee to be spread over the remainder of the surgeon's life.

The implications of the 1960 ruling on the competitive advantage of large established companies over their less well-financed competitors deserve attention. The ruling also tends to give an advantage to employment over self-employment, because, as suggested, deferred receipt of fees from individual clients is subject to risks and, if the risks are removed by funding, the deferral of tax is defeated.

If the unintended competitive advantages which the present rules permitting postponement of tax on deferred compensation give to large and well-established employers ever turned out to be significant, the law would probably be changed. This could be done by applying a more strict interpretation of constructive receipt, though it would present many administrative problems. Alternatively, the law could be made more liberal to permit funds to be set aside and turned over to third parties to assure payment of future obligations without making the compensation currently taxable. This latter change would also raise administrative problems, because the deduction should be available to the employer only as the income is taxable to the employee, and any accumulation of interest on the funds set aside should be currently taxed to the employer. Unless this were done, deferred compensation contracts would have all the tax advantages of nondiscriminatory qualified pension plans. Also, if funding were permitted on deferred compensation contracts, the present restrictions on nonqualified pension plans, discussed in the preceding section, would in effect be waived since funded deferred compensation contracts are really nonqualified pension plans for the individuals involved. It is thus possible that future modifications in the law to prevent discrimination against small business will permit widespread deferral of compensation income and the tax thereon, even when the income is fully guaranteed by an intermediate financial institution.

Employees of Tax-Exempt Organizations

A special rule applies to employees of organizations exempt from taxation under section 503(c) and employees of public schools or universities (par. 1207(d)). The employees are not taxable currently on purchases of individual annuities so long as payment does not exceed an exclusion allowance which is defined as 20 per cent of the employee's pay for the last twelve-month period, multiplied by the number of years of past service, less any amounts contributed by the employer which were excluded in prior years. Under this provision, most professors, for example, in their last years before retirement when family education expenses are finished and consulting income is at its highest, may choose, if the employer agrees, to have a part of their regular salaries used to purchase individual annuities on their behalf, with the proceeds to be received in postretirement years when applicable tax rates will presumably be lower. The calculation of the maximum exclusion is not simple. One cannot choose to have all the pay to which one is entitled used to purchase an annuity because the exclusion allowance is based on 20 per cent of the pay (other than that used for the purchase of an annuity) and too great a shift from current to future income would lead to a vanishing allowable exclusion.

The benefit is nonetheless very real and can serve to hold employees with an existing employer because of the importance of the factor of years of service. Employees of the specified organizations in effect can secure funded deferred compensation contracts, with the additional benefit of the income earned on the sums funded. All other employees, as noted in the preceding section, are currently taxable if amounts due under individual arrangements for deferred compensation are funded.

This provision of the law was not adopted to give special favoritism to teachers and employees of tax-exempt organizations (section 403(b)). It was enacted in 1958 to limit what had become a significant loophole under the general provisions of the law. It was apparently originally presumed that the pay scales of employees of tax-exempt organizations were so low that there would be no incentive for tax maneuvers and that neither the requirement for qualification of pension plans nor the rules regarding taxability of employer payments were applied to them. Thus, prior to 1958, it was possible for such employees to have all of their current compensation used by the employer to purchase annuities due in postretirement years, and in some situations this was done for part-time teachers who had other sources of current earned income. The limitations imposed by the new section in 1958 seemed adequate to the Congress to prevent spectacular abuse while still relieving tax-exempt organizations of the need to make their pension plans qualify under the general provisions of the law.

STOCK OPTIONS

Prior to 1946, stock options were ordinarily not subject to any special tax rules. Neither the grant nor exercise of an option was a taxable event. Sale of the stock purchased under an option gave rise to a capital gain or loss based on the difference between the purchase price and the selling price, in the same manner as did the purchase and sale of stock in the open market. On the basis of a court decision, the regulations were changed in 1946 to provide that the difference between the option price and fair market value at the time of exercise of an option was to be treated as compensation, taxable as ordinary income (par. 1310(b)).

This new tax rule virtually stopped the issuance of stock options, which had previously been used fairly widely to give key officers and employees a basis for securing a proprietary interest in a company and to provide management incentives for long-term corporate growth. With high tax rates, stock options had been the only way executives could secure substantial stock interests (and substantial personal estates) through employment in large corporations.

Because of their tax advantages, it is impossible to dissociate business from tax purposes in stock option plans. The existence of real business purposes is indicated by the extensive use of stock option plans many years ago when tax rates were lower and tax advantages not sufficiently important to justify their adoption on tax grounds alone. The desire of many investors to have key officers have an appreciable proprietary interest in a company is real and significant. Stock ownership by officers is considered by many long-term investors to be superior not only to ordinary salary arrangements but also to bonus or profit-sharing plans, which may lead to undue emphasis on short-term profitability.

In 1950, the Congress changed the tax law to provide capital gains treatment for stock options which qualified as "restricted stock options" (par. 1311(c)). For such qualification, the option price had to be at least 95 per cent of the fair market value when the option was granted (or 85 per cent, with less favorable tax treatment), and certain other conditions had to be met regarding the holding period, with safeguards to prevent dominant stockholders from using options to increase their percentage of control. In general, the limitations in the tax law were no more than would seem reasonable in the interests of stockholders in a stock option plan to be presented for ratification by stockholders. In fact, the relatively short holding period (24 months, of which 18 could be applied to the option prior to its exercise and 6 to the stock after its purchase) provided opportunities for quick turns in stock. Prompt sales defeated the objective of long-term proprietary interest which alone justified the use of stock options for business purposes and was the basis for favorable tax legislation in 1950.

In 1964, the requirements for favorable tax treatment of stock options were changed and a new category of "qualified stock options" was established (par. 1311(a)). Restricted stock options granted before 1964 may continue to be exercised under the rules under which they were established, but options granted after 1963 must meet the new requirements, which are tighter in two major respects and more liberal in one.

Options cannot be granted at less than market price at time of grant. Many companies even under the old law established option prices at market price rather than at 95 per cent of market price, and this change in the law was not resented even by the strongest advocates of options. But at the same time the period between grant and exercise of option was reduced from ten to five years. This inevitably forces management to concentrate on a shorter time span insofar as their own interests regarding growth and increased profitability of the company are concerned. In this respect, stock options have been brought closer to profit-sharing plans in their emphasis on short-term improvement which may be at the expense of long-term growth.

Also a new requirement for qualified stock options provides that an option cannot be exercised while an employee has a prior outstanding option unexercised. This change probably was intended to prevent an abuse of the option privilege through a succession of grants until one turned out to be a "winner" simply because of fluctuations in market prices and regardless of improvement in a company's own position, and on that basis it was understandable. But it also struck at the effectiveness of quite bona fide bonus-option plans in which employees had a choice to take an option instead of a cash bonus with, over the years, a general expectation that options would be taken and exercised and stock interests of executives increased. The right to take cash or an option in each year was in the nature of an escape clause which is effectively closed under the new requirement of the law, unless the stock price rises continuously.

The result of the requirement seems unfortunate in that it forces attention on the selection of a particular year for granting options. Instead of concentrating on the long-term growth of the company with reasonable confidence that over the years the price of the stock will reflect that growth and any interim adverse fluctuations can be ignored, it is now necessary to try to guess which year is the best to adopt an option plan from the standpoint of general market fluctuations as well as the company's own prospects for the next five years. This shift in emphasis was regretted by those who favor long-term executive stock ownership as a means of making personal pecuniary advantages coincide with the long-term growth and increased efficiency of the corporations for which they are responsible, which in turn will ordinarily lead to growth and greater efficiency of the nation's economy.

But the 1964 legislation removed a barrier in the old law which frequently prevented the use of stock options in closely controlled companies where options were most needed to secure the services of a new management and assure the continued independent existence of the company. In such companies, if there had been no recent arm's-length transfer of stock or valuation for estate tax purposes, it was virtually impossible to have any confidence in valuation of the stock, and a figure conservatively adopted in the best of faith might be considered too low at some later date after an option had been exercised. Under the restricted stock option rules, if the option price was held to be less than 85 per cent of fair market value at the time the option was granted, the entire difference between option price and fair market value when the option was exercised was taxable as ordinary income at the time of exercise. This harsh treatment might easily call for more cash to pay the tax than to buy the stock; the risk precluded the use of options in instances where the unavailability of options might mean either the employment of an unimaginative management or a merger with another company.

The law now mercifully and wisely provides that when the option price is set at less than fair market value in good faith, there will be ordinary income at the time of exercise of the option equal to the lesser of 150 per cent of the difference between option price and fair market value at the time of grant or the difference between option price and fair market value at the time of exercise. This treatment assures a penalty for a misjudgment, but the penalty is not catastrophic. There is no inducement to undervalue stock, but closely controlled companies can use options to secure new dynamic executives.

The present stock option provisions of the tax law are criticized by some as loopholes, on the ground that they are essentially compensatory and that profits from them should be taxed as ordinary income. Others, though agreeing that options are compensatory, believe that the economic advantages of having corporate managements own substantial amounts of stock are great enough to justify a special tax on them.[2]

A great many option plans were adopted immediately after the change in the tax law in 1950. Options have been a subject of much use, publicity, and controversy ever since. The 1964 legislation represented a compromise between advocates and opponents, and the subject is still controversial. Many of those who support the idea of special tax treatment of options object to what they regard as abuses in practice. Stock purchased under an option is too frequently sold as soon as enough time elapses for the profit to qualify as a capital gain. In some instances, the management then proposes another option plan because the key officers hold so little stock. Such grab-and-run practices discredit the whole concept of stock options by permitting them to be used as indirect compensation without securing the personal interest of the management in long-range growth, which is the only justification for the special treatment. Tighter rules, requiring long holding periods, are regarded by many as fair and reasonable to prevent abuse and also as necessary to forestall complete repeal of the stock option provisions.

A comparison of the relative benefits to the recipient of an option and the costs to the corporation raises interesting analytical problems. Superficially, the problem is simple. The difference between the option price and the market price at the time of exercise is a form of compensation, though taxable only when the stock is sold and then as a capital gain. Ignoring for the moment the time factor, one can say that the benefit to the optionee is equal to the difference between his marginal tax rate on ordinary income and his capital gain tax rate, which does not exceed 25 per cent. By granting an option, the corporation foregoes the receipt of the spread between option price and market price at time of exercise which amount could have been a deductible expense if an equivalent compensation were paid in cash. With a corporate rate of 48 per cent and a maximum spread between a top marginal individual rate of 70 per cent and a capital gain rate of 25 per cent, or 45 per cent, it would appear that the tax benefit to the individual was less than the tax cost, in terms of a deduction foregone, to the corporation. It might be argued that only if the spread between the individual tax rates on ordinary income and capital gains exceeded the corporate rate would options be mutually advantageous.

The problem is, however, more complicated than the foregoing

[2] For some years, some lower courts distinguished proprietary and compensatory options, but the Supreme Court struck down this legalistic concept. It is generally agreed that options are justified only if the corporation giving them receives something of value in return, which must be past, present, or future services.

analysis suggests. The time factor can be very important. A postponement of tax may be more important than a difference in applicable tax rates, and the postponement may be indefinite. If the stock is held until death, there is no capital gains tax and the rate advantage to the recipient is his full marginal tax rate.

From the standpoint of the corporation, the use of options presumably produces a difference in executive attitude from that achieved by ordinary compensation. If this is not so, that is if all option stock is sold as soon as permitted under the tax law, then options become only a tax gimmick and favorable tax treatment for them is unjustified as a matter of public policy. The reality and significance in the difference in attitude of executives probably cannot be determined with complete confidence, let alone measured.

Furthermore, the "cost" to the corporation is not measured by the difference between option price and market price at the time of exercise of the option. The option may never be exercised because market price never exceeds the option price, and yet the incentive effect may still exist and be effective. A general decline in the market may make the option ineffective though the status of the company has improved, partly on account of the inducement of the option, or increased efforts may have limited a deterioration in a company's position which would otherwise have occurred.

One final complicating factor in the use of options and in attempts to calculate their advantages and costs occurs when executives have little capital, as is typically the case. It may be necessary to give options for more stock than it is expected they will retain. Unless the spread between the option price and the market price becomes very large, the loan incurred to purchase option stock may be unreasonably high to continue for a long period. The profit on a sale of some stock as it becomes possible at capital gains rates can be used to reduce the debt on the remaining stock. This problem of making possible purchase of a sufficient stock interest to have a significant effect on attitudes is a very real one; it appears to be the only valid argument, from the standpoint of public policy, against a requirement for a very long holding period on stock acquired by options. To the extent that some stock is sold to realize a profit which in turn is used as the "equity" for continued holding of the remainder of option stock, the process may indeed appear costly to the corporation, but this cost must be viewed as part of the entire option package.

3

Personal

Exemptions and Deductions

A chapter on personal exemptions and deductions has no necessary place in a book on tax factors in business decisions. It is included simply to give full coverage on the federal income tax. Brief comments here on the recurring questions of "Why" and "So what" will permit a consistent approach to the entire subject.

EXEMPTIONS

The use of a uniform $600 exemption for each taxpayer and dependent represents a triumph for administrative convenience over refined equity in the tax law (par. 1106–07). For almost thirty years after the adoption of the individual income tax in 1913, the deduction or exemption for a dependent was much less than for a taxpayer or his spouse. At times the combined exemption for a couple was greater than the exemption for two single taxpayers; at other times it was less.

To meet the urgent needs for revenue during World War II, the bottom bracket rate, which had been 4 per cent in 1939, was raised to 23 per cent by 1944, and over the same period, the exemption, which had been $1,000 for a single taxpayer, $2,500 for a married couple, and $500 for each dependent, was reduced to $500 for a taxpayer and a dependent.

The reduction in exemption converted the individual income tax from a class to a mass tax, and the withholding of tax on wages and salaries was considered necessary both to assure collection and to avoid hardship on people who were not accustomed to setting aside substantial funds to meet a future liability. The use of a uniform exemption allowance simplified the calculations on tax liabilities and the amount to be withheld.

The size of the exemption is related to the amount of revenue needed. Attempts to base it on a minimum, or normal, or desired standard of living, with adjustments for difference in costs for families of different sizes, may be interesting, but when the income tax is relied on as the principal tax in a modern state, the revenue simply is not available if taxes are imposed only on middle and upper incomes. When government is expensive, support of the government is part of the cost of living.

The definition of dependents has been narrowed at various times to prevent abuse. The extreme example involved the "adoption" under the laws of a foreign country of an entire orphanage, with the per capita cost of support considerably less than the saving in taxes from each extra $600 exemption at a high-bracket tax rate (par. 1110). Various special rules have been adopted to cover appealing situations arising from adoptions by members of the armed forces while abroad or even to give continuing exemptions for known specific situations which would have been excluded under new and tighter general rules.

Additional exemptions for people who are over 65 or blind are simple though not very logical devices to give tax relief in situations where income is likely to be limited (pars. 1108–09). At various times, proposals have been made to extend the additional exemptions to people with physical handicaps other than blindness, such as cardiac cases or amputees. But the degree of impairment of earning power varies so much with the occupation of the individual that the Treasury and Congress have always concluded that the addition of these categories of exemptions would be as likely to create new discriminations as to relieve existing ones.

The rule that students who are dependents and who also earn income may still be counted as dependents, with a personal exemption for their parents, while at the same time using their own personal exemptions in computing their own taxable income is not logical, but it was adopted in 1954 as preferable to a preceding rule which had quite perverse effects (par. 1110.1.b). Under the previous rule, as soon as a student became taxable on his own income, his parents could not continue to claim him as a dependent. Thus, an extra dollar of income after he had earned $600 (ignoring deductions) meant that the parents lost a $600 exemption with a consequent increase in taxes of at least $120 to the parents at the then bottom tax rate of 20 per cent.

An increase in taxes of $120 because of an increase of one dollar of income seemed ridiculous. Parents discouraged children from earning above $600. It seemed especially unfortunate for young people to discover on their first involvement with the principal federal revenue source that it had such a capriciously inequitable result and such a perverse economic effect. The continuation of the deduction for a parent who continued to provide over half of the support of a child seemed the simplest solution (par. 3506). However, it is immediately apparent to students that they give rise to a double exemption while their parents continue to support them, but if they support themselves or, if married, are supported by the joint efforts of themselves and their wives, they are entitled to only a single exemption for themselves. This seems and is illogical as a matter of equity. But at least the perverse economic effects of an absolute tax penalty against further work do not arise. The idea of a double exemption for all students, regardless of their source of income or support, was rejected because there were so many others urging double exemptions for themselves on grounds of need or important social activities that it seemed impossible to select one group for this form of relief.

The existence of an exemption in an individual income tax makes even a proportional income tax progressive in fact. For those whose income is just above the exemption, the effective rate of tax on total income is very low. It becomes higher as the taxable income increases as a fraction of the total income. For many years, the beginning income tax rate was 20 per cent, applicable to the first $2,000 of taxable income ($4,000 on joint returns). Even with no progression through higher rates, this single rate assured progression from a rate of zero to something approaching 20 per cent. In 1964, additional steps were introduced in the rate scale, with intervals of $500 of taxable income. Ostensibly this was done to secure progression at the bottom of the income scale. In fact, the progression already was provided by the exemption; the smaller intervals simply increased the degree of progression and gave a lower marginal tax rate at the threshold of taxation.

SPLIT INCOME

The provision of the tax law which permits married couples to split their income arose as the most acceptable solution politically to a discrimination which had developed under the different property laws of the various states (pars. 1104–(b), 3504–05). Several states have community property laws under which each spouse is deemed to have an equal interest in the income of either of them while married. Under the wording of the federal income tax law, this splitting of income was recognized for tax purposes as giving rise to two equal incomes taxable as such. A large income split and taxed as two separate incomes pays much less, under the progressive rate schedule, than when taxed as a single income.

Efforts to amend the law to ignore the community property concept for federal tax purposes were blocked by representatives from those states. The tax advantages were so great that other states switched to the community property concept to give their residents the tax advantage of splitting incomes, often with confusion if not chaos on other aspects of property law. Various administrations proposed legislation to require all married couples to file joint returns with only a single tax rate schedule. This would have eliminated the tax advantages of income splitting under community property laws, but it would have had the effect of an annual tax on maintaining a state of marriage for all those who had bona fide separate incomes.

The income of the spouse with the lower income, instead of being taxed at the bottom of the progressive rate schedule, would have been added on to the income of the spouse with the larger income and taxed at whatever rates were thereby reached in the progressive scale. Some regarded this proposal as reasonable and appropriate; others, including the author, regarded it as immoral and indeed antisocial. The Congress always rejected it.

In 1948, the present split income provisions were adopted. For couples with a small taxable income which, even after splitting, is still taxable at the bottom rate, there is no benefit. And for couples with very large incomes, most of which even after splitting is taxable at the top rate, the benefit of splitting is minor as a fraction of total tax. The benefit exists largely in the middle income brackets where the effective rate of tax on two incomes is much less than that applicable to a single income of twice the size. This distribution of the benefit of income splitting is not defensible on grounds of equity or logic. But so long as it is not possible to ignore the community property concept and tax each individual, whether married or single, on his own separate income, the present rules seem the most acceptable.

The special rules for heads of households were adopted to give partial relief to those who, though not married, have financial responsibilities because they maintain a home for others (par. 1104(c)). A surviving spouse with children is likely to be harder pressed financially then was the married couple, and it seems harsh to impose the full progressive rate scale applicable to a single person. (A surviving spouse can continue the full benefits of split income for two years, but indefinite continuation contradicts the purpose of the split income provision which was to give all married couples the benefits available to those in community property states, and the community property concept gave no relief to surviving spouses.)

The head of household approach was a pragmatic compromise. It is not confined to surviving spouses, but is available to those who maintain households for specified relatives. An interesting interaction of social policy and tax law occurred in 1954 when at the recommendation of the Treasury the requirement for residence in the household was waived when a father or mother was, supported by a child. This was proposed in recognition of the fact that both generations often were happier when the parents lived in their own home community; it seemed improper to give a tax advantage to those who uprooted elderly parents and brought them into the home of a working child. This recommendation, made on the basis of general familiarity with family situations, turned out to be particularly appreciated by members of the Congressional staffs, many of whom were single people from other parts of the country whose parents were happier in their home towns, and the "grass roots" support for the relief measure did not come entirely by correspondence.

PERSONAL DEDUCTIONS

Some of the so-called personal deductions are entirely what the name implies. Charitable contributions and medical expenses, at least those for one's family, are quite unrelated to the earning of income; in no sense can they be considered costs which should be deducted to determine a true net income. Deductibility of some of these expenditures in computing taxable income reflects social policy rather than inherent equity.

In other personal deductions, there may be elements of cost with a fuzzy demarcation between the personal and quasi-business aspects. For example, interest on an installment purchase of a refrigerator seems as purely personal as the higher cost of a deluxe model. So does the interest on the mortgage on a home. But if the home site includes extra land which was purchased with the thought that it might appreciate and be sold prior to or even at the same time as the home itself, the interest attributable to the extra land might be regarded as a carrying charge of an investment to be treated as a current expense or capitalized as part of the cost of the land. So too with the taxes on a residence, though the deductibility of certain taxes in computing taxable income also reflects to some extent a desire to avoid conflicts between federal and state levels of government, as well as some mystique about an inherent inequity of "a tax on a tax," whatever that may signify.

Whenever any deduction is authorized, it must be adopted for a specific outlay or expenditure, and whatever the definition there will be borderline situations. For each of the personal deductions, there are numerous borderline cases with consequent litigation. The statute has sometimes been amended to prevent abuses or unintended benefits and at other times to authorize deductions for specific forms of expenditures in response either to a general sense of fairness or to the effective insistence of a pressure group. The definition of each of the personal deductions has become increasingly complicated because of the increasing complexity of personal and business affairs and because of continuing attempts to convert nondeductible expenditures into forms which qualify as deductions.

Deductions from Gross Income and from Adjusted Gross Income

The distinction between deductions from gross income to determine adjusted gross income and deductions from adjusted gross income to determine taxable income is intended to cover certain of the costs incurred by an individual in getting his income (par. 1103(b)). By setting up this special category of deductions, it is intended to put taxpayers in a comparable position to benefit from the other itemized deductions, some of which have a floor or ceiling related to the income before the itemized deductions. Consider, for example, a so-called outside salesman who himself incurs $3,000 of expenses in carrying on his activities and who earns $13,000 of commissions which are intended to cover these expenses. He is really in same position as a salesman with a salary or commission of $10,000 who has had $3,000 of expenses reimbursed by or charged directly to his employer. But if the outside salesman had to treat all his deductions in the same category, the first $390 of his medical expenses would not be deductible under the 3 per cent floor, in contrast to $300 for the man with reimbursed expenses. But the outside salesman would be permitted to take a larger charitable deduction. The use of the two sets of deductions, with the intermediate step of adjusted gross income, gives more nearly uniform treatment to taxpayers with substantially similar taxpaying capacity.

Furthermore, and equally important, the separate treatment of deductions to secure adjusted gross income is necessary to make the standard deduction equally available to all taxpayers. The 10 per cent allowance as a standard deduction is intended to permit everyone to get at least that amount to cover presumed outlays on medical expenses, contributions, interest, taxes, and casualty losses. Even if one has actual outlays of only 5 per cent, he still gets the benefit of the 10 per cent presumption up to the $1,000 ceiling. If a salesman with expenses of 5 per cent of his income could not deduct them separately, he would not be able to get the full benefit of the 10 per cent presumption for the itemized personal deductions; if he had actual outlays of another 5 per cent on itemized deductions, he would get no additional benefit from the standard deduction.

Standard Deduction

For purposes of simplification, a standard deduction is authorized as an alternative to itemized deductions (pars. 1103(d) and (e), 2420–23). The figure of 10 per cent of adjusted gross income was selected as being somewhat above the average of itemized deductions, in order to induce its use by people with small incomes. But it is not significant for those with large incomes who almost inevitably will have deductions in excess of that figure. Various proposals have been made to increase the ceiling to $2,000 or $2,500, but they have been opposed openly on the grounds that this tax relief would not be shared by those with the smallest incomes and more quietly by various charities which fear a loss of contributions if tax deductibility were no longer significant.

The minimum standard deduction was adopted in 1964 as a form of special relief for taxpayers with the smallest taxable incomes, with no benefit to others. An increase in the personal exemption would give some relief to all taxpapers, with an increasing dollar advantage, but decreasing proportionate advantages to those in the higher brackets. By contrast, the minimum standard deduction gives relief only to those whose ordinary deductions do not reach the minimum. It does not benefit even those with the smallest income if they have large itemized deductions for medical expenses, charitable contributions, taxes or interest. Its adoption, in fact, was a form of selective tax relief with effects which were not universally regarded as logical.

With the increase in home ownership, and the consequent greater prevalence of deductions for interest and taxes, the standard deduction has become less widely used. A person carrying a large debt on his home, with interest and taxes, is very likely to have total deductions in excess of 10 per cent of adjusted gross income if he makes appreciable charitable contributions or incurs substantial medical expenses.

Charitable Contributions

By authorizing a deduction of up to 20 per cent or 30 per cent of adjusted gross income for contributions to specified educational, charitable, and religious organizations, the percentage depending on the nature of the organization, the tax law recognizes the importance of private support for social services. The law here is more liberal in this respect than most if not all foreign tax laws. The significance of the deduction may be described in two somewhat contradictory ways. The higher the marginal tax rate of an individual, the greater would be the sacrifice of making a specified contribution in the absence of deductibility. However, the deductibility reduces the net cost of any given contribution as the marginal tax rate gets higher. Thus, contributions of $1,000 from a taxable income of $100,000 represent a net contribution of 1 per cent in the absence of a tax deduction. With a 62 per cent marginal tax rate, the net cost of the deduction is reduced to $380 or .38 of 1 per cent of the before-tax income. But this $380 would still be almost .7 of 1 per cent of the after-tax income of $54,820. The progressivity of the tax rates reduces the net cost of any deductible contribution as a fraction of after-tax income. The greater the spread between the marginal and the average tax rate, the greater is the reduction in the net cost of a contribution when it is stated as a fraction of after-tax income.

The first set of problems involves the definition of deductible contributions. Over the years, the percentage of income allowed as a deduction has increased to the present level of 20 per cent, with an additional 10 per cent for contributions to educational and religious organizations, hospitals, and many other general charities supported by a governmental unit or the general public, as distinct from private foundations (pars. 1941, 1943). The extra 10 per cent deduction was established in 1954 when the Congress gave statutory approval to two-year charitable trusts (par. 3020(a)(1)). It was pointed out at that time that the two-year trusts permitted a potential donor with investment income to exceed the 20 per cent ceiling by placing part of his capital in trust for two years and thereby having income from it go directly to the qualified beneficiary. As a gesture to reduce this "advantage" of donors who might put capital in trust, the extra 10 per cent deduction was authorized for all donors, but beneficiaries for this extra deduction were first quite closely restricted to schools, hospitals, and churches, which were felt to be in greatest need and least subject to criticism.

There is a somewhat involved relationship between the deductibility of contributions to organizations and the tax status of the organizations themselves. Contributions are deductible only if made to organizations which are themselves tax-exempt. But by no means all tax-exempt organizations qualify as recipients of tax-deductible contributions, as is indicated by a comparison of section 170, which lists the organizations to which contributions are deductible, and section 501, which lists tax-exempt organizations (pars. 1943(a) and 3134). A critical distinction is made between organizations operated exclusively for "religious, charitable, scientific, . . . literary or educational purposes, . . ." in section 170(c)(2)(B), and repeated with a minor addition in section 501(c)(3), and organizations for "the promotion of social welfare" in section 501(c)(4), the latter also receiving tax exemption but not qualifying for tax-deductible contributions. The distinction between education and charity on the one hand and social welfare on the other seems somewhat elusive on first acquaintance. Rulings and litigation over the years have developed a workable line of demarcation, though it is by no means always agreeable to, or even understandable by those who establish an organization which is held to have a social welfare rather than an educational or charitable purpose. Education is conceived very broadly and not confined to schools.

A limitation in section 501(c)(3) provides that an otherwise exempt organization organized and operated exclusively for "religious, charitable . . . or educational purposes," will lose its qualification if a substantial part of its activities involve "carrying on propaganda, or otherwise attempting to influence legislation." The various state and local Leagues of Women Voters have become classic examples of the difficulty of deciding what aspects and how much of a total program constitutes a "substantial part" of activities to influence legislation. Rulings have varied with the emphasis in the activities in the different local organizations from year to year. On the whole, the deductible status has been recognized unless a major campaign was underway to influence specific legislation, since the ultimate purpose of much educational activity is to influence legislation, perhaps even a specific aspect of legislation, as in birth control. But the disqualification of an organization which attempts to influence legislation has been applied to many situations in which one individual attempted to push his favorite cause by setting up a nonprofit corporation or trust to make his expenditures tax-deductible.

When an organization, such as an art museum, gives valuable services to members which are not available to the general public, such as free admission, bulletins, or special exhibitions, the basic membership fee is not deductible as a contribution. Many organizations note on their listing of dues that only the amount above the ordinary membership fee, that is, the difference between an ordinary and a sustaining or contributing membership, is deductible, but others do not make this distinction, perhaps because they regard the benefits of membership as having nominal value. The room for abuse is apparent if one thinks, for example, of an organization to secure and exhibit old motion pictures, with admission limited to members. Most people would regard the memberships as season tickets, as does the Internal Revenue Service, but a good deal of ingenuity has been devoted to attempts to qualify similar groups as education organizations.

Decisions on some of the borderline organizations, whether favorable or unfavorable, may be extremely delicate and have substantial political overtones. A failure to qualify will lead to charges of adverse discrimination, while qualification leads to charges of favoritism by those who may oppose the particular educational or charitable activities. The power is indeed a rather awesome one, the exercise of which is not relished either by career or appointed officials in the Treasury. The lines have become fairly clear, however.

The Internal Revenue Service publishes a list of organizations to which contributions are deductible, with supplements. Organizations receive rulings after application, though a year of operation may be required before a ruling is issued. In spite of the difficulties with borderline cases, most familiar organizations which would be thought of as charitable or educational qualify for deductible contributions.

Certain qualified organizations may lose their exempt status by engaging in specified prohibited transactions, involving loans, payment of unreasonable compensation or rendering services or making sales on a preferential basis to a substantial contributor or a member of his family (par. 3134(d)). Not only does the organization lose its tax-exempt status, but contributions to it thereby are also made nondeductible. This restriction is designed to apply to family charitable trusts and foundations.

One should note also that many exempt organizations, other than churches, are taxable on unrelated business income from operating a business activity or from a purchase and lease-back of property with borrowed funds (pars. 3435-40). The imposition of this tax does not disqualify the deductibility of contributions to the organization.

A second set of problems arises in measuring the value of a contribution which is made in the form of property. The general rule is market value, but this is an invitation to abuse, and several restrictions have been developed, with others probably still to come. A few examples will indicate the problems in tax administration.

First, there may be uncertainty about market value, as in the case of unique art objects. High appraisals are important to donors if they are accepted for tax purposes and donees are not adverse to the publicity attending "valuable" gifts. A rapid appreciation in appraised value after acquisition may make the purchase of an art object for subsequent gift to a museum a profitable investment for a person in a high bracket. Donated real estate may present similar problems. Some universities refuse to specify any figure in acknowledging unique gifts and merely report the sales price when and if the property is sold; by adopting this policy, they at times forego gifts which are made to less fastidious institutions.

In contributions by business concerns, the use of market price as the measure of a gift seems reasonable, as in the case of a computer given to an educational institution. The costs of production in the year of making the gift must, of course, not also be taken as a deduction; or if the article was on hand at the beginning of the year, it must be removed from the opening inventory to avoid a double deduction. But what is the market price of spring hats contributed to a church bazaar held after Easter, or of fresh strawberries which were stocked in excessive amounts and given to a charity supper just before they spoiled?

And what are the possibilities of profit through production with the expectation of giving products away if the cost is only 25 per cent of market price and the corporate tax rate is about 50 per cent? The potential criticism of "profit through gift" has led some companies with high gross margins to limit the claimed market value to a break-even figure when large gifts were made in some emergency relief campaigns.

It has been suggested that the amount of a deductible contribution be limited to cost, but the adverse effect of such a rule on universities, hospitals, and other major charitable organizations which receive much of their capital gifts in appreciated securities has been felt to be much more serious than the remaining tax abuses. Even a limitation to cost would leave room for abuse in the value claimed for the gift of an old television set to a rummage sale, or of a house full of expensive modern furniture to a qualified charity after the fashion in furniture or the mood of the donor has changed.

One favorite tax device combined a present tax benefit from a future gift by contributing an art object with a reserved life interest, or a reserved interest for part of each year. This was blocked in 1964 by the addition of section 170(f), which specifies that a gift of tangible personal property is deductible only when all intervening interests and rights to actual possession or enjoyment have expired.

The law permits deductions for out-of-pocket expenses in connection with services to a qualified organization, as for example, the expenses of attending a meeting of trustees. But no deduction is granted for the value of services or gifts in kind, as for one's time in attending such a meeting, or for the commercial value of one's blood given to a blood bank (par. 1942).

An unlimited charitable deduction is allowed if, in the taxable year and in eight out of the ten preceding taxable years, the amount of charitable contributions plus income tax exceeds 90 per cent of taxable income, subject to certain adjustments to income and limitations on the activities of the qualifying organizations. This section was originally adopted as a special relief measure for one or a very few people who entered religious orders to which they gave all their income. For anyone with an effective tax rate well under 50 percent, only great generosity would permit qualification. But when the top-bracket rate went to 91 per cent with a ceiling overall rate of 86 per cent, a very wealthy person could qualify with gifts from appreciated capital and, once qualified, one had almost a free choice between income tax payments and charitable contributions up to 90 per cent of taxable income. With a reduction in the top marginal rate to 70 per cent, the net cost of qualification again became substantial.

Medical Expenses

The deduction for medical expenses has been changed many times, both as to the amounts and definitions (pars. 1945–46). The purpose is to give relief in hardship cases where medical expenses are unusually large (and with no associated pleasure involved). But trivial abuses are possible by inclusion of ordinary toothpaste-type expenditures, and major abuses may occur if one manages to be told to go to vacation areas for reasons of health.

The allowance of a deduction for the cost of medicines and drugs only to the extent that they exceed 1 per cent of gross income is intended to help exclude casual purchases of drugstore items and should be regarded as a simplification by most taxpayers who would otherwise be tempted to keep records or estimate the amount of trivial purchases. There is also a limitation as to the specific types of items allowable, but the insertion of the quantitative floor removed a temptation to be careless about the exact nature of purchases. The floor of 3 per cent of adjusted gross income, including the excess over 1 per cent for medicines and drugs, is also intended to give the relief only to distress situations, though the figure chosen seems low for acute financial distress. from sickness.

Casualty Losses

The deduction for casualty losses is designed to give tax relief to a person because of damage to his property from an unusual event over which he had no control. By authorizing a deduction in computing taxable income up to the amount of the loss, the law provides that to that extent there is presumed to be no real taxpaying capacity. This is not a common relief provision in the tax laws of other countries; it is purely a reflection of social policy in this country. Problems arise both in defining and in measuring the deductible losses (par. 2205).

The emphasis in definition is on unusual, extraordinary, and "act of God" casualties. Slow deterioration through rot and rust is ordinary and to be expected; it is not a casualty. So are losses of trees from lack of moisture in areas where lack of moisture is a common occurrence. But the line of demarcation is vague when one must distinguish between an unusually severe drought and normal dry spells. Termite damage has been held to be a normal risk of owning wooden structures, but in at least one case the damage was held to be so sudden and improbable that a property owner got the benefit of a casualty loss deduction.

Sometimes both ordinary and extraordinary circumstances combine to create damage to a single article. A rusted-out automobile fender which is also bent in a collision is a good example. When casualty losses were deductible in full, before the addition of a $100 nondeductible floor for each casualty event, the casualty loss deduction placed a great strain on the consciences of taxpayers and of garagemen to decide how to allocate the cost of automobile body repairs between normal wear and tear and a small bump which could qualify as a casualty. The adoption of the $100 floor significantly simplified the record keeping of taxpayers and removed an attractive temptation for petty chiseling.

The deductible loss is measured by the decrease in the value of the property, which may be much less than the cost of restoring property to its previous condition. This is notably true when old trees are lost in hurricanes. The cost of replacing old trees by transplanting is extremely high and typically much greater than the loss in market value of the property on which the trees stood. It is the latter which measures the deductible loss, though the former may be taken as a measure of the latter, as is true when an otherwise good used car has a fender crushed.

It must not be forgotten that the deductible loss is also limited to the adjusted basis of the property for determining loss on a sale. If the basis is trivial, as would be true for example on a painting made and still owned by a prominent artist, the loss in market value from destruction by fire would not be the measure of the casualty loss; it would presumably be limited to the cost of canvas and paint. In all instances, only the net loss is deductible. Insurance proceeds or other forms of reimbursement must be first applied against the loss.

Taxes

The deduction in computing taxable income for other taxes paid during the year has been narrowed at various times. Originally, all taxes, including even the federal income tax on the previous year's income, were deductible in computing the current year's taxable income. (This deduction of the federal income tax itself lasted only three years after 1913. Such a deduction raised interesting possibilities; at a 100 per cent tax rate, which might be expected to satisfy any political pressure for high rates, the effective rate would approach 50 per cent for a person with a steady income. The income tax is deductible in computing taxable income in Denmark and Belgium. But to get an effective rate of over 50 per cent, the statutory rate in Denmark was pushed above 100 per cent, with catastrophic results for anyone in the first year that his income went into that bracket.)

Subsequently, all federal taxes were made nondeductible except as business or investment costs, a change vigorously protested at the time but one which simplified record keeping and made unnecessary rough estimates of amounts paid under the various excise taxes (par. 1910–11). Thereafter, in 1964, the deduction for state and local taxes was limited to income, property, general sales and gasoline taxes, eliminating such taxes as those on drivers' licenses and miscellaneous excise and sales taxes (par. 1912). To eliminate the need for records on general sales taxes, the Internal Revenue Service provides guidelines showing acceptable amounts of deductions for families of various sizes at various income levels in different states (pars. 20, 21, 1917).

The definition of deductible taxes authorized in the law is explicit, and there are few if any uncertain areas similar to those arising in charitable contributions and casualty losses. The only real complication arises in allocating property taxes, assessed and paid on an annual basis, between a buyer and a seller of real estate (par. 1920). The rules as to when a tax becomes due depends on state law, and the appropriate allocations are familiar to tax and real estate specialists in each jurisdiction.

Interest

The deduction for interest is allowed in computing individual taxable income as well as in determining net business income (par. 1901). Thus, it is not important to determine whether indebtedness is incurred for personal or business purposes so long as it is a bona fide debt of the taxpayer (pars. 1902–03). If interest were deductible only when a debt arose in connection with a business or investment, there would be difficult problems of definition and an invitation to convert personal debt into ostensible business debt.

The principal area of abuse in interest deductions has occurred in some highly unusual insurance or annuity policies issued by a few insurance companies. In the extreme cases, after a small initial cash payment, all subsequent premiums were borrowed from the insurance company itself, along with an amount sufficient to pay current interest on the indebtedness, giving rise to a current deductible expense with a saving in taxes and a net increase in one's after-tax income. The premiums and loans were tied to the increase in cash surrender value. When one took account of the present value of the tax saving, it actually paid to borrow at a higher interest rate than that used by the insurance company in its actuarial calculations in building up the policy reserves. Most of the exceptions to the general rule for deductibility of interest are related to insurance policies (par. 1901). They represent successive amendments to the law which were regarded as necessary to prevent the tax law and insurance from being brought into disrepute by artificial "interest" deductions.

The other major exception is for interest on debts incurred to carry tax-exempt bonds. A deduction of interest against other taxable income, with the borrowed funds used to secure tax-exempt income, would produce a high tax leverage in favor of such investments. Though the disallowance is sound in principle, the enforcement is difficult except in extreme cases because if one has other assets against which to borrow, it is difficult to argue convincingly that a particular loan provides funds for a particular use.

The only really complicated aspect of the calculation of an interest deduction arises from installment sales in which no specific interest factor is apparent (par. 1905). A formula was added to the law in 1954 to permit the calculation of an assumed interest expense. This is an extreme example of a deduction for a purely personal expense. It is questionable whether the improvement in equity justifies the additional complication in the law.

Combined Effect of Deduction for Taxes and Interest on Home Ownership

Since interest and real estate taxes constitute a substantial part of the cost of home ownership, the fact that both are deductible makes ownership substantially better than renting from a tax standpoint. The higher the marginal tax rate, the greater the advantage of the deduction. A person renting a home or apartment must pay for it from after-tax income; the interest and real estate taxes paid by the owner which are included in the rent cannot be passed through to the tenant.

The tax advantages of ownership are quite properly emphasized by real estate agents and the developers of cooperative apartments and condominiums, and have doubtless been a significant factor in inducing people to switch from the status of tenants to owner. Some critics of the present law regard the discrimination in favor of owners as so unfair that they propose that the presumed rental value, or some other measure of annual value, of owner-occupied homes be regarded as imputed income and be included in computing taxable income. The administrative problem of determining rental value for distinctive properties is formidable, and the probable reaction of taxpayers has made this change in the law unlikely. For a very long period, the British income tax law did indeed include a schedule for such imputed income, but in recommending its repeal the Chancellor of the Exchequer noted that while most taxes were paid with resignation that part was paid with rage.

An alternative way of restoring equality of treatment would be to disallow a deduction in real estate taxes and mortgage interest on owner-occupied dwellings. This would be much simpler administratively. It would still leave a tax advantage to the home owner who had purchased for cash or had built up a large equity because the income-in-kind from the use of capital invested in a house still would be nontaxable. Others, including the author, argue that encouragement of home ownership is desirable for various reasons as a matter of public policy and, since the discrimination works in the right direction, the inequity is not great enough to justify additional tax complications.

4

Business

Expenses and Accounting Rules

Questions about the deductibility of business expenses in computing taxable income turn around the two words "What" and "When". In general, the same sort of expenses and costs are allowed in computing taxable business income as are required for a proper measurement of income for the use of management and for public reports. But since accounting is not an exact science there is room for differences of opinion as to whether some items should be treated as capital outlays or current expenses, and as to how rapidly other items should be written off. Where there is room for judgment, one can predict the probable attitude of the various parties involved on the basis of their interests and traditions.

Taxpayers naturally want to take deductions as soon as possible and postpone the realization of income. Unless they anticipate a change in tax rates, a dollar saved in taxes is worth more this year than next, a fact which is recognized even by those who have never heard of the concept of present value. But from the standpoint of the Treasury, the disposition is to postpone the allowance of the deduction and to hasten the realization of income. Revenue in the current year is more important than revenue in a later year, and perhaps the taxpayer, individual or corporate, will not be around to pay taxes in the later year.

In contrast to these inclinations for tax purposes, a general disposition in business is to want the current situation to be at least not unfavorable; growth is important but so is the present. This means that where there is room for discretion, recognition of costs and expenses may be postponed and realization of income speeded up. Professional accountants, on the other hand, in auditing and certifying business reports to the public, resist these tendencies because conservatism has traditionally meant that if there is a doubt the current net income should not be overstated. For public reports, accountants prefer an earlier recognition of expenses, and a later recognition of income items.

These contradictory desires and inclinations pervade virtually all aspects of income determination. In brief, businessmen have different points of view regarding taxable income and income for public reports; within limits, they prefer to minimize the former and maximize the latter. But the outside agency in each case has the contrary approach; tax officials prefer to maximize current income at the expense of future income, while public accountants prefer to minimize the former even if this means maximizing the latter.

There is no general requirement under the Internal Revenue Code that tax and book deductions or income items must coincide. In many of the continental European countries, no tax deduction is allowable for an item that has not been currently, or previously, charged as an expense on a company's own accounting records. Section 446 appears to require conformity between tax and book accounting with the statement that "taxable income shall be computed under the method of accounting on the basis of which a taxpaper regularly computes his income in keeping his books" (par. 2701). But taxpayers have not been able to use this section to enforce acceptance of their own methods when it runs counter to specific statutory provisions or any of the several rules which have been adopted by the Internal Revenue Service and upheld by the courts. Least of all, it is not effective in sustaining taxpayers' claims on the speed of depreciation or amortization or the need for certain reserves for estimated expenses or the size of other reserves even though they are accepted in principle, such as those for bad debts.

This chapter covers the tax treatment of various expenses which are not treated elsewhere as part of a general discussion of some aspects of business. Thus, depreciation, the distinction between repairs and capital expenditures, and rent are all considered in the chapter on the acquisition, use, and disposition of capital assets. Deductions for salaries, entertainment and travel expense, and contributions to pension funds are covered in the chapter on tax factors in compensation, and the special deductions for farmers and the extractive industries are described in sections or chapters devoted to these activities. The tax rules for interest and taxes, which are deductible whether incurred for business or personal reasons, are discussed in the chapter on personal exemptions and deductions. The remaining business deductions considered here constitute a somewhat miscellaneous group.

The first section of the chapter is devoted to expenses incurred by individuals in their personal or professional activities in seeking income.

The second section covers business expenses, which are equally relevant whether the business is incorporated or unincorporated. Business expenses relevant only to corporations are discussed in the chapter on the taxation of corporations. A third section covers various aspects of accounting, including alternative methods, inventories, and changes in methods. The comments throughout this chapter are relatively brief. The tax rules typically are identical or very close to familiar accounting rules. Thus, there is little need to explain the "why" of this part of the tax law. And since they exert little influence on major business practices and policies, the "so what" aspect of the discussion, which runs through most of the book, can also be covered briefly.

PROFESSIONAL, BUSINESS, AND INVESTMENT EXPENSES OF INDIVIDUALS

Though many professional, business, and investment expenses of individuals are allowed as tax deductions, there is a constant temptation to try to convert an outlay for personal enjoyment into a professional or investment expense (par. 1804). Travel expense to inspect and confer with the manager of a large ranch is deductible, but a long trip to a favorite mountain resort area is not made deductible by ownership of a piece of land which produces a few tons of hay in a good year (par. 1803). A teacher's expenses, including travel expenses, for summer courses which maintain or improve one's skills are deductible, but how long must a "course" held in Europe be to justify the round-trip travel which gets one to the course and incidentally to a place where one spends the rest of a summer vacation (par. 1831). These and similar situations present broad areas of uncertainty rather than a narrow range of borderline cases.

For many years, the educational expenses of teachers were deductible only if the courses were required by a school board or other employer to retain a job or to secure normal in-grade pay raises. But since the policies of school boards differed greatly on these requirements, teachers who took courses as a matter of choice to maintain their standing with teachers under other jurisdictions felt that the tax law discriminated against them. After extensive conferences with the various groups concerned, the regulations were amended in 1958 and again in 1967 to include expenses to "maintain or improve skills required by the taxpayer in his employment or other trade or business" as well as to meet the "express requirements of the individual's employer" (reg. 1–162–5(a)(1)–(2)). It was recognized that this discriminated in favor of a person who was established in a profession and therefore was already in a position to earn a professional income, as compared with a taxpayer who was still in the process of qualifying and hence had less income and was even more in need of relief. But this could not be provided unless the basic law was changed to make all educational expenses deductible.

The liberalization in 1958 by an amendment to the regulations produced more equal tax treatment between employees and self-employed people, and between various categories of the latter, but it emphasized the contrast between those who incurred educational expenses to maintain or improve a skill in an existing activity and those who took courses to qualify for a higher job. Neither the expenses of an undergraduate taking courses to secure a teacher's certificate nor those of a principal taking graduate work to qualify for a position as superintendent are deductible.

One should always remember three key words—"ordinary," "necessary," and "directly"—which are used in section 162 of the tax law authorizing deductions for both business expenses and those nonbusiness expenses related to self-employment or investment activities. Each of the three words has been a subject for interpretation in many litigated cases. Typically, the interpretation has been a fairly strict one, though an advertising expense does not become nondeductible because the advertisement is extraordinary, nor does an investment counsel's fee become nondeductible because, far from being "necessary" to earn income, it actually led to a loss even greater than that which would have been secured by a random selection of securities.

Sometimes the distinctions seem overly refined. Legal expenses are deductible if connected with the receipt of income or income taxes, but not if they are connected with capital (pars. 1803, 1824). Fees for the preparation of a will, for example, are not deductible.

Rent for an office is deductible for a professional man (par. 1826). If part of a rented residence is used for some or all of one's professional activities, a pro rata part of the rent is deductible, as is a part of the cost of maintaining a residence which one owns and occupies. But a professor's claim for a deduction of one-quarter of his residence expense with the assertion of a need for an upstairs study and a downstairs study in his eight-room house to carry out his duties as a professor will presumably be as summarily and contemptuously rejected by the university authorities from whom he asks for certification of need as by the tax auditors who review his tax return. However, the expense of one study in which books are written and from which consulting work is done is often regarded as an acceptable deduction.

The deduction for child care was adopted in 1954 in response to numerous representations on behalf of working wives and widows (par. 1833). The Congressional discussions of the proposal revealed a great range of opinion as to the desirable activities of wives and mothers. The law has since been liberalized in various respects. No one would assert that all the distinctions are logical; they represent a general desire to give relief in true hardship cases where a widow has to work and to do so must pay for the care of a child and, beyond that, legislative compromises on situations between hardship and those where a wife works to "buy a fur coat"—to repeat a favorite phrase used by those who were unsympathetic to any but the most limited deductions.

An individual may take a deduction for losses on bad debts, regardless of whether the debt was incurred for business or nonbusiness purposes (pars. 2301–03). However, if the debt was incurred for nonbusiness purposes, the loss on it is treated as a short-term capital loss (par. 2304). By placing the loss in this category, the law makes the deduction much less significant than casualty losses or the other nonbusiness itemized deductions allowed individuals in computing their taxable incomes, since a capital loss is useful only in reducing capital gains and, up to the $1,000 annual maximum, as a loss to be deducted against ordinary income. A loss on a loan is not disqualified merely because it is made to a relative, but the bona fide character must be solidly established (par. 2305). The temptation to seek a two-fold tax gimmick through a bad "loan" is obvious. The initial transfer of funds as a "loan" would avoid the gift tax, and the later "loss" would create a short-term capital loss; a maneuver which adds a reduction in tax on top of an escape from a tax is indeed an attractive shenanigan. To prevent abuse, the debt must be genuinely worthless; forgiveness of a debt does not establish a loss (par. 2311). The general rules on bad debt losses are discussed in the next section of the chapter, along with other business expenses.

OPERATING AND BUSINESS EXPENSES

The general requirement that expenses to be deductible must be ordinary, necessary, and directly related to the business has already been noted, but repetition is justified to make these three requirements a part of one's thinking. On the whole, outlays which would be regarded as business expenses for public reports are acceptable for tax purposes (par. 1802). Exceptions include bribes or fines, and expenditures where the benefit is remote, such as payments to equip a village baseball team, as distinct from the cost of outfitting a team to represent the company itself.

In addition to the distinction between capital expenditures and current expenses on buildings and machinery discussed elsewhere, the same distinction must be made on such matters as the costs of an investigation of a new business, which must be capitalized (par. 1805, cf. 1825). The costs of acquiring an existing trademark is also a capital expenditure but, under section 177, the expenses of protecting or expanding a trademark, or acquiring one other than by purchase of an existing one, may at the taxpayer's option be amortized over a five-year period.

The fact that a business is illegal does not make the income from it nontaxable. A corollary of the taxability of income of the illegal business is a deduction for ordinary and necessary expenses, though not for expenses which are themselves illegal (par. 1808). The deduction is allowable only against the income from the expenses of the illegal business; an excess of expenditures cannot be charged against other income as is permitted for other business activities.

The option to deduct research and experimental expenses currently or over a period of five years or more was added to the law in 1954 to encourage such outlays in the interests of economic growth and as a relief to small business (par. 1841). Prior to that time, there had been frequent instances in which taxpayers had been required to capitalize such expenditures. Small companies especially were likely to be subject to this requirement because their research activity might be confined to a single identifiable product or process for which the outlays could be deemed to be a capital investment. Large companies whose research laboratories were active on many things might be permitted to take the total expense as a current one.

The intent of Congress and the Treasury was to remove any tax barrier to expenditures in research and experimental work. The option for current deduction was the most favorable treatment which could be given to a profitable company, short of an outright subsidy. The further option to treat the outlays as deferred expenses over a period of five years or more was designed to let a company which was not currently profitable select whatever period it chose in which to take the deduction; it presumably would select a period in which the combination of profitability and expected effective tax rates would make the deduction most beneficial. The authority to use these same options for expenditures incurred for this purpose through a commercial or tax-exempt research organization was specifically directed to small business which may not have its own research facilities and hence has to get its work done by contract.

The options for treatment as current deduction or deferred expenses do not extend to the equipment or buildings used for research. With the removal of the possibility of abuse through depreciation write-offs against ordinary income with subsequent sale at capital gains rates in 1962, it might be reasonable to lend further encouragement to research by giving this liberal tax treatment to the outlays for a property used in research. There would still be a problem if equipment originally used in research, after being expensed or written off, were converted to regular production activities, but the opportunities for such conversion do not seem great and adjustments would be no more difficult to enforce than those required when an investment credit turns out to be excessive because property is disposed of sooner than had been expected (par. 2019(e)).

It has also been proposed that a deduction be allowed for some amount in excess of the actual outlay on research; a deduction of 150 per cent of the expenditure against a tax rate of 50 per cent would reduce the net cost of research to 25 cents on the dollar. Canada gave this sort of inducement to research outlays for some years, but the United States tax law has thus far not been used to give subsidies in this way. Additional depreciation allowances have also been proposed for certain real estate investments in slum areas.

Bad debt deductions generally follow the rules used in ordinary business accounting (par. 2301). Both direct charge-offs and the use of a bad debt reserve are authorized (pars. 2303, 2308). The addition to a reserve is limited to an amount which is reasonable on the basis of experience. Extreme conservatism, which may be considered good business practice, is not permitted for tax purposes. But a deduction for partial worthlessness is allowed (par. 2303(a)). And a write-down required by bank examiners is accepted for tax purposes (par. 2310(b)).

Recoveries of bad debts previously charged off must be either credited to income or to the bad debt reserve, depending on the method used (par. 2309). A credit to the reserve, of course, has the effect of reducing the deduction for regular additions to the reserve, either in the year of the recovery or subsequently. But a rather complicated rule provides that a recovery of a bad debt previously charged off directly need be included in income only to the extent that the charge-off actually reduced taxes (par. 2309(b)). This tax benefit rule was established in litigation and subsequently was incorporated in section 111 of the law. The complications arise from the need to trace the effect of the original deduction through loss carrybacks and carryovers. This relief is seldom applicable, but when it does apply can be important.

The distinction between business and nonbusiness bad debts is important to individuals carrying on a trade or business, but is seldom relevant for corporations (pars. 2304–05). Note, however, that a loss on worthless bonds is treated as a capital loss for all taxpayers, individual or corporate, except banks and in some instances parent corporations holding bonds of certain subsidiaries (par. 2310).

Losses are generally deductible in computing taxable income so long as they arise in connection with a trade or business or from transactions entered into for profit (pars. 2200–3). Since corporations typically are created and operated to carry on a trade or business or to make a profit, virtually all of their losses qualify as deductible. But for an individual, there is a temptation to allege that a purely personal transaction is one on which there was an intention to make a profit. For example, the owner of a house with expensive features who discovers when he comes to sell it that no one else will pay enough to cover his costs would like to be able to rent it, or try to rent it, and then claim a loss on its sale. The law was amended to provide specifically that the basis against which the loss could be calculated cannot exceed the value at the time a residence is converted to use as a rental property; original cost is irrelevant (par. 2204).

Various types of losses with special rules, such as casualty losses, losses on investments in stocks and bonds, and losses on "hobby" businesses, are discussed in other sections.

To reduce the tax penalties against business activities which show losses in some years, the tax law permits a net operating loss arising from a trade, business, or profession to be carried back three years and forward for five years. In the absence of such an allowance, the total tax over a period of years might exceed the total net income. During some of the depression years of the 1930's, no carrybacks or carryforwards were allowed, and even at the corporate tax rates of less than 20 per cent then applicable, the net effect in some instances was for a tax to be paid though over a period of several years a business operated at net loss. The carryback and carryforward provisions complicate the tax law, but they exist purely as relief measures.

The carryforward is especially important to new companies for which, by definition, a carryback is meaningless. Since losses in early years are likely to occur in new ventures, if a carryforward were not permitted income taxes would impede the restoration of the original investment after the business became profitable. But for an established company, the carryback is more important because it provides funds immediately—a feature of the carryback which is also attractive as a part of a compensatory fiscal policy. The Treasury and the Congress have been sympathetic to the extension of the time periods for carrybacks and carry-forwards whenever it became apparent that the existing intervals were inadequate for any substantial group of taxpayers. The carryback has thus been lengthened from one to three years, and the carryforward from five to seven years for certain industries and to ten years for losses from expropriations.

For individuals, an operating loss is significant not only as a carry-back or carryforward, but as a deduction against other income. This result arises from the fact that individuals are taxed on their net incomes from all sources; only capital losses have to be segregated. This feature of the law makes it attractive to operate a new venture in which only losses are expected as a proprietorship or partnership, or as a subchapter S corporation, until it becomes profitable. The carryback and carryfor-ward is an additional benefit (par. 2241).

A series of adjustments is necessary to convert the net loss shown on a tax return into a real measure of economic loss. The adjustments appropriate to individuals and corporations differ somewhat, on account of the distinctive features involved in the computations of their net tax-able incomes (pars. 2242, 3217). For example, individuals are allowed a deduction of one-half of net long-term capital gains in computing taxable income, but this is a means to secure a lower rate of tax on such gains. To get a proper measure of the real results of a year's operations, which should reasonably be carried back or forward, the total net gain should be taken into account; this is done by adding back the half of the gain previously deducted. For corporations, the deductions for intercorporate dividends are designed to give a low effective tax rate on such dividends; it also must be added back to get a reasonable measure of the net result of a year's operations.

Some adjustments previously required have been eliminated in the interests of simplicity by successive amendments to the law. A perfec-tionist approach to convert loss in terms of taxable income into an accurate measure of economic loss would become a rather elaborate cal-culation. Convenience has taken precedence over refinement.

For both individuals and corporations, a net operating loss must be applied to the earliest open year under the loss carryback and then successively to subsequent years (pars. 2242(b), 3218–19). This is the most favorable treatment possible to assure the full utilization of a loss carryback and carryover. It also prevents the offset from being used at the taxpayer's option against income subject to an unusually high tax rate, which might be advantageous for an individual.

ACCOUNTING METHODS

The tax law recognizes most of the accepted general methods of accounting (par. 2701). Either the cash or accrual method may be used, though the accrual method must be used for businesses operating with inventories of goods for sale (pars. 2702–03). A general provision of the law, section 446, provides that the method must clearly reflect income for the taxpayer, and section 482 gives authority to reallocate income and deduction items among taxpayers controlled by the same interests. As noted at the beginning of this chapter, the requirement that taxable income shall be computed under the method of accounting used by a taxpayer for his own books does not mean that all entries made on the books will prevail in determining taxable income.

In some instances, it is necessary to prescribe specific rules to prevent avoidance of tax. The concept of constructive receipt, for example, is necessary to prevent postponement of tax by a taxpayer on a cash basis who might otherwise neglect to deposit his bond coupons or his salary checks (par. 2702(c)). Specific rules have been established as to when various items of income must be reported (par. 2715). In some instances, these are necessary to prevent unreasonable postponement of tax, as with the unclipped coupons just referred to. But in other instances the rule seems a harsh one, as in the requirement that most prepaid income is taxable when received, even for taxpayers on an accrual basis (par. 2715(e)). A payment for the last as well as for the first year's rent when a long-term lease is signed would be an example. This position is apparently based on a not too defensible pragmatic ground rather than on any theory of income determination. If the income is not taxed when it is received, the taxpayer may not be there to pay the tax when it later accrues. Some taxpayers have secured special statutory relief from this general rule for particular forms of prepaid income, such as prepaid subscriptions or membership dues (par. 2715(f)).

Repayments of amounts previously reported as income can lead to hardship if the income was taxed at a high rate and a large repayment occurred in a year when income was relatively low, or when the repayment wiped out the other income. Special relief is granted if the repayments exceed $3,000, a figure selected as sufficiently large to include any situations in which there would be any appreciable tax advantage from an adjustment. This is another complication in the law, but it is there to be used or disregarded at the taxpayer's option (par. 2715(o)).

A general relief provision was added to the law in 1964 to permit income averaging over a five-year period (par. 2717). To preclude averaging for minor revisions in tax liabilities, the averaging provision can be used only if the averagable income for a tax year exceeds $3,000 and the adjusted taxable income is more than one-third higher than the average income for the four preceding years. Several adjustments must be made in the taxable income of all the years involved though, except for those involving long-term capital gains, they will seldom be applicable, dealing as they do with such items as net wagering income and income from gifts and inherited property. The purpose of the adjustments is to deny the benefits of averaging to fluctuations arising from property acquired by gift or inheritance (which may be thought of as a windfall and hence not in need of relief) or from wagering (perhaps in the same windfall category or at least not worthy of special treatment), or capital gains (which already have the benefit of a lower rate of tax).

The basic idea of averaging is appealing on grounds of equity. Those concerned with tax policy have always been confronted with a difficult choice between fairness and simplicity. The five-year averaging provision is relatively simple, at least in comparison to some of those proposed in public finance literature. But some of the adjustments seem overly refined and, though seldom applicable, must make the procedure seem unduly formidable to one about to embark on the calculations.

The tax law has accepted several methods of postponing the recognition of gain when payments on sales are received in installments or on a deferred basis. The simplest procedure is the regular installment sale for tangible personal property. The tax law permits the profit to be taken into account pro rata as the installment payments are made (par. 2801). Of course, if notes are received for any balance due and are then transferred to a finance company, the profit is immediately recognized; since cash is available, there would be no reason to postpone a tax.

The installment method, involving a pro rata recognition of profit, is also available for sales of real property and casual sales of personal property for more than $1,000, provided that the payment in the year of sale does not exceed 30 per cent of the selling price (par. 2812). The use of this method is subject to precise rules and definitions, which require care in drafting a contract. Payments on the principal of a mortgage accepted by the seller are treated as installment payments. Even if the payments in the year of sale exceed 30 per cent of the selling price, it is possible to postpone recognition of some of the profit if the fair market value of the obligations of the buyer are less than their face value (par. 2813).

In all situations involving postponement of recognition of profit and tax, specific rules are provided to cover the tax significance of repossessions of property (pars. 2804, 2821, 2823).

Special rules also fix the time when various deductions may be taken for tax purposes (par. 2721). The most significant limitation is the denial of deductions for amounts credited to reserves for future liabilities (par. 2721(f)). The denial of such a deduction is one of the major reasons for differences between taxable and book income, and it has been emphatically criticized by various business and professional groups. For business purposes, for example, it is reasonable and indeed desirable to set up a reserve to meet the costs of repairs on products sold under guarantees.

In 1954, two new sections were added to the law to permit deductions for estimated losses and expenses, and to postpone the recognition of prepaid income. The original estimate of the revenue loss in the transition year, when both actual outlays and an estimate for future outlays could be deducted, was $50 million. However, so many new forms of reserves for future expenses were suddenly developed, including reserves for overhaul of airplane engines and relining of blast furnaces, that the estimate of the probable revenue loss rose to $1 billion, with a prospect of almost endless litigation. The sections were repealed, with the repeal in process before the date when tax returns were due in 1955.

It was contemplated at the time that a revised and strictly limited allowance would be adopted for such reserves as those for liabilities for repairs on products sold, with a further restriction to prevent a full double deduction in the transition year. But some of the most vigorous protagonists for what had been thought of as a reform to bring the tax law into closer conformity with business accounting concepts said that if there were to be no immediate double deduction, they really did not care to pursue the matter. At that point, both the Treasury and the Congress lost interest in the subject. Hopefully, it may be revived again.

An individual on a cash basis owning a corporation on an accrual basis has an obvious opportunity to get the best of both tax worlds by having the corporation take a deduction for an accrued liability to himself, for salary or royalty payments, while neglecting to collect the money and avoiding any drawing of a check or other act which would make the income taxable to him through the concept of constructive receipt. The law accordingly denies a deduction when a debtor on an accrual basis does not actually make payment to a related creditor on a cash basis within two and a half months after the close of the debtor's tax year (par. 2723).

The tax law for many years recognized only the first-in-first-out (fifo) method of inventory accounting (pars. 2600–03). In 1937, the use of the last-in-first-out (lifo) was authorized, subject to the very stringent constraint that if lifo was used for tax purposes, fifo could not be used for any purposes, including even financial statements prepared for creditors. At that time, the lifo method was considered desirable to smooth out cyclical fluctuations in profits arising from cyclical price changes even when the quantity of goods in inventory was constant.

The prohibition against the use of fifo calculations for other purposes was relaxed in 1939, just in time to permit a shift to lifo accounting for tax purposes at the start of the permanent rise in most prices under the inflation of World War II and subsequent years (par. 2603(f)). In the absence of this optional method of valuing inventories, the cash squeeze on companies with large and rapidly appreciating inventories would have been serious. The lifo method ignores the paper profits which are brought into existence by the fifo method when, even with a constant amount of inventory, each year's ending inventory is higher than the beginning inventory, with a consequent artificial reduction in cost of goods sold and increase in profits. The availability of the lifo method was extended, after litigation by taxpayers, to nonhomogeneous inventories on the so-called "dollar value" method.

The tax law has become quite broad in the variety of inventory methods permitted (pars. 2604, 2607). However, the base stock method, which is in many respects similar to the lifo method, is not permitted, nor are the deductions for expected changes in value of the sort which are authorized in several continental European countries. It has been proposed that the lifo method be combined with cost or market value evaluation, instead of being based entirely on cost, but both the Treasury and the Congress rejected the idea as being unduly liberal and inconsistent.

The rules governing a change in an accounting method seem and are quite complex (pars. 2704–06). They can best be understood if one realizes that a change in method may involve a double deduction or a failure to get a deduction, or a double inclusion of an income item or complete escape of an income item. For example, on a shift from a cash to an accrual method, accrued but uncollected income items would escape taxation since the opening statement on the new method would show them as already accrued while for the last statement on the cash method they were not collected.

To prevent double deductions or escape of income taxes, the Treasury for many years was reluctant to force a change in accounting methods, even after the existing method was clearly wrong, as was the continued use of the cash method after a taxpayer was carrying inventories. The situation had become intolerable by 1954, and a special provision was adopted as part of the new Code that year.

As a result of extensive hearings and deliberations in the Congressional committees, various transition rules were established, including a waiver of adjustments for items arising prior to 1954 if the change is initiated by the Internal Revenue Service. With the passage of time, the pre-1954 items have become of less practical significance and the existing transition rules are designed to include all deductions and income items once and only once, but with an opportunity to spread the impact over more than one year.

5

Gains and Losses
on Sales and Exchanges—
Capital Gains

The tax statutes have consistently taken full advantage of the all-inclusive concept of income authorized under the Sixteenth Amendment to the Constitution. Income is defined in section 61 of the Internal Revenue Code as: "All income from whatever source derived, including (but not limited to) the following items:" among which are included "gains from dealings in property."

Exchanges as well as sales of property can be a source of income. Though one might not immediately think of an exchange of one item of property for another as giving rise to a taxable gain if no prices are set and no cash is involved, a moment's reflection indicates that if gain were not recognized on exchanges there would be a premium on barter transactions (par. 1602). Intermediaries and brokers would go to great length to work out swaps between owners of various items of property, and by exchanges of property one could realize the benefits of an indefinite succession of good investments or purchases of property with an indefinite postponement of tax. As long as there is a tax on the gains from sales of property, a tax on the gains from exchanges of property is necessary to prevent widespread avoidance of the tax (pars. 1401–02). The law provides, however, that the tax on gains arising from certain forms of exchanges may be postponed, in ways which are described below.

Along with the recognition of gain on sales and exchanges of property, the tax law provides for a recognition of losses in an almost comparable fashion. But the symmetry is not complete because losses generally are recognized only when they occur in a trade or business or from a transaction entered into for profit. This limitation may seem harsh, but again it is apparent that a complete recognition of losses for tax purposes would mean that much personal consumption could be charged as a deduction in computing taxable income. The loss on a personal automobile, refrigerator, or residence reflects the use that the owner has made of it since purchase; it is an expenditure on consumption spread over time. There is no more reason to allow the loss as a deduction in computing taxable income than there would be to allow the rental paid for similar items.

Gain and loss generally are calculated as the difference between the fair market value of what is received and the basis of what is sold or given up on an exchange (par. 1401). The tax basis of property ordinarily is original cost plus any additional investments or outlays on it which are not treated as current expenses and less any sums realized from it other than income, and any charges to income made because of it, such as depreciation (pars. 1501–02). This concept of tax basis is substantially similar to the accounting concept of book basis. It is simply what a taxpayer has "tied up" in a piece of property, taking account of original cost and any subsequent events, including write-off of the property, which involve additions to or partial recoupments or recoveries of the investment on the property.

It must be emphasized that the tax basis is not necessarily the same as the basis on a company's books. The cost of an improvement which was treated as an expense on the books may have had to be capitalized for tax purposes because it increased the value and had a long life, or the depreciation taken on the books may have been different from that allowed for tax purposes. The concepts are the same, but not necessarily the amounts.

If cash is received on a sale, there is no problem in fixing its value; if other property is received, the determination of its fair market value may involve controversy and, in the last analysis, litigation (pars. 1503–04). Only in rare instances is it impossible to get some determination of a fair market value; where it is impossible, gain is not recognized and the basis of the old property carries over and becomes the basis of the new property. Thus recognition of gain or loss is postponed.

When property is received in a taxable exchange, its fair market becomes its basis. This is the value against which the taxable gain or loss was calculated on the old property, and it is, in effect, the cost to the new owner.

The tax law establishes special rules for basis of property acquired in a few particular ways, some of which are discussed in more detail in subsequent chapters concerning major areas of business decision. The principal exceptions are on property acquired from a deceased person, in which case the property takes the value at date of death, or one year after death if the estate tax is calculated on values at that time (par. 1508). In contrast to this treatment for inherited property, the basis for computing gain for all gifts made after 1920 is the basis to the donor; the donee for purposes of determining gain is put into the position of the donor, but with an upward adjustment for any gift tax paid under an amendment to the law in 1958 (par. 1510–11). If the market value at the time of the gift is less than the basis to the donor, this market value becomes the basis to the donee for computing loss. A gain cannot escape taxation, but some losses may not give a tax benefit to anyone. As an historical relic, any appreciation in value up to March 1, 1913, the date when the first income tax became effective, is considered as not subject to tax and hence the basis for calculating gain is cost or value at that date (par. 1507).

In all the rules concerning both gains and losses and the tax basis of property, adjustments are made for the liabilities assumed or associated with properties sold or exchanged (pars. 1512(f), 1409). On first acquaintance, the reasons for these rules may not be apparent. But when one is relieved of a debt by passing it on to someone else, there is a gain comparable to the receipt of money with which to pay the debt. And the debt may be incurred just before a sale or exchange, with money received in that way. When this indirect form of realization through borrowing against property is once fully understood, the rules prescribing the effects of liabilities on gains and losses on sales and exchanges and on the tax basis of property will be seen to be not only reasonable but necessary.

One may, in fact, realize disposable funds on any property, including a greatly appreciated asset, by borrowing against it, with no tax liability for this sort of realization. The tax law makes no attempt to tax currently this sort of indirect realization when no sale or exchange is involved. Recognition of the assumption of the liability as the equivalent of cash at the time of even a tax-free exchange provides for ultimate taxation of the amounts previously realized indirectly (par. 1409).

NONTAXABLE SALES AND EXCHANGES

The tax law permits several forms of exchange of properties to be made without immediate recognition of tax; some of these are discussed in more detail in subsequent chapters on aspects of business to which they are relevant. In general, the nontaxable exchanges are either those in which the exchange is for property which is only nominally different, as stock for stock in the same corporation, or those in which no free funds arise from the exchange and where the imposition of a tax would put a financial squeeze on a continuing business activity. Examples of the latter are transfers of property to a corporation controlled by the transferors, exchanges of stock and securities in certain precisely defined corporate reorganizations, and exchanges of property held for productive use in a trade or business (pars. 1403–06, 3304).

A tax-free exchange is intended to postpone tax until some subsequent transaction or event in which funds become available. There is no intent to forgive tax. The postponement is accomplished by requiring all parties to keep the old tax basis of property and compute subsequent gains or losses on the new property against this old basis of the previously held property.

Principal Residence

A special rule is applied in the sale of a person's principal residence (par. 1415). Consistent with the concept of postponing tax when no free funds arise from a transaction, there is no recognition of gain on the sale of one's principal residence to the extent that an equal or greater amount is spent to buy another principal residence within a period beginning twelve months before and ending twelve months after the sale. If a new residence is built, the period following sale is extended to eighteen months. To the extent that the cost of the new residence falls short of the sale price of the old residence, any gain is recognized. The basis of the new residence takes the tax basis of the old, with various adjustments to assure that tax is postponed and not forgiven (par. 1519). Any number of these tax-free sales and purchases may be made, so long as each successive purchase is used as a person's principal residence. The basis to the estate or heirs of whatever residence is held at death, of course, becomes the value at date of each; if one continues to own a residence until death, the tax on previous gains is forgiven.

In recognition of the fact that older people often give up a house and move into an apartment and need the income from all of the proceeds of the sale of the residence to pay the rent on the apartment, any person 65 or over may elect to exclude the gain on a residence occupied for at least five out of the preceding eight years. However, gain may be excluded only if the sale price is $20,000 or less; if the sale price is greater, the fraction of the gain which can be excluded is determined by the ratio which $20,000 bears to the sale price (par. 1415(j)). This low ceiling figure seems rather harsh since the income from $20,000 would provide only very modest rental quarters indeed and fall far short of luxury standards. But the exclusion of gain in this instance is an absolute one; the tax basis of the investment securities acquired from the proceeds of sale do not have to be reduced by the amount of gain excluded. And if another principal residence is purchased by a taxpaper over 65, the limited exclusion of gain is still made absolute; taxpayers 65 or over do not reduce the basis of the next residence by the amount of gain which they can exclude (par. 1519).

Involuntary Conversions

A final set of circumstances under which gain is not recognized is described under the general term of involuntary conversions, the most self-evident example of which would be the proceeds of a fire insurance policy (pars. 1410–14). Though cash is immediately in hand, it is not freely available if one proposes to replace the destroyed property with similar property of equal value. Thus, to the extent that the amounts received are used for replacement of similar property within prescribed periods, the gain is not recognized regardless of the fact that the sum received exceeds the tax basis of the property.

Over the years, the concept of involuntary conversion has been the subject of litigation, and numerous amendments to the law have been proposed, and some adopted, to cover particular distress situations. For example, sale of livestock because of drought conditions followed by subsequent repurchase was made to qualify for treatment as an involuntary conversion by an amendment in 1956.

Other amendments have been necessary to prevent what were regarded as abuses, as when the owner of property on which there is an unrealized gain intentionally acquires a second property in order to be forced to dispose of one or another under the rules of a government regulatory agency. If the owner can claim involuntary conversion, using the proceeds of the sale of the first property, without recognition of gain, to buy other properties, there is an open invitation to maneuver into a position to be forced to do, without tax, what one wants to do anyway, but which if done voluntarily would be taxable. For this reason, section 1071 provides that nonrecognition of gain or loss on sale of property required by the Federal Communications Commission is granted only if the Commission certifies that the sale is necessary to effectuate a change in its policy or the adoption of a new policy. But relief is given by the tax law for certain distributions pursuant to the Bank Holding Company Act of 1956 and in obedience to orders of the Securities and Exchange Commission (secs. 1101–03, 1081–83).

Similar problems and possibilities have arisen in connection with disposals of property required under the antitrust laws, which have also had new applications. In one instance, it was apparently presumed by a taxpayer that the sale of a hotel after the antitrust laws were extended to service industries could be treated as an involuntary conversion if the proceeds were reinvested in another hotel in a different city. But the concept was held not to be applicable, and the Congress did not adopt relief legislation which was proposed. Similarly, relief legislation was not adopted to cover cases when privately owned water companies were required to be sold to municipalities and, in the absence of other opportunities for investment in private water companies, the proceeds were invested in widely owned utility company stocks. But relief legislation of a somewhat different sort was adopted when the du Pont company was forced to dispose of its holdings of General Motors stock; in the absence of this legislation, the distributions of stock would have been treated as ordinary income with a penalty tax of a billion dollars or more on the shareholders. The Congress, in adopting section 1111, agreed that the operation of the general rule of the law taxing distributions of stock in other companies as a dividend in kind would not be fair when the distribution was forced by a new application of the antitrust laws made a generation after the stock to be distributed had been acquired.

CAPITAL GAINS

The detailed definitions and significance of capital gains, as they apply to particular forms of investment, are discussed in later chapters. This section will introduce the subject with some comments on the general concept of capital gains and the principal arguments for and against a differential tax treatment of them.

The fact that long-term capital gains of individuals are taxed at no more than 25 per cent is significant for many types of investments. The tax treatment of capital gains is a major point of controversy in tax policy in many countries. A discussion of the subject in general terms will provide an introduction to the consideration of the significance of the differential tax rate for specific investments.

Many people insist that an increase in the price of land or securities arising over many years, and perhaps reflecting no more than the decrease in the value of the dollar through inflation, does not represent income. According to this point of view, any tax on the difference between original cost and selling price when an investor sells one piece of property or security to buy another should be regarded as a capital levy rather than a tax on income.

Others feel that the concept of "net accretion" gives the best and fairest definition of income. An individual's net accretion for a year is measured by the change in his net worth, positive or negative, plus his consumption. For a person with no assets at the beginning of a year, income under this concept would be the same as under the familiar concept of income. The total flow of wages, interest, dividends and net rents would be either consumed or saved. If it was all consumed, income would be measured entirely by consumption; if part was saved, the increase in net worth from zero to the amount of the savings, plus the consumption, would equal income as ordinarily defined.

If one has some assets at the beginning of the year, the measurement is a bit more complicated though the concept is still clear. If the value of the assets does not change and all wages, interest, dividends and the like are consumed, consumption alone measures the net accretion. If some of the flow of ordinary income is saved, it is reflected in an increase in assets, and consumption plus that increase represent income under the concept. The distinctive feature of the concept appears when existing assets change in value. If values increase, this is then taken into account along with income as ordinarily defined. A salary of $10,000 all of which was consumed plus an appreciation from $15,000 to $20,000 in the value of securities or real estate would add up to an income of $15,000 under the net accretion concept. If the assets decreased in value from $15,000 to $13,000, the net accretion income would be $8,000. The concept of net accretion takes as the measure of one's income his increment of economic power over a period, combining the ordinary payments for his services and the use of his assets with the changes in the values of the assets themselves.

The problem of measuring annual changes in value of assets has been recognized as creating almost insuperable administrative difficulties by most of those who regard the net accretion concept as the ideal definition of income. The theory is worth noting, however, because of its great appeal to many writers on public finance who, when they reluctantly have to forego inclusion of annual changes in net worth as part of income, feel even more strongly that realized capital gains should be taxed in full along with other income. Since postponement of tax until realization is itself a forced concession on practical grounds from this ideal of annual taxation of each year's appreciation in value, any further concession through lower tax rates on realized gains in their view merely adds to the inequity.

One's opinion on the fairness of a lower rate of tax on capital gains will be based on subjective grounds, as is true on all matters of tax equity. Feelings can become quite strong regarding the proper taxation of capital gains. Those who regard any tax on appreciation in capital value as a capital levy can become indignant at the net accretion concept. They feel especially strongly about taxing realized gains which are reinvested and insist that the fruit in an orchard must be distinguished from the growth of the trees themselves. But those who favor the net accretion concept are equally indignant at the thought of those who already have some property becoming wealthy through appreciation in values without paying at least as much in taxes as those who are trying to accumulate property by saving from salaries and wages. Both points of view should be understandable. The author quite emphatically happens to favor the former position.

Quite apart from matters of equity, a lower rate of tax on capital gains may be justified on economic grounds. The realization of a gain usually is a voluntary act. It may be postponed indefinitely. The fact that a tax will be due on a realized gain means that a capital sum is reduced when it is changed from one investment to another. A share of stock purchased at $50 and worth $100 represents $100 of capital, but if the stock is sold subject to a capital gains tax of 25 per cent and the proceeds are used to buy a second stock, there will be only $87.50 available for the purchase after the tax on the sale. The investor must not only prefer the second stock over the first to induce him to make the sale and purchase, he must like the second stock enough more than the first to prefer to have $87.50 worth of it to $100 of the stock he already holds and can continue to hold. The capital gains tax has a "freezing" effect on all investment in which there is a gain and thus reduces the liquidity of the capital markets.

The extent of the freezing effect is not known. Tax-conscious investors and many financial advisers insist it is large. Some statistical studies indicate that it is minor. The psychological impact is regarded as important by some who note that when the act of selling investments makes one subject to a tax perhaps greater than one's living expenses for a year there is a strong barrier to performing that act. And the depressing psychological effect of paying such a tax, if it is once incurred, is likely to discourage a person from voluntarily subjecting himself to that mental anguish a second time. But anyone who expects to live on investment profits as well as salary and investment income will happily seize on low-taxed profits in preference to high-taxed dividends or interest and have no qualms at all about realizing and spending gains.[1]

A second economic argument for a lower tax on capital gains is that it is probably paid out of capital to a greater extent than any other tax except the estate and gift taxes. Whereas one typically fixes his consumption on the basis of his after-tax income, one is not likely to reduce consumption to restore his net worth when it has been reduced by a capital gains tax. Hopefully, the shift in investment will make the ultimate net worth greater than it otherwise would be, and a pattern of consumption and current savings ordinarily would not be much modified.

The economic significance of imposing a tax which falls especially heavily on capital depends on the relative importance of consumption and investment in a country's economy. This basic question affects many aspects of fiscal and monetary policy. It is enough to note its particular relevance to capital gains taxation.

From the standpoint of equity, one might want to distinguish between capital gains which are reinvested and those which are spent on consumption. Probably many of those who regard the capital gains tax as a capital levy do so because they presume that gains will be reinvested and would regard consumption of a realized gain as imprudent, at the very least. They would not be concerned about full taxation of gains spent for consumption. And probably many of those who object to the low tax on gains do so because they see examples of conspicuous consumption based on realized gains, or perhaps even based on funds borrowed against appreciating assets with no realization and no tax at all. The full taxation of gains which are not reinvested should be favored by both groups. If this were done, those who believe that capital should be respected by both its owners and the state will be content and those who think that all sources of increased economic well-being should be taxed will be partially though not completely satisfied. The author advocates full taxation of realized capital gains which are used for consumption and

---

[1] The highly personal character of reactions to capital gains taxes was most surprisingly revealed in a conversation with a man active in the management of a family fortune probably running into the hundreds of millions of dollars, with many beneficiaries in several generations. He remarked that he could never understand the so-called psychological barrier of the capital gains tax. When it was described to him in the foregoing terms, he said, "Yes, I suppose I would feel that way if I regarded things personally. But we just consider the alternative investment possibilities and sell what we do not like and buy the things we like better." Perhaps the psychological barrier exists only for those with enough capital to be subject on occasions to a tax that is large in comparison with their regular taxes and net incomes, but without enough to put their investments in the hands of managers who may regard them impersonally.

a tax-free roll-over of all other gains, but this book is not the place to argue tax policy.

But whenever there is no tax or a lower rate of tax on capital gains, it must be expected that a great deal of ingenuity will be devoted to converting ordinary income into capital gains. The greater the spread between the tax rates, the greater the advantage of contriving ways to throw receipts into the favored category and the greater the diversion of human effort from productive activity into tax manipulations. Much of the complication in the tax law has been inserted to prevent or reduce what are regarded as unintended and unjustified uses of the capital gains provisions. Even those who are indignant at the thought of full taxation of reinvested capital gains are offended by the maneuvers which bring the concept of capital gains into disrepute. Throughout this book reference will be made to special forms of capital gains, genuine and contrived, arising from various forms of investments and business transactions and to the special provisions of the law which are necessary to prevent abuse of the lower rates of tax on capital gains. One example here will indicate the ingenuity of taxpayers and the resulting complications in the law.

Bonds issued at a very large discount could, in the absence of a special provision of the tax law, give rise to artificial capital gains. If the going market rate is 5 per cent, a 3 per cent bond could be sold at a discount at a price to yield 5 per cent to maturity. The total income would consist of the current interest and the difference between issue price and face value which, with constant interest rates, would be realizable by a steady increase in market price as the bond approached maturity. But the appreciation would simply be a substitute for normal interest. To prevent abuse of the capital gains provisions, the law was changed in 1954 to provide that if bonds were issued at an original discount in excess of ¼ of one per cent times the number of years to maturity, any gain on sale or redemption due to original discount should be taxed as ordinary income. The margin for small discounts was allowed to permit ordinary pricing of bonds with stated interest in multiples of normal fractions of one per cent (par. 1622). Similarly, it has been necessary to amend the law to prevent the sale of bonds with future coupons detached, thereby converting what would be ordinary interest into capital gain.

6

Tax Factors

in Investments by Individuals

Almost any reasonably sophisticated investor, when he thinks of municipal bonds, real estate, oil and mining ventures, farms, life insurance, new businesses, and closely controlled corporations, realizes that each of them is subject to special tax rules which may make investment in these areas more attractive from a tax standpoint than the more familiar investments in bonds, whether of the federal government or corporations, stocks of widely owned companies, and savings bank deposits. Some of the preferential provisions have been adopted by the Congress for the purpose of encouraging investment in a particular form or to give a tax break to a favored or powerful group. Others arise out of the operation of general provisions of the law which have turned out to have a special significance for particular forms of investment, and the Congress has not seen fit to take away these tax benefits even though they were unintended.

This chapter covers the principal distinctive tax factors in various forms of investments available to individual investors, other than the extractive industries and new business ventures which are discussed in later chapters. As in the other chapters, there is no attempt to make this an exhaustive treatise or, least of all, a tax guide for people active in the area. Consistent with the general objective of the book, the emphasis will be on the two recurring questions "Why?" and "So what?" The relevant provisions of the law can be better understood if one understands the reasons for their existence. Thus, some history is given to describe the "why" of the law. And certainly most people handle their investments differently because of the tax law and the many features in it which give distinctive treatment to various forms of investments. These influences on the acts of investors constitute the "so what" of the analysis.

Common Stock

Income received from dividends on corporate stock is taxed in full to individual stockholders, with a $100 exclusion for each taxpayer. The dividends are paid from corporate income which has already paid the corporation income tax. Thus, dividend income received by an individual has been subject to double taxation. No other form of income received from a corporation is subject to double taxation since wages, salaries, interest, rent, and royalties are all deductible by corporations and taxable only to recipients.

The price of corporate stock, however, reflects its net income after the corporation tax and the dividends paid from this after-tax income. Stock is bought subject to its double tax burden at prices which make it competitive with other forms of investment subject to only one tax. The discrimination, to the extent that the tax is not shifted by the corporation in higher prices to customers or lower prices to labor and suppliers, is on those who own stock when the corporate tax is raised. Historically, major increases in the income tax on corporations have usually occurred when corporate profits were also rising, and the effect of the higher taxes has been to keep net profits and the price of common stock from rising as much as it otherwise might have done rather than to reduce profits and stock prices. The significance of the corporate tax is discussed in more detail in Chapter 9; here it need be mentioned only as a factor influencing investment decisions.

Though some deplore the double taxation of dividend income, others refer to the "corporate tax loophole." This phrase is based on the fact that the corporation tax rate is less than the highest individual tax rates and it is therefore cheaper from a tax standpoint to have a corporation earn income than to earn it as an individual, so long as the corporation retains it. But so long as the corporation retains income, that is, so long as the tax advantage lasts, the funds are not directly available to the individual stockholders. They get an indirect benefit (in the form of an increased personal net worth) only to the extent that the price of the stock reflects the retained income, and they can get a direct benefit (funds in hand for consumption or other use) only by selling some of the stock; and if they do so, the capital gains tax enters into the calculations. But there will be a break-even at only one level of individual and capital gains tax; at present rates, the highest-bracket individuals would pay less total tax by realizing gains equivalent to retained corporate income.[1]

[1] For an individual in the top bracket of 70 per cent, $100 of business income received directly would give a net income of $30. If earned by a corporation, $52

Of course, stock prices do not reflect retained earnings dollar for dollar and there are many reasons, ranging from matters of control to inconvenience, why ordinary stockholders do not think of selling small amounts of their investments to get indirectly the equivalent of the cash dividends they might have received directly. Even regular stock dividends, discussed in a later chapter, do not seem to be regarded as a ready alternative to cash dividends. But the advantage of corporate retention and later sale of the stock or liquidation of the corporation can be attractive for high-bracket owners of closely controlled corporations and has made it necessary to prevent abuses through the use of personal holding companies and unreasonable accumulation of surplus for the purpose of avoiding individual income taxes. Provisions to prevent these abuses are discussed in Chapter 15.

For the ordinary investor, considering alternative investments in stocks, taxable bonds, or real estate, dividends are treated like all other forms of income with the minor exception of the $100 exclusion.

Real Estate

One of the most obvious ways to secure a capital gain instead of ordinary income is to build up the value of an asset to the point where it is about to produce its maximum income and then, instead of receiving the taxable income, sell the asset for its capitalized value, paying a capital gains tax. Perhaps as dramatic an example as any would be an investment in land on which one plants fruit trees. While they are growing there is no income. There will in fact be expenses, and the ideal arrangement from the tax standpoint will exist if the expenses can be deducted currently instead of capitalized and if the investor has enough income from other sources to absorb the deductions against high tax brackets. In such cases, the cost of the property is reduced by the saving of tax on other income, which reduces the net cost to much less than half of the actual cost. The present value of the income stream is realized in a lump sum as a capital gain at the point in time when it is about to be significant and taxable. Investments in orchards are particularly featured for professional men in their last years before retirement, when their incomes are at a maximum, with the full productivity of the trees timed to coincide with the year of retirement. Of course, it may even be desirable to hold the property

---

could be retained after the corporate tax of 48 per cent; if stock increased in price by that $52 and that amount of stock were sold subject to a capital gains tax of 25 per cent, the final net realization would be $39. The break-even point at present rates would be an individual marginal tax rate of 61 per cent.

and receive the income in the post-retirement years subject to lower tax brackets. But these and other uses of real estate in farming are discussed in the next section of this chapter.

Another way to build up value in property is to write it off through depreciation more rapidly than it falls in market value. If property purchased for $100,000 could be depreciated to zero, with the depreciation deducted from high-bracket taxable income, while its market value was falling only to $50,000 and then sold at a capital gain for that price, the juxtaposition of tax rates would create a substantial after-tax gain from an otherwise unprofitable transaction. If one assumes that the property was purchased entirely from borrowed funds and the income from it just covered the expenses other than depreciation, the depreciation deduction would save $70,000 in taxes for a top-bracket taxpayer over the years of ownership. If the $50,000 on sale were taxed as a capital gain at 25 per cent, net proceeds of $37,500 plus the $70,000 tax savings would leave a margin of $7,500 over the debt of $100,000, plus the income earned by the use of the funds arising from the annual tax savings through depreciation over the period. To the extent that annual depreciation exceeded the required amortization of the loan, there would be a further source of income through the interim use of the excess funds "arising from" depreciation. A large debt due in the remote future under a purchase money mortgage is sometimes desired to increase the basis for interim depreciation deduction. The use of "borrowed basis" requires continuing attention to prevent abuse. Only under a peculiar tax law could a buyer prefer to purchase at a higher rather than a lower price.

If market value of the property actually increases with the passage of time or declines only to a negligible extent because of inflation, the tax saving from depreciation is all net and does not have to be regarded as partly needed, along with the net proceeds of sale, to pay the debt on the property. The frequent availability of such situations has led to the apparently ridiculously contradictory phrase "tax-free depreciation income" sometimes used in advertising real estate. The operation of the tax law, in fact, does make depreciation a source of net income, to the extent of the marginal tax rate against which it is deducted, if there is no actual decline in market value. If the final tax on disposal is at capital gains rate, it can be a minor offset to the interim advantage of the savings in taxes. Even if the gain is taxed at the same rate as that applicable to the depreciation deduction, there will still be an advantage in time through having the use of funds between the years when taxes were reduced and the final year when an equivalent tax was paid.

The tax law has imposed some limitations on extreme capital gains in real estate investment. Not all outlays on property are deductible at the option of the owners. The cost of a building must be capitalized, along with the cost of major improvements.

The other limitation on the conversion of ordinary income into capital gain in real estate investment was adopted in 1964 when some or all of the profit on sale of depreciated real estate up to the original purchase price was made taxable as ordinary income if the sale is made within ten years of the purchase (par. 1613(b)). All the gain up to purchase price is taxable if the property is held less than twenty months. After that a sliding scale is applied with one per cent of the profit being shifted to the capital gain category for each month of ownership until, after ten years, the entire profit becomes capital gain. This provision of the law, section 1250, is much less strict than section 1245 adopted in 1962 applicable to the sale of all depreciable property except livestock and real property. That section provides for a full recapture of amounts previously allowed as depreciation deductions, regardless of the length of time the assets were held (par. 1613(a)). Other countries, even those which do not tax capital gains at all, have similar provisions to recapture depreciation to the extent that it turns out at the time of sale of property to have been in excess of the actual decline in market value. The fact that the excess depreciation on real estate is recaptured only when property is sold within ten years, and then only on a sliding scale, gives a continuing tax preference to long-term investment in depreciable real property so long as rising costs and the pressure of population expansion continue to keep the market value of buildings from falling as rapidly as the buildings may be written off under allowable depreciation.

The Treasury proposed full recapture of all excess depreciation on all property in 1961, at the same time that it recommended the investment credit and announced plans to allow faster depreciation. The Congress adopted the full recapture for tangible personal property, such as machinery, equipment, automobiles, trucks, and airplanes, in 1962 when the new depreciation guidelines were established, but made no restrictions on real estate. The limited recapture of excess depreciation on real property came only after renewed urging by the Treasury.

Prior to the recapture provisions, one sometimes had the impression that depreciable property was acquired more for depreciating and selling through a succession of owners than for productive use. Even commercial airplanes were owned by individuals or syndicates of individual investors and leased to airlines. Ownership was changed when an owner "ran out of depreciation" or, under the declining balance method, when depreciation became small. After a capital gain which represented a recovery of a good part of the deductible depreciation, a new owner would start the process all over again. The juxtaposition of tax rates could be a major source of net gain even for corporations owning fleets of rental automobiles. In real estate investment, the turnover of ownership has merely been slowed down. So long as a property can be written off faster than its market value declines and is held for more than ten years, once it has been written off it will be worth more to a new owner than the existing owner and we can expect to have continued sales and purchases of buildings for tax purposes.

SPECIAL PROVISIONS OF THE TAX LAW
OF BENEFIT TO FARMERS

The most significant tax advantage of small farmers is that income in kind from one's own efforts and the ownership of one's own residence are not taxable. Thus, housing and in many instances a considerable part of the value of food (to the extent that it is grown on the farm) are not included in taxable income. This situation arises out of general rules of the tax law rather than special provisions intended to benefit farmers; these tax advantages of farming arise from the nature of farming rather than from legislation intended to benefit farmers. But a strict rule is applied, and the value of goods received in trade for farm products at a store is taxable income. So long as home-grown eggs are eaten on the farm, tax is not involved, but if eggs are traded for cake mix at the local store the value of the cake mix is, naturally, regarded as taxable income.

But a glance at the index of a tax manual reveals the existence of numerous special provisions relevant to one or another aspect of farm operations. In the first group are authorizations for immediate deductions for various outlays which, under general provisions of the law, would be regarded as capital expenditures, deductible if at all through depreciation or amortization. Soil and water conservation expenses are the most conspicuous example (par. 1836, sec. 175). As the name implies, the deduction applies to conservation outlays which are deemed to be in the public interest. The same treatment is given expenses of land clearing (par. 1836(c), sec. 182). In view of the continuing problems of surplus crops and the various programs to discourage the cultivation of existing agricultural land, the public policy served by the tax deduction for clearing land is less apparent. Both of these deductions are subject to limitations of 25 per cent of the year's income from farming to prevent their use by investors who are simply developing land for investment or later use but are not active farmers at the time.

With these exceptions, the rules distinguishing business from personal expenses in farming, and current expenses from capital expenditures, are generally consistent with ordinary accounting and business concepts, which are discussed along with other accounting problems in Chapter 4 (par. 1835). However, one other option is available which can be very important to both farmers and investors in farm properties. Development expenses "prior to the time when the productive state is reached" may be regarded as investments of capital (reg. 1.162–12). This option is significant for anyone starting a farm with no income against which to deduct current outlays. But the implied observe is vastly more important, allowing as it does the deduction of development expenses against other income from any source and with no requirement that the taxpayer be an active farmer. The opportunity for an individual with high earned income to develop an orchard or a farm and charge the expenses against his salary or professional fees in years immediately before retirement, with the property becoming productive at about the time his earned income ceases, makes farm development relatively inexpensive for nonfarmer investors.

The other major tax advantage available to farmers is the option to combine a cash method of accounting with capital gains treatment for breeding livestock. All expenses of growing the livestock are currently deductible under the cash method, thus offsetting income taxed at ordinary rates, while the values developed by the outlays are taxed as capital gains (pars. 2607, 1616(a)). To be sure, farmers may use an accrual method of accounting, with several special options available for valuing inventory including a "farm-price" and a "retail-livestock-price" method, but the cash method is so clearly preferable when it is combined with sales of some of the farm livestock for capital gains that for some time the Internal Revenue Service refused to permit farmers to change to it from the accrual method. The Congressional intent was clear, however, and in 1953 the previous administrative difficulties placed in the way of farmers were removed.

If a farm is operated for recreation or pleasure at a net loss rather than on a commercial basis, the expenses will be disallowed as personal expenses, and the income if any need not be reported (par. 1835(c)). The courts have applied a rather strict interpretation of pleasure, and disallowances of deductions have been upheld only in quite clear instances of hobby farming.

Under a general provision of the law, even when an activity qualifies as a trade or business, if losses exceed $50,000 a year for five consecutive years the excess over $50,000 can be disallowed (par. 2202(c)). This is equally applicable to hobby farms and other businesses, such as newspapers or antique furniture shops, and is designed to prevent a high-bracket taxpayer from financing his hobby by tax deductions from other income. In most activities, perhaps especially in farming, it seems possible so to conduct an affair that the loss will fall short of $50,000 at least once in five years. The limitation on hobby losses is effective only against the truly spectacular hobby activities.

TAX-EXEMPT SECURITIES

The interest on bonds of states and all subordinate units of government is exempt from the federal income tax (par. 1314(b)). It is argued by some that these bonds are tax-exempt under the Constitution, but this has never been tested in the Supreme Court. The fact that salaries paid by states and municipalities have been held to be taxable under a non-discriminatory income tax makes many feel that interest on municipal obligations would be similarly treated, but since the statute has given tax exemption since 1916 there has been no basis for a test of constitutionality.

The advantage of tax exemption is related to an investor's marginal tax bracket. For anyone in a 70 per cent tax bracket, a 3 per cent municipal bond gives the same net return as a 10 per cent taxable bond, or stated another way, a 3 per cent tax-exempt bond gives three and a third times as much net income as a 3 per cent taxable bond (3 per cent compared to .9 of 1 per cent). Tax-exempt investors such as pension funds and educational and charitable organizations get no benefit from tax exemption and hence have no rational basis for including municipal bonds in their portfolios. When the full corporate tax rate became applicable to the net taxable income of life insurance companies in 1955, instead of a low flat rate on all investment income, they became interested in municipal bonds.

Investment bankers and brokers regularly issue tables showing the equivalent net returns of taxable and tax-exempt bonds at various income brackets. For high-bracket investors, it is virtually impossible to find a taxable interest income which with any reasonable safety gives the same net return as is available on tax-exempts. The availability of tax-exempt bonds for the fixed-income fixed-dollar section of an investment portfolio has led many higher-bracket individual investors to consider tax-exempts and investments with potential capital gains as the only worthwhile holdings for other than very liquid assets.

Exhibit 1 gives the yield on high-grade municipal bonds and corporate bonds for selected dates. The changes in the differential are as conspicuous as the fact that not only the higher-bracket individual investors but corporations subject to the full rate of corporate tax could at all times have secured substantially higher net returns from tax-exempt bonds. In spite of this fact, corporate investors including banks and insurance companies regularly hold large amounts of investments with taxable interest. The explanation is found, among other things, in liquidity preferences and traditions on portfolio diversification. Many very high-grade municipal bonds are issued in relatively small amounts and customarily bought to be held to maturity. Markets are thin and underwriters do not stand ready to absorb large fractions of an issue.

EXHIBIT 1

YIELDS ON HIGH-GRADE MUNICIPAL
AND Aaa CORPORATE BONDS

Year	High-Grade Municipal (Aaa)	Corporate (Moody's Aaa)	Municipal Yield as Percentage of Corporate Yield
1946	1.64%	2.53%	65
1947	2.01	2.61	77
1948	2.40	2.82	85
1949	2.21	2.66	83
1950	1.98	2.62	76
1951	2.00	2.86	70
1952	2.22	2.96	75
1953	2.82	3.20	88
1954	2.46	2.90	85
1955	2.18	3.06	71
1956	2.51	3.36	75
1957	3.10	3.89	80
1958	2.92	3.79	77
1959	3.35	4.38	76
1960	3.26	4.41	74
1961	3.27	4.35	75
1962	3.10	4.34	71
1964	3.09	4.40	70
1965	3.16	4.49	70
1966	3.67	5.13	71
1967	3.74	5.51	68

Source: *Federal Reserve Bulletin.*

The "compartmentalization of the money market" is effectively shown by the changes in differences in yield under constant tax rates, and, by definition, with no changes in relative risks. In one month in 1946, the rate on tax-exempts actually exceeded the market rate on corporate bonds, presumably reflecting a flood of issues in the immediate postwar period after an extended interval when local capital expenditures were cut back because of shortages of labor and material for everything other than war needs. Studies of changes in the yield differential reflect, among other factors, the shifts in availability of funds and the scale of new issues, along with any changes in expectations concerning tax rates and the tax law with respect to the continuation of tax exemption on outstanding issues.

If there were only a few outstanding tax-exempt bonds, perhaps $100 million, with complete confidence in their continued tax exemption, they would presumably all be in the hands of the highest-bracket investors as part of the fixed-dollar segment of their portfolios, with the price bid up to a point where the yield reflected the tax advantage of their marginal tax rate, modified by any uncertainty regarding continuation of these tax rates. But with the very large volume of tax-exempt bonds, the yields have had to rise to attract buyers subject to much lower tax rates, giving disproportionate tax advantages to the higher-bracket intramarginal purchasers. It follows that the savings of interest to the borrowing state and local governments is less than the savings in federal taxes by higher-bracket individual investors and corporate investors.

ANNUITIES AND LIFE INSURANCE

In recognition of both the distinctive nature of life insurance companies and the social importance of life insurance, the tax law gives relatively favorable treatment to life insurance and annuity policyholders and to life insurance companies. The most significant tax advantage is that the interest which an insurance company has assumed that it will earn on the investment in insurance and annuity policies is not taxed currently either to the company or to the policyholders. It can be earned and compounded tax-free at least until the maturity of policies. If a life insurance policy matures by death of the insured, the accumulated interest is never subject to any income tax; for all other policies interest when received by the beneficiary generally is taxed in one way or another, subject in some instances to presumptions under which actual interest may not exactly equal taxable interest. But the tax-free accumulation before maturity of a policy is a clear and unqualified tax advantage, the immediate importance of which varies with the marginal tax rate applicable to alternative investments by potential holders of life insurance and annuity policies.

Before describing the principal provisions of the tax law relative to life insurance and annuities, a brief review of the essential characteristics of insurance will provide perspective for its tax treatment.

Nature of Life Insurance and Annuities

The simplest form of life insurance conceptually is a one-year term policy. On the basis of the statistical probability of death, from mortality records of the past, and with a sufficiently large number of people insured to let the average experience be realized, the necessary premium can be calculated to pay the face value of policies to the beneficiaries of those who die. With an expectation that one out of fifty people of an age group will die within a year, a premium of $20 would provide $1,000 of insurance, ignoring the costs of operating an insurance company and ordinary safety margins. Actual premiums are set above the amount based on the probability of death to allow for costs, profits (in case of a stock company), and margins; the latter are sometimes provided by using a mortality table which does not fully reflect increasing longevity. Term life insurance is thus essentially similar to fire and other forms of casualty insurance involving simply a pooling of risks.

But term life insurance by its nature becomes increasingly expensive as the years pass, and at advanced ages, when the chance of death is high, premiums become prohibitive. Furthermore, a person may cease to be insurable and hence be without insurance when he needs it most. To give some latitude, insurance companies offer term insurance policies with guaranteed renewability regardless of health, or guaranteed convertibility into other types of policies. Five- and ten-year term policies are also available which give uniform premiums for the period covered, with the premiums in the first years a little above and those in the later years a little below the amounts indicated if the years were regarded as separate units.

Term insurance is the cheapest form of insurance and is especially attractive to younger men to provide funds in case of death for education of children or for a surviving widow before the values in a pension fund have accumulated. Term insurance for a group of employees is often provided by an employer as part of fringe benefit package plans up to retirement age for a multiple of from one to three times annual compensation. Group term insurance is usually available without medical examinations.

At the other extreme is ordinary life insurance, which provides uniform premiums throughout one's lifetime for a stated amount of insurance to be paid at death. These policies may provide that no premiums are due beyond a very advanced age, such as 90, to relieve those few people who live far beyond their expectancy from having to pay indefinitely; the funds foregone are negligible in the aggregate, but can be very burdensome to very old people or those who support them. Uniform premiums during a lifetime require higher premiums in earlier years than those needed to cover the current expectation of death, while in later years the premium is less than that so needed. The earlier premiums, to the extent that they exceed the amounts required for current death losses, constitute a sum which can be invested to produce income. And this investment income is available, along with subsequent premiums, to build the fund to pay the face values of policies as they become due or, in the delightfully unsentimental phrase used in the industry, mature through death. In the later years of a policy, the accumulated amount, referred to as the policy reserve, becomes a substantial sum, approaching the face value, and the interest on it is also substantial.

In establishing premiums, each company makes its own assumptions on future interest; and this interest is taken into account, along with life expectancies and the various expenses of running the company, in setting premiums. To assure adequate margins of safety, the interest assumed to be earned in setting the terms of the insurance contract is somewhat less than that which it is reasonably hoped will be earned, just as the assumed mortality is likely to be a little greater than the mortality actually expected. The interest which is assumed to be earned and taken into account in building the reserves against the insurance policies is deductible in computing the taxable income of insurance companies. Nor is this interest currently imputed to policyholders in computing their taxable incomes.

One must remember that not all the premium is accumulated; the reserve is built up only from the excess of the premium over the cost of current insurance. Furthermore, it should be noted that the interest on the reserve is in a sense fungible with current premiums to provide current insurance and increase the reserve. It is a matter of allocation as to which source of funds is presumed to provide which benefit. The allocation may be important in determining the tax status of certain insurance benefits. For example, the presumed cost of current insurance under group permanent life insurance which is taxable to employees becomes progressively less than the cost of term insurance because the Internal Revenue Service has ruled that the interest on the policy reserves should be deemed to reduce the cost of current insurance which is taxable to the employee, rather than be added to the reserve; the reserves are increased by the excess of the premium over the net cost of current insurance after first applying the interest element to the cost of current insurance (par. 1306).

Ordinary life insurance thus involves investment as well as insurance. A capital sum is accumulated by the insurance companies consisting of the excess of the premiums over the amounts needed to meet current death claims and the compound interest on these capital sums which exist for all policies other than term life insurance policies. Most insurance contracts provide that an insurance policy which has a reserve accumulated against it may be turned in for a cash surrender value, usually somewhat less than the reserve value. And policyholders may borrow against the policy, at an interest in excess of that assumed to be earned on the reserve funds, up to the cash surrender value, thereby reducing the "net insurance" to an amount approximately equal to the difference between the face value and the accumulated capital sum. Exhibit 2 shows the buildup of cash surrender values of a typical policy.

EXHIBIT 2

GUARANTEED COST LIFE INSURANCE

Cash or Loan Value per $1,000

Age at Which Policy was Issued	Years After—Ordinary Life				
	5	10	15	20	65
30	$ 43	$120	$202	$289	$560
60	139	296	440	569	139
Limited Pay—25 Years					
30	72	182	306	446	716
60	145	312	474	647	145
Limited Pay—15 Years					
30	122	295	495	549	716
60	207	472	814	854	207
Life Paid Up at 65					
30	53	141	236	341	716
50	185	427	716	767	716
Endowment—20 Years					
30	172	404	676	1,000	
60	174	386	631	1,000	
Endowment—Age 65					
30	71	179	300	436	
50	253	584	1,000		

Many other forms of policies are offered in addition to term and ordinary life policies; most of them are variations of ordinary life policies, involving an even larger element of investment and larger premiums.

Many people would like to stop paying premiums when they retire and their incomes are reduced. To meet this demand, policies are designed to be fully paid for at 65, or at some other age; since the premiums will be paid for fewer years by those who live beyond that age, they must be larger. Policies are also designed to be paid up after a specified number of years rather than at a certain age. Here again, the premiums must be larger and the investment element greater.

Endowment policies are paid up after a specified number of years and may be surrendered for their full face value at that time, even if the insured person is living. These policies are a form of saving, with an insurance element added to assure that the planned amount will be available at the time of death if that occurs before the date when contractual payments cease. Exhibit 3 indicates the range of premiums for different types of policies.

EXHIBIT 3

GUARANTEED COST LIFE INSURANCE

Rate per $1,000

Annual Premium

Type of Policy	Age						
	30	35	40	45	50	55	60
5-year term convertible	$ 6.91	$ 8.05	$ 9.86	$12.34	$17.33	$23.56	$32.84
5-year term renewable	7.28	8.58	10.61	13.47	18.96	25.82	36.13
10-year term convertible	7.49	8.74	10.81	14.31	19.74	26.93	
Term to age 65	11.73	13.52	15.74	18.54	22.49		
Ordinary life	18.01	21.24	25.17	29.95	36.53	44.36	55.02
Limited pay, 25 years	24.59	27.62	31.08	35.07	40.36	46.62	55.82
Limited pay, 15 years	35.74	39.88	44.41	49.32	55.37	61.91	70.45
Life paid up at 65	20.71	25.05	31.08	40.22	55.37		
Endowment, 20 years	46.04	46.71	47.74	49.20	51.87	55.33	61.59
Endowment, age 65	24.24	29.87	37.52	49.20	67.69	105.54	

Both stock and mutual companies write life insurance and annuity policies. Since by their nature, mutual companies do not accumulate or distribute profits other than for those who do business with them, the excess of premiums over those which turn out to have been necessary, along with gains from more favorable mortality experience or lower costs than those assumed, are in one way or another eventually paid to policyholders in the form of dividends. Commonly these are applied to reduce current premiums, and on policies fully paid up to increase the amount of insurance. They are not regarded as taxable income, except in the highly improbable case when total dividends exceed total premiums paid (par. 1213). Stock companies, to meet the competition of mutual companies, offer participating policies which typically have higher premiums than nonparticipating policies offered by stock companies but also pay dividends based on more favorable results than those assumed in setting the premiums. Nonparticipating policies offer lower contractual premiums, but with the company taking all risks and receiving the full benefit of all gains.

Annuity policies, in a sense, are the reverse of insurance policies. Premiums are accumulated, along with interest on the accumulating capital sum, until the date when annuity payments are to begin under the contract. The annuity payments are set at a figure which will absorb the total accumulation, including the interest earned on the declining capital sum during payments, over the life expectancy of the annuitant. An insurance element is thus present because the aggregate payments to the very long-lived people will exceed the amounts to which they are individually entitled on the basis of their own accumulations, with these excesses being made good by the amounts by which those who die before their life expectation fail to recover the accumulations against their policies.

With a pure annuity policy, if the policyholder dies before the annuity begins, he will recover nothing. But that risk, like the risk of no return from term life insurance for those who do not die while the insurance is in force, is the price paid for maximum returns for those who live. To obviate that sense of loss, annuity policies can be written with a guarantee of a specified number of annuity payments even if the policyholder does not survive that long or with a return of the actual investment. Such policies give lower benefit payments or require higher premiums for a given annuity. Here also under the tax law, the interest assumed in the actuarial calculations of premiums and benefits is not taxed to the insurance company, nor is it imputed currently to the policyholders.

Taxation of Life Insurance

The tax treatment of life insurance is quite simple. Premiums paid are not deductible (pars. 1804, 1830(a)).[2] Consistent with the nondeducti-

---

[2] The only exception is the special case of payments by employers on policies in which the employees are the beneficiaries. The premiums for such policies are

bility of premiums, the proceeds of life insurance policies arising from the death of the insured are not included in taxable income (par. 1210). (Life insurance proceeds are included in an estate for estate tax purposes if the decedent owned the policy or had any of the "incidents of ownership," but this fact has nothing to do with income taxation. Estate tax aspects are discussed briefly in the chapter on estate and gift taxation.)

If an insurance policy matures or is turned in for its cash surrender value before death, the excess if any of the amount received over the premiums paid is taxable income (pars. 1211–12). Only death can give full tax exemption to the accumulated interest on a life insurance policy. But it should always be remembered, as noted previously, that some of the interest on the accumulating reserve may be regarded as helping to pay for part of the current insurance, and this part of the interest is never subject to income tax. In a very real sense, the policy reserve is a segregated fund, the interest on which pays for various things; only to the extent that the interest is in fact added to the reserve and compounded may it enter into taxable income.

Prior to 1954, the exemption from income tax on proceeds realized because of the death of the insured was applied without qualification and included the interest earned subsequent to death and included in any installment payments. This gave a strong inducement for high-bracket beneficiaries to leave insurance proceeds with an insurance company and have the policy paid in installments extending over many years. To remove the tax discrimination in favor of this form of investment, the law was changed to make such interest taxable but with an exemption of up to $1,000 a year of interest for a surviving spouse if the interest was included in installment payments of life insurance policies (par. 1210). The $1,000 annual amount was left free of tax to encourage surviving spouses with modest capital to leave their insurance money where they would not be in danger of squandering it. There is, however, no comparable tax inducement to convert the proceeds of insurance into an annuity.

The excess of the amount received from a policy over premiums paid, except in the case of death, is taxed as ordinary income. If an endowment policy is converted into an annuity when or within a short period after it matures, there is no immediate tax; the subsequent annuities are taxed in the ordinary fashion with the cost of the insurance policy

---

deductible if the insurance is group term, or as a payment to a pension trust if the latter takes out the insurance as part of its financing. On policies for individual employees who own the policies, the premium may be deductible as compensation if within the limits of reasonable compensation, and taxable to the employee. But these special cases of employer-employee insurance relations are described in detail in the chapter on compensation policies.

becoming the cost of the annuity contract. The law has been tightened at various times to prevent the realization of the compound interest as capital gain. The fact that the amount is realized at one time makes the interest no less ordinary income than the compound interest on savings bonds which is also received in a lump sum after as long as twenty years.

The selection of the correct tax rule for annuities is more difficult. Three different rules have been applied, none of which is completely satisfactory. Under the present law in effect since 1954, the cost of an annuity, that is the premiums paid for it, is divided by the life expectancy of the annuitant, or the joint expectancies of the annuitant and any surviving beneficiary, and this amount is deducted from each payment (pars. 1205–06). If the annuitant lives just to his expectancy, he will recover his investment tax-free and everything above that will be taxed. The result seems eminently fair. But if he lives less than his expectancy, he will have been taxed on part of each annuity payment though as it turns out he will not recover his investment tax-free. This seems unduly hard. However, if he lives beyond his expectancy, he will continue to receive part of his annuity tax-free, and in the aggregate will receive more than his investment. And this seems unduly generous. The two tax inequities balance each other in the aggregate, though not for any one individual.

The present tax treatment is consistent with the inherent inequities of annuities themselves, by which, it will be remembered, the long-lived annuitants benefit at the expense of those who died before they reach their life expectancies. It was this consistency of the tax treatment with the very nature of an annuity which convinced the responsible officials in the Treasury and the members of Congress that the present treatment was reasonable and less bad than two alternatives which had been used previously. As a refinement of the present rule, if an annuity provides for a definite number of payments or recovery of an investment regardless of survival, the amount to be deducted as a return of capital from the annuity payments is adjusted to correspond to the changed actuarial probability of recovering the investment over the life expectancy.

Under one prior method of taxation, the first annuity payments were deemed to be a return of capital until the investment was recovered, after which all payments were deemed to be income. This may seem fairer, but it had what came to be regarded as a fatal defect because annuitants after receiving their annuities tax-free for many years were suddenly confronted with a tax on the full amount. This was hard to explain and produced some hardship in providing funds to pay a tax on an income which had previously been tax-exempt.[3]

[3] A present survivor of this earlier treatment exists in the rule that when the employee's investment in a contributory annuity plan set up by his employer will

Because of objections to the sudden shift from tax-free to taxable status, the law was changed to provide a presumption on the amount of interest received in annuity payments. This was fixed at 3½ per cent of the investment in the annuity as it stood at the time the first annuity payment was made. This amount was taxable as each payment was received. The balance was considered to be a return of capital until the cost was fully recovered, after which the entire payments were treated as taxable income.

A little reflection will indicate that for various reasons this rule permitted the tax-free recovery of the investment only in rare cases. First, the capital sum decreased as annuity payments were made. The original investment was not earning interest over the life of the annuity and even if the insurance companies used a 3½ per cent interest factor, as inevitably some of them did not, the sum to which the interest was applied varied. To be sure, during the period prior to payment of premiums, the interest factor was also at work and this fact might roughly offset the decreasing capital sum during the period of payments. The result was most conspicuously unfair for a person who purchased an annuity to begin immediately with a single premium payment, a not uncommon action at the time of retirement. But it became apparent that under the policies and interest rates then existing, annuity holders commonly would have to live beyond their life expectancies to recover their investment free of tax. The present rule was adoptd as a substitute for the 3½ per cent presumption.

Taxation of Life Insurance Companies

The taxation of life insurance companies is discussed briefly in a later chapter devoted to the tax treatment of various special forms of corporations. But since the taxation of the companies themselves bears so directly on the tax status of life insurance and annuity policies, a few paragraphs on the development of the tax law regarding life insurance companies will round out the subject.

Life insurance companies have traditionally enjoyed lower effective rates of taxation than most corporate enterprises. The principal problem in life insurance taxation has always been to define net income in such a

---

be recovered in three years or less by the annuity payments, he does not have to allocate his investment over his life expectancy; this exception to the general rule was made for convenience to obviate allocations which would result in only small deductions from a total annuity some part of which would be taxable from the start anyway (par. 1207 (c) (2)).

way that legitimate additions to policy reserves are not included in net income. The problem is further complicated by the rivalry between mutual and stock companies and by the socioeconomic importance of life insurance and life insurance companies.

From 1921 to 1959 life insurance companies were taxed only on their net investment income as defined by the tax law.[4] Until 1942 net investment income was determined by allowing specified rates of interest on the reserves each company individually held for its policyholders. Any investment income above the amount imputed by the specified rate was subject to normal corporate taxation. In 1942 Congress adopted an industry-wide formula for dividing the investment income between policyholders and individual companies. This formula, commonly called the Secretary's ratio, deemed a certain percentage of investment income to be taxable income without regard to the individual company's investment experience. The ratio for 1942 was 93 per cent.[5] Between 1942 and 1947 the Secretary's ratio gradually increased until the ratio exceeded 100 per cent. In 1948, when it became apparent that life insurance companies were no longer paying any taxes on investment income, Congress passed a "stopgap measure," which in effect taxed all life insurance company investment income at a 6½ per cent rate.

For the period 1949 through 1957 various stopgap taxes on life insurance companies were applicable. These taxes were enacted on a year-to-year basis while the Treasury and the Congress endeavored to work out a basis for permanent tax legislation. A flat 6½ per cent tax was applied from 1949 until 1955. From 1955 through 1958, the tax rate was the normal corporate tax on 15 per cent of the investment income or an effective rate of about 7½ per cent on total investment income.

In 1959 the present insurance company tax law was passed (par. 3434(a)). The law provides a three-part tax base for life insurance companies consisting of (1) a portion of their investment income based on the individual company's reserves and investment experience; (2) one-half of underwriting income [6] as earned and (3) the remaining half of underwriting income to the extent that it was distributed to stockholders. This total income less certain tax credits and deductions is subject to the normal corporate tax. The net capital gains of the insurance company are also taxed. Perhaps the most significant change in the 1959 act was the taxation

---

[4] Net investment income is that portion of investment income not required for reserves or other policy liabilities, i.e., the company's share of the investment income.

[5] This percentage of investment income was imputed to the policyholder's policy reserves and other policy liabilities. The other 7 per cent of investment income was subject to the normal corporate tax.

[6] Underwriting income consists of premiums collected in excess of necessary reserves; in essence it is the operating income of the insurance company.

of underwriting income. This element of income had not been taxed since 1921, and it constituted a major portion of total income for certain insurance companies. Congress also refined the definition of investment income to eliminate some inequities in the older laws.

Uses of Life Insurance

This is not the place for a general discussion of the value of life insurance or annuities as investments, or the extent to which an expectation of inflation modifies the traditional analysis. It is sufficient here to note that the higher the marginal tax bracket of an investor, the greater the attraction of a tax-free accumulation. A 3 per cent interest factor in an insurance policy seems unattractive, but for a person subject to a 70 per cent tax rate, it would take 10 per cent taxable interest to give the same net return for compounding. The fact that the accumulation of interest in a life insurance policy is never subject to income tax if the policy is held until death is a major attraction, as noted by insurance salesmen in their solicitations of wealthy individuals.

Life insurance is often used by many smaller companies and their owners to provide liquidity for business and estate settlement purposes. For example, a company can take out a policy on the life of a stockholder, whether an employee or not, with itself as beneficiary so that upon his death the proceeds will be available to redeem any notes or stock of the company he may have held. A policy can also be taken out on a key executive or stockholder so that the company will receive an immediate cash consideration in the event of his death. This cash can be used to help carry the business along until an adequate replacement can be hired or trained.

Under either plan the company receives the death benefit tax-free and as long as the insured person or his family is not the beneficiary, the premiums paid by the company are not taxable income to the insured. This is true even though the proceeds of the policy may ultimately go to his estate through retirements of any outstanding notes or redemptions of stock, to the extent of estate and inheritance taxes, with no risk of having the payment in stock redemption treated as a taxable dividend (par. 1710(b)). The full significance of this provision is discussed in the chapter on corporate distributions.

Two or more owners of a business at times cross-insure themselves rather than have the company make financial plans as described above. In this case, the premiums are paid by the individual and are not tax-deductible. Under this plan, the owners cross-insure each other so that the surviving owner is the beneficiary of a policy on the life of the deceased owner. The surviving owner then applies these proceeds to purchase the decedent's equity in the business. This plan provides liquidity in the decedent's estate and allows the surviving owner to retain control of the company. If the policies are surrendered before death, the difference between the amount received and the net premiums paid is taxable as income to the recipient.

The chief difficulty with the use of insurance for estate tax purposes, whether carried by the company or as cross-insurance, is that it can be very expensive, especially if the insured lives to a normal age. In the case of cross-insurance of two owners, they are paying for twice the amount of insurance actually needed because it is impossible to tell who is going to die first. A further problem exists in that at some point in life everyone becomes physically uninsurable. While this obviously does not affect any insurance already in force, it may mean that additional insurance will not be available at any cost when it becomes necessary as the value of stock in a company increases.

7

Estate
and Gift Taxes
and Estate Planning[1]

The federal estate tax, at rates ranging from 3 per cent to 77 per cent, and the federal gift tax, at rates from $2\frac{1}{4}$ per cent to $57\frac{3}{4}$ per cent, impose substantial capital levies on the transfer of property within a family as well as to all outsiders except qualified charities. Transfers between spouses, whether made during life or at death, receive the benefit of marital deductions which may also substantially reduce the effective tax burden on transfers between generations.

This chapter describes the principal provisions of these two taxes and indicates the major procedures which may be adopted, and the considerations to be taken into account, in planning for the transfer of family property during life and at death.

GENERAL ASPECTS OF ESTATE AND GIFT TAXES

The federal estate tax is imposed not only on all property owned by a decedent at the time of his death, but also on property which he may have previously given away in contemplation of death, as defined in the law, and even on some property which he has never owned, as for example property held in a trust under which the decedent had the right to designate who should receive the property under a general power of appointment (pars. 3904–17).

[1] All paragraph references in this chapter are to the Prentice-Hall *Federal Tax Course,* unless otherwise indicated.

103

The law concerning the inclusion or exclusion of various property rights in a taxable estate is as complex and varied as is the law concerning property rights itself. Joint tenancies, tenancies by the entirety, tenancies in common, community property, property subject to dower and courtesy, general and special powers of appointment, transfers in contemplation of death, transfers reserving the right of use or enjoyment of income, transfers taking effect at death, transfers reserving a power to alter, revoke, amend or terminate, and transfers for inadequate consideration are among the property rights for which the tax law makes specific provision. A tax practitioner, and especially anyone concerned with estate planning, must be familiar with the rules regarding all of them. It will be sufficient here, however, to note the general concepts on which the rules are based and their application in the more common forms of property ownership. But first a brief comment on the gift tax will be useful since these two taxes, the estate tax and the gift tax, complement each other.

The gift tax is imposed on gratuitous transfers of property during life, in contrast to the estate tax, which is imposed on the transfer of property at death, whether by a will or by the operation of law in the absence of a will. Each tax is imposed on the transferor, as an excise tax on the privilege of transferring property, with the tax base being measured by the value of the property. The gift tax was enacted primarily to prevent escape from the estate tax by gifts before death. (Not all countries with death duties have gift taxes. In the United Kingdom, for example, there is no gift tax, and if one can guess the sequence of deaths correctly, it is possible to maintain family property intact by gifts between spouses and successive generations.)

The rates of the gift tax are three-quarters of those of the estate tax (pars. 3934, 4027). Neither tax makes any distinction in rates based on the degree of relationship of the heir or donee, or of the number of specific bequests or gifts. The tax is thus based on the aggregate estate or the aggregate of cumulative gifts made by a donor during his life. The progression in each rate scale is separate, however. Though the estate tax rate schedule is higher than the gift tax rate schedule, it is better not to give away all of a large estate before death because the lower brackets of the estate tax are, of course, much lower than the higher brackets of the gift tax, and the fact of previous gifts is irrelevant in the calculations of the estate tax on any property remaining to be transferred at death.

The estate tax is imposed on the total estate before tax; that is, the amount to be paid in tax is included in the base on which the tax is calculated. The gift tax, by contrast, is on the net gift; the tax is not in the tax base. A taxable estate of $10,000,000 pays a tax of $6,088,200, with a net estate for heirs of a little less than $4,000,000. But if one starts with the same $10,000,000 and proposes to give it away, something over $7,000,000 may be given with a gift tax on that amount of slightly under $3,000,000. Thus, though the rate scale of the gift tax is three-quarters that of the estate tax, the dollar amount of the gift tax is considerably less than would seem to be indicated by the relationship. One must always remember the extremely important difference that the estate tax is imposed on the amount of the estate before tax, while the gift tax is imposed on the amount of the net gift after tax.

Each tax has its own set of exemptions. For the estate tax there is a specific exemption of $60,000; for the gift tax the specific lifetime exemption is $30,000 for each donor, regardless of the number of donees (pars. 3928, 4021). There is also an annual exemption of $3,000 for each donor for each donee, which does not count toward the $30,000 lifetime exemption for each donor for all gifts (par. 4020). In addition there is a marital deduction in each tax, which, however, operates quite differently in the two taxes.

Marital Deductions

The marital deduction in the estate tax permits up to half of the adjusted gross estate (to be defined later) to go to a surviving spouse tax-free (pars. 3929–31). Thus if the spouse owning all the family property dies first, half of the estate can go to the surviving spouse tax-free and in turn be passed on to the next generation as a separate estate with another $60,000 exemption and a fresh start on the progressive rate scale. If the spouse with property dies first, an estate of $10,000,000 can become two estates of $5,000,000 each, with a saving in tax of over $1,000,000 in the final transfer to succeeding generations. The marital deduction is designed to reduce the tax burden on bequests to surviving spouses, but the capricious result in the total tax imposed on the transfer of property to children and grandchildren, depending on the sequence of death of parents, seems highly inequitable.

In the gift tax the marital deduction works differently. One-half of any gift to a spouse is exempt (par. 4023). This means that only one-half of any gift is exempt, and only if one gives all of his property to his spouse will he be able to give half of it without tax. By contrast, the marital deduction in the estate tax permits any amount up to one-half of the total to be transferred tax-free to the spouse. The marital deduction in the gift tax also permits the $30,000 lifetime exemption per donor and the $3,000 annual exemption per donee to be doubled, if there is a living spouse who consents. Thus even if the property is all owned by one spouse, gifts of $6,000 per year may be made tax-exempt to each donee, including of course children, children-in-law, and grandchildren. With sizable families a significant fraction of even an appreciable estate may thus be transferred by lifetime tax-exempt gifts. The marital deduction in the gift tax does not, of course, permit each spouse with separate property to double his or her annual tax-free gifts; the effect is rather to provide that the couple will be allowed a $6,000 annual exemption per donee and a $60,000 lifetime exemption for all donees, over and above the annual exemption per donee, even if only one of the spouses owns property or makes the gifts.

Property Subject to Estate and Gift Taxes

The gift and estate taxes together are designed to impose a tax on all gratuitous transfers of property, whether by gift inter vivos or at death. The law has become complicated to prevent avoidance by various ingenious forms of transfer through trusts or piecemeal transfers. It will probably become even more complicated to meet the problems created by the use of multiple trusts and trusts extending over several generations. Sometimes property is subject to both taxes, as in the case of a gift in contemplation of death, but there is no double tax burden since the gift tax may be credited in full against the estate tax (par. 3935). There is in fact a great tax advantage in making deathbed gifts even with the certainty that they will be held to be in contemplation of death with the estate tax also applied. The advantage arises from the fact, noted before, that the gift tax is not included in the tax base in computing the gift tax, and since it is either paid or payable to the Treasury, the fact of a gift means that the amount of the gift tax is removed from the estate tax base as well.

Gifts in Contemplation of Death

Since 1950, the tax law has mercifully provided that any gift made more than three years before death cannot be held to be in contemplation of death, regardless of any facts and circumstances existing at the time of the gift or subsequently (par. 3911(a)). Prior to that date, there was a great deal of litigation concerning motives. Generally the courts have been rather generous in their recognition of motives associated with life and have ruled against contemplation of death even for gifts from elderly and feeble donors when there was evidence of specific objectives associated with life, including a desire for children and grandchildren to have a sense of financial independence, or to secure investment experience, or to provide funds for a specific purpose such as the purchase of a house or an assured fund for education. These same motives still may be used to overcome the present presumption that any gift within three years of death is in contemplation of death; the three-year rule provides assurance that the passage of three years will give certainty and prevent any assertion of contemplation of death [2] (par. 3911(b)).

Property Owned Jointly

On property held as joint tenants or tenants by the entirety, the entire value is included in the estate of the decedent unless the surviving joint owner can prove that he paid for part of the cost of the property (pars. 3905–07). This can be a nuisance, at best, and may be very difficult if, for example, property was purchased by funds from a joint general purpose bank account with frequent deposits and withdrawals for many purposes. The balance in a joint bank account itself is subject to the same rules. If one holder of a joint account withdraws funds deposited by the other, a gift is presumed to have been made; this is a necessary rule to prevent general avoidance of the tax through joint bank accounts but it can be a great nuisance. When withdrawn funds are all devoted to household expenses, there is of course no attempt to impute gifts between spouses or children and parents. But the complications of tracing and identifying the source of funds are sufficient to make many couples keep separate bank accounts for their separate investment funds, with a joint account only for household purposes. Reciprocal powers of attorney will permit each to draw on the other's account in case of incapacity or emergency.

Prior to 1955, when a husband and wife took title to a residence as tenants by the entirety or as joint tenants with right of survivorship, the spouse paying all or more than half of the cost was deemed to have made a gift to the other. And if on subsequent sale the spouse who originally made the entire payment took all of the proceeds, he was

[2] In the United Kingdom, where a similar time rule applies, it is alleged that a prominent, elderly individual who had given most of his property to his heir to avoid the death duties was so scandalized by the heir's use of the property that he committed suicide shortly before the expiration of the time period to assure that the government would step in and take most of it under the contemplation of death rule; socialized use was presumably considered less bad than private misuse.

deemed to have received a gift back from his wife. These gifts, reportable and taxable if they exceeded the exemptions, and absorbing the lifetime exemption even if not taxable, were apparently often not recognized as such even by some experienced conveyancers. There apparently was a good deal of quite unintentional violation of the law arising from the purchase and sale of family residences. The law was changed in 1954 to provide that in purchases of real estate (the special rule probably should have been limited to real estate occupied as a residence) the taking of title jointly by a husband and wife does not constitute a gift, except if the purchasers so elect (par. 4016). If the election is not made, a gift is deemed to be made when the real estate is sold, unless the proceeds are divided in the same proportion as the original purchase price was provided by the husband and wife. This treatment of real estate simplifies the gift tax with respect to purchases of residences and prevents the imposition of tax where no gift is intended; it is one of the few simplifications in the gift tax since its adoption in 1932.

Tenancy in common, as distinct from joint tenancy and tenancy by the entirety, does not involve gift and death tax complications, since each owner has a separate fractional interest in the entire property, which interest he can dispose of to his heirs as he chooses; only the value of the fractional interest is included in his estate (par. 3905(c)).

Property in Trusts

The major complications in determining property to be included in an estate come from trusts and from incomplete transfers. The tax law has been made increasingly strict, that is, the range of property rights subject to inclusion in the estate tax base has been made increasingly broad, to prevent avoidance of the estate tax through partial or incomplete transfers before death. It is for this reason that transfers intended to take effect at death, that is, transfers in which the transferee can secure propery only by surviving the transferor, do not serve to remove property from an estate, no matter how long before death they may have been made.

Property in trust is owned by the trustee and hence is not in any literal sense among the assets of the grantor when he dies. The tax law recognizes a transfer to an irrevocable trust as removing property from a grantor for estate tax purposes, if the transfer is complete with no rights reserved, and of course subject to the three-year rule on contemplation of death (par. 3912(a)). But if the grantor reserves the right to receive income or in any way to change the trust conditions, the trust property will be included in his estate. It is in this area that the law is especially complicated; it deals with special reservations of powers which have never occurred to most people. For example, a right to revoke a trust by joint action of the grantor and the beneficiaries (not included in an estate) is distinguished from a situation where the trustee has the right to revoke or alter a trust with the consent of all the beneficiaries if the grantor also has the right to remove the trustee and appoint himself as successor-trustee (included in an estate) (par. 3914).

Generally a gift tax is applicable for a transfer to an irrevocable trust, and the income from the trust is then taxable to the trust if it is not distributed, or to the beneficiary if it is distributed. However, even though the trust is irrevocable, if the trust property will revert to the grantor within ten years, the income from the trust is taxable to the grantor and the gift tax applies only to the present value of the income for the period of the trust, according to actuarial tables. If the trust is revocable, the income is taxable to the grantor and the gift tax applies only to the annual income distributed to the beneficiaries.

The exercise of a power of appointment under a trust established by someone else may constitute a taxable gift if it is done during life or may bring trust property within an estate if the power is exercised by will at death. The mere existence of some powers of appointment, even if they are not exercised at any time, may bring property within an estate. If, for example, a person leaves his property in trust, with his child to receive the income for life and the principal to go to whomsoever the child directs, including the child's estate, but in the absence of any action by the child the principal is to be divided equally among the grandchildren at the child's death, the entire principal will be included in the child's estate even if he does not exercise his power to designate who shall receive the principal.

A general power of appointment is one which includes the right to exercise the power in favor of oneself, his estate, his creditors, or the creditors of his estate (pars. 3909–10). Thus the failure to exercise a general power is in effect the renunciation of the right to personal use of property; it seems reasonable that the existence of such a power should bring property within the estate of the person having the power. This has not always been the case, however; for general powers created before October 22, 1942, only the exercise of a power will bring the property into the possessor's estate. A release of a general power of appointment, or the lapse of a power, may give rise to a taxable gift. Distinctions are made for powers created before and after October 22, 1942, for releases of powers before and after June 1, 1951, and in connection with lapses of powers to invade principal depending on whether the authorized invasion exceeds $5,000 or 5 per cent of the principal, whichever is greater. Anyone becoming involved with the existence, regardless of actual use, of powers of appointment needs specific legal advice regarding the tax consequences of his actions or inactions.

One major point, however, stands out. Property may be left in trust for as many generations as is permitted under the governing state law, usually for the duration of specified lives in being plus twenty-one years, with each succeeding generation having the right to income from the property, and with no estate or gift tax other than the original estate or gift tax when the property was transferred to the trust. Even the right to invade principal to maintain an ascertainable standard of living will not necessarily bring the trust property within the taxable estates of the intervening generations. This tax treatment of trusts is a major factor, perhaps the most important single tax factor, in estate planning. The opportunity to skip the estate and gift taxes in intervening generations gives a strong inducement to leave property in trust for as many generations as is possible without violation of the rule against perpetuities.

Life Insurance and Annuities

Life insurance owned by a decedent regardless of the beneficiary, or payable to his estate regardless of the owner of the policy, is included in his estate (par. 3916). Thus, if a person has the right to change the beneficiaries, or to borrow against the policy, he is deemed to be the owner of the policy. The fact that he may not have had an opportunity to exercise the right to change a beneficiary, as in an airflight insurance policy purchased just before takeoff, does not remove the proceeds from the taxable estate. But a policy purchased by a wife or her husband, on which she paid all premiums from her own funds and owned all right to change beneficiaries and assign the policy or borrow on it, would not be in the husband's taxable estate when he dies. And since 1954, the fact that a husband pays the premiums on a life insurance policy owned by his wife on himself will not bring the proceeds into his estate. Prior to that time, the "premium-payment-test" made the proceeds of insurance taxable where one person paid the premiums directly or indirectly, even if he had none of the usual incidents of ownership.

The payment of premiums on a policy owned by someone else constitutes a taxable gift to the extent of the premiums, subject to the regular exclusions and exemptions, as does the gift of a life insurance policy itself. If a policy is given, the value for tax purposes is deemed to be the replacement cost of a similar policy, not the premiums previously paid.

An annuity for a surviving wife or children purchased by a decedent is included in his estate, at a figure based on its actuarial value taking into account the life expectancies of the annuitants. The basis to the survivor may be less than the amount subject to estate tax, in which case relief is given by a complicated calculation which in effect allows the excess of estate tax value to be offset in computing the taxable income of the survivor over the life expectancy of the survivor (par. 3917).

A special rule applies, however, for annuities to survivors under a qualified pension plan (par. 3917(b)). In such cases, the present value of the future expected annuities, to the extent that it is based on the employer's contributions, is not included in the taxable estate of the decedent, and consequently there is no "cost" basis for the beneficiaries. Thus, all subsequent annuities are taxed in full as income is received. This special rule, adopted in 1954, was designed to relieve the hardships which arose when an estate consisted almost entirely of a survivor's annuity from a pension plan. In the absence of the relief provision, there might be no way to secure funds to pay the estate tax, especially since it would be impossible to borrow against the annuity if it had no guarantee provision and ceased with the death of the survivors. The concept underlying the special rule for annuities from qualified pension plans is that the entire amount is deemed to be deferred compensation, rather than in part income from an investment, with the compensation spread over the duration of life of any member of the family unit rather than confined to the life of the wage earner. Another special rule applies to annuities for survivors based on the contributions of tax-exempt employers who may not have qualified pension or profit sharing plans.

Foreign Real Estate

Until 1962, foreign real estate was not included in the taxable estates of U.S. citizens and residents. This gave a strong inducement to purchases of foreign real estate; even death bed purchases could be attractive with a prospect of loss on later sale, if the prospective loss was less than the estate tax saved. This provision of the U.S. estate tax law led to quite unusual forms of real estate ownership in places where there was social and political stability, currency stability, and no local death taxes. In at least one place, very small pieces of real estate were created "to die with" and sold subject to involved repurchase agreements, though the property was quite unsuitable for any use during life. Tax legislation in 1962 removed the exemption of foreign real estate.

Valuation

The valuation of property for estate and gift tax purposes follows the usual rules of fair market value (par. 3919). For such items as listed securities, cash, and savings bonds there is no problem of valuation. For real estate, art objects, personal effects, and interests in closely controlled businesses, valuation may be complicated, expensive, and finally determined only after litigation.

The valuation of stock in a closely controlled business can be especially troublesome and important (par. 3922(a)). No rule or formula has been established, nor should it be. Book value, replacement value of net assets, liquidating value, and capitalization of earnings (with adjustments for cyclical variations and any indicated trends) are all relevant, with adjustments for the effects of the death of the owner of stock if he is a key man in the management of the company. There may be, indeed there is likely to be, a considerable range of opinion regarding value among equally dispassionate experts based on the relative weight they attach to different factors in the valuation. But the relative importance of all significant factors will vary with circumstances, and it is inevitable that opinions will differ as to the weight to be assigned to each factor in any particular set of circumstances.

To minimize problems of valuation, the owners of some closely controlled businesses have made secondary distributions of some stock, or issued new stock, thereby assuring the existence of a market valuation. Some investment banking firms have stressed the usefulness of a market for purpose of valuation in their solicitations for stock offerings. In the 1930's and 1940's, when stock commonly sold at less than book value, a market value on such terms could be very attractive in terms of its absolute level as well as for the objective' evidence it provided. But with the great increase in stock values and high price earnings ratios after the middle 1950's and continuing into the 1960's, the market values often exceeded the figures that could have been secured by valuation in the absence of a free market figure, giving another example of the fact that action to minimize taxes may frequently backfire.

It is well established that when a large block of stock is included in an estate, the value per share may be substantially reduced to take account of the depressing effect of a large offering on the market (par. 3922(b)). This rule is applied fairly generously in some instances. Conversely, a block which carries control may have greater value per share than the market value of casual sales of small lots of stock.

Bona fide buy-and-sell agreements among partners or stockholders in a closely controlled corporation will usually be recognized (par. 3923). When the agreements are between members of a family, however, they will be reviewed critically to determine whether they involve hidden bequests, as would occur if an elderly father had a buy-and-sell agreement with his son and heir under which the son acquired a large block of stock, to add to his own previous small holding, at an unreasonably low price. The attraction of the nominal valuation for estate tax purposes would more than offset the risk that the son would predecease the father.

The estate tax law also gives an option to value an estate twelve months after the date of death (par. 3920(a)). Since the tax return is not due until fifteen months after death, executors regularly keep the valuation date open for a year, to get the benefit of any decrease in market values. Property sold, distributed, or exchanged during the year takes the market value on the date of sale, distribution, or exchange, if the optional date is used. Thus, if an estate uses the optional date, certainty can be secured on any items where controversy is expected by sale during the year or exchange for property of known value.

Credits Against the Estate Tax

The first step in figuring the estate tax is to reduce the gross estate, based on valuations, by all debts and expenses, including funeral and administrative expenses (par. 3926). This gives the adjusted gross estate against which the marital deduction is calculated, if applicable. The tax rates provided by law are then applied to the taxable estate, which is equal to the gross estate less all debts, expenses, deductions, and exemptions. The tax as thus determined may be reduced by crediting against it certain state inheritance and estate taxes, certain federal gift and estate taxes, and certain foreign death duties.

The allowable credit for state inheritance and estate taxes gives some recognition to the prior claim of the states to death duties in this country (par. 3936–37). As the federal tax rates were raised and the exemptions reduced subsequently, the allowable credit was held to the original figure with a complicated calculation necessary to determine the tax under the 1926 law, subject to the credit, and the additional tax not subject to the credit. The method of calculation was changed in 1954, to get the same result in a simpler manner. Since the exemption in 1926 was $100,000, there is no credit allowable on the lowest segment of a taxable estate, subject to the present $60,000 exemption.

Virtually all states have enacted "mop-up" estate taxes to absorb any allowable credit, to the extent that their regular inheritance and estate taxes do not amount to the credit. This situation is possible because many states rely primarily on inheritance taxes which are taxes related to specific bequests, with exemptions applicable to each. An estate large enough to be subject to the federal tax might thus not be subject to state inheritance taxes if it was spread out among many descendants. Conversely, the absolute level of exemptions is usually lower in the state taxes than in the federal tax, and if there is only one or a very few heirs, or if the state tax is an estate tax, there may be a substantial state tax even though there is no federal tax against which to credit it. On the average, about one-third of the total state death taxes is credited against the federal tax; the remainder arises from state taxes on estates below the level of federal taxability and state taxes in excess of the amount allowed as credit. And in a typical year, credits against the federal tax for state taxes are about 10 per cent of the total federal tax.

A credit against the federal tax is also allowed for the gift tax previously paid on gifts which are held to have been in contemplation of death (par. 3935). As previously noted, the amount of the gift tax is removed from the base on which the estate tax is calculated, thus making gifts attractive even when it is certain that they will later be held to have been in contemplation of death. The gift tax credit is allowed even if the gift tax is paid after the donor's death and even if the gift tax is deductible from the gross estate as a debt of the decedent. The credit is limited to an amount which bears the same ratio to the estate tax as the value of the gift bears to the value of the entire gross estate, less the charitable and marital deductions. The credit is also, of course, limited to the gift tax actually paid. It is not necessary that the property received by gift be separately identifiable or even that it still be held, but if identifiable its value for estate tax purposes will be taken into account in calculating the first limitation on the credit, if that value is lower than the value on which the gift tax is calculated.

A credit against the estate tax is also allowed on property in an estate received from a previous decedent (par. 3939). The credit is on a sliding scale ranging from 100 per cent of the previous estate tax attributable to the property in the estate of the second decedent when the interval between deaths is within two years. The credit is reduced by 20 per cent for each additional two years between deaths and vanishes if the interval is more than ten years. There are again two limitations on the credit. Under the first limitation, the credit cannot exceed the proportion of the prior decedent's estate tax that the value of the property received by the second decedent bore to the total adjusted taxable estate of the first decedent. The second limitation provides that the credit cannot exceed the proportion of the estate tax of the second decedent which the property received from the first decedent bears to the total estate of the second decedent. The credit for prior estate taxes is intended to reduce the impact of the estate tax in reducing a family's property when successive deaths occur at unusually short intervals.

The final credit against the estate tax is for foreign death taxes on property located abroad (par. 3938). This credit is also subject to limitations which, in effect, restrict the credit for foreign taxes in the proportion that property located in the foreign country imposing the tax bears to the total estate, and it requires an allocation of the charitable and marital deductions over the entire estate including the property located in foreign countries. Estate tax conventions with some foreign countries give additional special treatment to property located abroad and the taxes paid on it.

Deferral of Payment of Tax Attributable to Investment in Closely Controlled Businesses

The estate tax not infrequently requires the sale or liquidation of a closely controlled business on the death of one of the principal owners, if his estate has no liquid assets. To reduce this pressure, the results of which are considered undesirable under almost any economic or social philosophy, the law was amended in 1958 to permit the payment of estate tax over ten years, subject to interest at 4 per cent, to the extent that the tax is attributable to an interest in a closely held business (par. 3944). The value of the interest must exceed 35 per cent of the gross estate or 50 per cent of the taxable estate, and the corporation or partnership must have no more than ten members, or if the number of members is larger, the value of the decedent's interest must be at least 20 per cent of the voting stock or partnership capital. Also, interest in two or more businesses may be brought within the 35–50 per cent rule if the decedent owns more than 50 per cent of the stock in each.

This special rule for interests in closely held businesses should be viewed in conjunction with section 303 of the law, which permits redemption of stock to pay estate taxes without danger of having any of the proceeds treated as a taxable dividend, when the same 35–50 per cent concentration exists in an estate (par. 1710(b), *Federal Tax Handbook*). The two provisions have not been completely conformed, as they should be, since the redemption must take place within three years and ninety days after the filing of the estate tax return, while the estate tax itself can be spread over ten years. These two relief provisions in the law, separately and together, can be very effective in preventing the need for liquidation or sale of family businesses. Since sales are likely to involve mergers, these provisions of the law help to assure the continued independent existence of business concerns. They were advocated and adopted for that purpose and have been effective. Their existence lengthens and complicates the tax law, but this is an almost inevitable consequence of relief provisons, a fact which critics of the length and complexity of the law too often forget.

FACTORS IN ESTATE PLANNING

No formula can be given for estate planning. Many variables must be taken into account in any specific situation. Above all, it should be recognized that an attempt to secure minimium taxes may lead to action which is thoroughly undesirable from a business standpoint and from the standpoint of relations between members of a family or the effects on individual members of a family. Subject to these limitations, the following principal tax factors may be noted as necessary for consideration in any plan for transfer of an estate through a combination of inter vivos gifts and testamentary bequests.

Annual Exclusion and Lifetime Exemption for Gifts

As a minimum, tax-free gifts should be made to the maximum extent allowable. Further tax advantages will arise if the donees are in lower income tax brackets than the donor; subsequent income taxes are then also reduced by gifts. The obvious nontax limitation on gifts is an excessive reduction of the estate of the donor during his lifetime, or excessively large accumulations by donees. A further difficulty comes in maintaining equality among grandchildren or great-grandchildren if a program of gifts is started before all members of a generation have been born.

Use of Estate Tax Exemption and Lower Brackets of Estate Tax Schedule

An enthusiasm for gifts should not be carried to the point that taxable gifts are made when the property, if retained until death, would fall within the estate tax exemption or be subject to lower estate taxes than gift taxes.

Time Factor in Payment of Gift and Estate Taxes

Though the gift tax may be lower than the estate tax, it must be paid currently, thereby reducing the capital in a family with a consequent reduction of subsequent income and potential capital gains. The appropriate discount factor to apply to a later and larger estate tax, to make it comparable to a present gift tax, will depend on the rate of return on the capital and the rate of income tax applicable to the income.

Marital Deduction

The marital deduction will presumably be utilized to convert one large estate into two smaller estates, thereby putting them lower in the progressive tax scale. If the surviving spouse has a substantial life expectancy, it is reasonable to let her receive the full marital deduction even if she has a substantial independent estate; the fact that the two estates are not of equal size and hence the combined estate taxes are greater than necessary may be more than offset by the advantage of minimizing the reduction in capital at the time of the death of the first spouse. The tax saved by taking full advantage of the marital deduction will remain available to earn income and appreciate over the remaining life of the surviving spouse. If the spouse with few independent assets is dying before the spouse with most of the family property, nothing can be done to secure the benefit of the marital deduction short of suicide, an act which even the most enthusiastic tax minimizers tend to reject.

Gift to Remove Gift Tax from Estate Tax Base

The fact that even an unpaid gift tax, from a gift in contemplation of death, is removed from the estate tax base can yield a major tax saving when the higher brackets of the estate tax are applicable.

Basis of Property to Donees and Heirs

The fact that property passing at death, including property brought into a taxable estate as having been made in contemplation of death, takes the value at death for purposes of computing subsequent gain or loss gives a strong inducement to hold appreciated property until death

(*Handbook*, par. 1508). Property transferred by gift carries forward its cost or other basis from the donor to the donee plus the gift tax paid on the gift (*Handbook*, par. 1510–11). But if property is expected to appreciate still further, it may be better to transfer it at present value than to hold it for inclusion in a taxable estate at a higher value. The applicable gift and estate tax rates, the applicable capital gains tax rates, and the contemplated disposition of the property by the prospective donee or heir must all be taken into account.

Use of Leverage Assets in Gifts

High leverage common stock in a closely controlled business may be created and given to members of succeeding generations. This reduces the value of property subject to the tax on transfers between generations while assuring that future appreciation will be concentrated on the stock which will not be in the estates of members of the older generation. This point is developed at some length in the chapter on capital structures of corporations. Similarly, property may be purchased subject to a mortgage with the equity given to younger members of a family; the mortgage might even be held by older members if the sale price of the equity is reasonable.

Use of Charitable Bequests

The net cost of charitable bequests is reduced by deductibility in determining a taxable estate. Control of a family business may be more readily retained if nonvoting stock is created, as it can be through a tax-free recapitalization, and transferred to a family foundation or to any other charity. Abuses of family foundations arising from employment of or transactions with family members or transactions with the family business are likely to lead to some modification of the law with respect to them.

Use of Trusts

The advantages of skipping generations in successive estate or gift taxes are so great that it is almost negligent not to create trusts extending over several generations, even for estates of no more than several hundred thousand dollars. If the property is sufficiently great to permit accumulation of the income, multiple trusts are desirable since each one has its own $100 exemption for income tax purposes and has the progressive individual income tax rate schedule applied to it separately. A number of trusts each consisting of no more than $50,000 to $100,000 can keep the income tax on accumulating income in the lower brackets.

Trusts extending over several generations have the unfortunate effect of making passive rentiers out of the members of the intervening generations; they as individuals and society might be better off if they owned their capital outright and played a more active role in the economy. Legislation to reduce the tax advantages of multiple trusts and of trusts which extend beyond one generation is not unlikely.

Conclusion

The foregoing listing of the tax factors relevant to estate planning will suggest the many assumptions and calculations which are necessary to work out alternative plans and to select the best plan in any specific family situation. Life expectancies, future tax rates, future incomes from existing family property and future incomes of all family members from all other sources, probable increases and decreases in the value of existing property, future needs for income by different family members, and the probable period over which existing assets will be retained in the family investment portfolio are among the variables for which assumptions must be made to estimate the tax consequences of alternative plans. A final decision must of course be determined by the many personal considerations of the appropriate amounts and sorts of property and income to be available to different family members at different ages and subject to different restrictions. Tax factors, though extremely complicated, constitute only one category of factors for consideration; an obsession with tax minimization may produce many unnecessary strains on personal relationships within a family and either undesirable restrictions or undesirable freedom in the use of segments of a family's capital.

8

Tax Factors

in the Choice of Form

of Business Organization

The choice between a partnership or corporate form of business organization is often conclusively determined without reference to tax considerations. The advantages of limited liability, the assurance of free transferability of interests, or an inherent fear of the unknown in a partnership relationship may make a corporation the only acceptable form of organization for a venture in which an active businessman seeks capital from someone outside his family. Conversely, on rare occasions, an individual or group may so distrust the idea of a corporation on the grounds that it puts a paper entity between themselves and their property that they insist on operating as a proprietorship or partnership. And some lines of activities by law may not be conducted in corporate form, though with the permission for stock exchange firms to incorporate the legal barrier to incorporation applies almost entirely to professional activities and not to business ventures requiring capital investments.

Differences in tax liabilities between partnerships and corporations can be very great, however, and when there is some freedom of choice in the selection of the form of organization, tax factors may be controlling. The Congress recognized the lack of neutrality in the tax law as unintended and undesirable and, in 1954 and 1958, did what it could to make the tax burden similar regardless of the form of organization by permitting certain partnerships to elect to be taxed in general like corporations and certain corporations to elect to be taxed more or less like partnerships. The option for partnerships to be taxed like corporations was repealed effective April 14, 1966; partnerships which had made the election could continue under it through 1968.

The major differences in the taxation of partnerships and corporations can be stated very simply, though the detailed provisions of the law regarding some transactions are even more intricate than the transactions themselves.

Basically, a partnership is not a tax-paying entity. For tax purposes, it is regarded as an aggregation of the interests of the partners. It computes and reports its separate income as a legal entity, but the individual members pick up and report their pro rata shares of income and expense items on their individual tax returns as though they were, to the extent of their respective interests, in business as individuals. Furthermore, the character of each income and expense item is preserved; ordinary income, capital gains and losses, even charitable contributions and foreign tax credits retain their character and are added to similar items which each individual may have from his direct activity and investments. These combined totals for each individual are then subject to whatever limitations or restrictions may be applicable.

Thus, a charitable contribution by a partnership may mean a tax deduction for one partner who as an individual has not reached his 20 per cent or 30 per cent limit, but for another who has already personally given his deductible maximum a partnership gift results in a wasted deduction. Similarly, a share of a partnership capital loss will have to be offset against realized capital gains by a partner who has personal gains, but to the extent of $1,000 can be offset against ordinary income by a partner who has neither capital gains nor loss on a personal basis.

Since all income and deduction items are taken into account for tax purposes currently, a partner's basis for his partnership interest reflects at any time not only his investments in and withdrawals of capital, but his share of the accumulated profits. With income and gain imputed and taxed annually, any income not withdrawn is equivalent in determining a partner's investment in a firm to a new investment by him of funds from other sources.

The tax treatment of a corporation and its stockholders is in virtually all respects opposite to that of a partnership and its partners. The corporation calculates its own taxable income and pays its own tax. The separate legal entity is fully accepted for tax purposes. In fact, a corporation is included in the definition of "person" for most aspects of the income tax law. The corporation income tax, in fact, preceded the individual income tax by four years. It was first imposed in 1909 as an excise tax measured by net income, prior to the adoption of the Sixteenth Amendment in 1913 which overcame the barrier to direct taxation in the original Constitution, the Supreme Court having held that an income tax was a direct tax.

The corporation income tax rates have been quite unrelated to the individual rates, except for a brief period following 1913 when the corporate rate and the normal rate for individuals were both at one per cent, with higher surtax rates on larger individual incomes rising to 6 per cent. The corporate rate or rates have always been below the top-bracket rates for individuals.

The taxable income for corporations is defined in substantially the same way as that for an individual's own business income, with certain obvious differences such as the allowance of deductions for salaries of owner-managers of corporations (within the limit of reasonable compensation) and for amortization of organization expenses and the absence of personal as distinct from business deductions. Corporations may also distinguish between ordinary income and losses and capital gains and losses, and interest on state and municipal bonds is also tax-exempt to them.

But all income and gains lose their identity and character after being received and taxed—or nontaxed—to a corporation. Distributions to stockholders are presumed to come from a fungible pool of earnings and profits, with all amounts received taxed as dividends to the extent the company has earnings and profits, regardless of the source of funds to the corporation. Some exceptions to the general rule are recognized in the tax law for payments to stockholders in partial or complete liquidations of corporations or other returns of capital, but these are rarely applicable and the exceptional payments must qualify under the rigid requirements of the law. The basis of a stockholder's investment in stock continues as his original cost, regardless of the payment of ordinary dividends or accumulations of retained earnings by the corporation. The only adjustment is for receipts from the corporation which are held to be returns of capital.

The relative attraction of partnerships or corporations from the standpoint of income tax burdens is self-evident from the foregoing description of their tax treatment. Income received by stockholders is subject to double taxation, first in the hands of the corporation and then to the stockholders as dividends, or as capital gains if they sell stock at a price above its basis to them. Thus, to the extent that income is to be distributed currently, there is a clear tax disadvantage to a corporate form.

To the extent that earnings are to be retained, there may be a tax advantage to the corporate form of organization. But the calculation on the extent of the advantage involves assumptions about the time and form of ultimate realization. If the stockholders' individual marginal tax rates are above the corporate rate, there is an immediate tax saving by using a corporation and leaving the income in it. Since the individual marginal tax rates of the stockholders will probably differ, there may be a conflict of interest among them as to the relative tax advantages of a partnership or corporation. Those with a marginal tax rate below the corporate rate would be better off to have the income taxed to them directly. But funds retained by the corporation are still one step removed from personal possession. When and if the income is later paid out as dividends, it will be subject to individual tax which, of course, may be at a higher or lower rate than the current rate.

However, retained earnings may never be paid out. If used for permanent corporate expansion, the value of the stock will presumably also grow, but whether by exactly the amount of retained income or by more or less cannot be predicted with confidence. In some closely controlled corporations, the owners have reciprocal buy-and-sell agreements based on book value; in these situations retained earnings are precisely reflected in value, and in some mergers book values are a major factor. But the market values of a stock traded in open markets seldom reflect book values closely. Market values may fall far behind rising book values if retained earnings do not lead to commensurate increases in earnings. Or in a dynamic growth situation, market values may rise much faster than the book value of the stock. Thus, in appraising the tax advantage of using a corporation instead of a partnership to get a lower tax rate on earnings left in the business, one must first decide what effect the retention will have on the value of the stock. But this is only the first step in the analysis.

One must also decide on the most likely form of ultimate realization. The possibilities include dividends at a later time, sale of stock with a capital gains tax, a tax-free merger with further postponement of tax, or continued ownership of either the existing stock or stock received in exchange in a tax-free merger until death with a step-up in basis and no capital gains tax on the increase in value up to that time. Thus, the retained earnings or whatever increase in value is associated with them may be taxed later as regular income, as capital gains, or not at all, and whatever tax is imposed will not be due until some time in the future and hence should be discounted to present value, at whatever rate is appropriate for the individual concerned.

In spite of the uncertainties in estimating the tax advantages of a corporation over a partnership, they are sufficiently great to be used for what the Congress has been convinced were purposes of tax avoidance. To prevent the use of corporations merely for accumulating income, the tax law imposes a severe penalty tax on the unreasonable accumulation of surplus for the purpose of avoiding income tax by its shareholders (pars. 3422–24). The application of this tax is discussed in Chapter 15.

TAXATION OF PARTNERSHIPS

If all partnerships involved simple arrangements, with each partner contributing cash to the venture, sharing profits and losses in proportion to their investments, dealing only with outsiders, and liquidating the partnership in cash when its affairs are wound up, the tax law concerning partnership would also be simple. But when some partners contribute cash and others property with a tax basis different from its market value, when gains are divided differently than losses, when some partners receive guaranteed incomes, when the partnership has business transactions with one of the partners as an individual and when the partners withdraw property as well as cash from the partnership, the tax treatment as well as the internal accounting of the partnership becomes complicated.

Partnership accounting is somewhat of a specialty, not usually covered in any detail, if at all, in introductory accounting courses. With this precedent, the discussion here of the taxation of partnerships will be confined to an explanation of the reasons for some of the principal rules which appear to be and are rather involved. Hopefully, when one understands the reasons for them, they will seem more comprehensible. And when one realizes that they are often necessary as relief measures to prevent taxes from being imposed on transactions which do not give rise to disposable cash, one should be less annoyed at the fact of their existence. The remainder of this section may be skipped by anyone unconcerned with the details of partnership agreements.

A basic concept in the taxation of partnerships is that transfers of property to a partnership and withdrawals of property from it by partners should not be subject to tax (par. 2917). If transfers of property to partnerships were taxable, taxation would be a barrier to their formation because at the very time when businessmen and investors were getting together to go into business or expand an existing business they might have to use some of their available cash to pay a large tax for the privilege. This would occur in the absence of tax relief if property transferred to the partnership by one of the partners had a low basis in comparison with its market value, as is likely to be the case with patents, land, buildings, or machinery. But with transfer to the partnership not subject to tax, to prevent tax avoidance the basis of the transferred property must be carried forward and used in subsequent calculations of depreciation and gain or loss (par. 2912(b)).

Since a partner takes into account in calculating his own taxable income his share of distributive partnership gain or loss, his basis must reflect these results. If partnership income already taxed to a partner were not added to his basis, it would be subject to a second tax when the partnership was finally sold or liquidated. Similarly, his basis must be increased by his distributive share of any nondeductible partnership expenses or nontaxable income. If tax-exempt income were received directly, he could invest it in the partnership and increase his basis; if the partnership receives it on his behalf, as it were, his basis must be similarly increased to prevent a tax penalty against receipt of tax-exempt income by a partnership.

Withdrawals from a partnership decrease a partner's basis in his partnership. Whether the withdrawal were deemed to be of an original investment or distributive shares of income previously taxed as earned, its withdrawal should not give rise to a tax, but should reduce the basis of the remaining investment; if basis were not reduced, final liquidation would show a loss where none existed. If property other than cash is withdrawn, to prevent any nontaxable step-up or loss of basis, the reduction in a partner's basis in a partnership is reduced by his basis in partnership property distributed to him.

A partner may acquire his interest in a partnership by rendering services to it, in which case the fair market value of the interest which he receives is deemed to be income currently taxable to him and in turn becomes the basis of his interest in the partnership.

A final very important rule concerning a partner's basis is that it is increased by his share of any increase in the partnership's liabilities and decreased by any reduction in the liabilities. This concept seems puzzling at first, implying as it seems to that one's investment and hence his net worth is increased by the mere act of borrowing. The rule means that for tax purposes a partner's involvement in a venture is equally great whether he puts his own funds into it or allows it to borrow from others, and this may seem strange. But a slight extension of the last sentence reveals the logic of the tax rule because when a partnership borrows it does so on behalf of its partners who are committed financially by its debts. The increased basis in the partnership because of its borrowing does not represent any change in the net worth of a partner's investment in it or in one's personal net worth. The debt is presumably matched by an equal increase in assets at the moment it is incurred, the two increases canceling each other insofar as net worth is concerned. The reason for recognition of an increase in basis by borrowing is to support the deductibility of depreciation on assets acquired with borrowed funds or expenses incurred with them. Furthermore, the deduction of losses by each partner is limited to his basis in a partnership. This limitation is imposed to prevent indefinitely large offsets of individual income by partnership losses. But if bona fide deductions are not to be nondeductible because incurred through a partnership, it is necessary to recognize that basis is increased to the extent of liabilities incurred.

Tax Status of Distributions of Partnership Property to Partners (pars. 2918–19)

As a general rule, when a partner withdraws money or other property from a continuing partnership, he has neither gain nor loss, and the property he receives has the same tax basis in his hands as it did in the partnership (par. 2918(a)). This is the counterpart of the absence of tax on transfer of property to a partnership. But the tax basis in his hands cannot exceed his basis in the partnership; otherwise there would be a step-up of basis with an eventual avoidance of tax. If he receives money in excess of his basis, the excess is currently taxable as capital gain. If the tax basis of other property, reduced by the amount of money received, exceeds the remaining basis of the interest, the basis of the other property must be reduced in proportion to its fair market value. This procedure produces two sensible results. It avoids any step-up in basis and imposes no tax until cash is available for payment.

Distribution by Partnerships

The tax rules regarding distributions by partnerships, or withdrawals from partnerships by partners, are greatly complicated by the need to prevent the conversion of ordinary income into capital gains by what are referred to as collapsible partnerships. This could occur, for example, if goods in an inventory, or even uncollected receivables, were distributed to partners with a tax at capital gains rates on the difference between the tax basis to the partnership and the current fair market value. The partners could then as individuals sell the property or collect the receivables with no further tax, because the basis in their hands would have been brought up to the prospective current value by payment of a the capital gains tax. If the sales and collections had been conducted by the partnership in the ordinary course of business, ordinary income would have been realized and taxed to the partners.

Collapsible partnerships are analogous to collapsible corporations, discussed in a later chapter. The word collapsible refers to a termination, partial or complete, of the business carried on by a legal entity before the final sales and collections which occur in the ordinary operations of a company carrying on a continuing business with its customers. The tax abuses first arose in connection with corporations, and led to new provisions of the law. Fortunately, it was found feasible to define collapsible corporations by objective tests and if a company does not fall within the definition no complications arise. In 1954, collapsible partnerships were being adopted to get similar results, and in the legislation adopted then to prevent the new abuse it was not found feasible to establish a definition for collapsible partnerships. The special rules apply to the distribution of certain defined classes of property by any partnership. Accordingly, each type of distribution or withdrawal includes complicating rules to be applied when the specified forms of property are involved. A similar problem arises in connection with the recapture of depreciation on sales of depreciated property and of the investment credit on property sold before the presumed life on the basis of which the investment credit was allowed.

Though the safeguards against abuses through collapsible partnerships complicate the law and indeed make it appear quite formidable, they are not applicable for partnerships which conduct their affairs in a normal way with the partnership itself carrying all transactions through to completion and the partners withdrawing only cash. Even when a partnership is converted into a corporation, as the business expands, the special rules are not applicable. After these preliminary comments, the following discussion will ignore the many special provisions and exceptions which have been found necessary to make sure that what would be ordinary income if business were conducted in the ordinary way is not converted into capital gains by extraordinary transactions between partnerships and partners.

Distributions by a partnership to a partner are generally not taxable, so long as they do not exceed his basis in the partnership (par. 2918). This seems reasonable because up to that point a partner is merely recovering his original investment or withdrawing the accumulated income which has already been imputed and taxed to him. When the distributions exceed basis, and if the distribution is in the form of money, the excess is taxed as capital gain. If the distribution is in other property, there is no current tax, but the basis in the partnership reduced by any money received, is allocated to the various items of property, which means that tax will be due when they are later sold.

Loss is not recognized unless a partner's interest is completely liquidated and the property received consists entirely of money, in which case a capital loss is recognized to the extent of the excess of basis of the partnership interest over the money received. (This is the first of numerous rules on which no reference is made to the exceptions and special rules for inventory, receivables and property which might lead to recapture of depreciation or an investment credit.)

The partnership itself also generally realizes no gain or loss on distribution of property to a partner. The basis of distributed property to a partner, other than property received in a complete liquidation of partnership interest, is the partnership's basis for the property so long as this does not exceed his own basis for his interest in the partnership (par. 2919). Thus, property can come out from the partnership with a carryover of basis, just as it can go in, but there is no chance for a step-up of basis. If the basis to the partnership of distributed property exceeds a partner's basis for his interest in the partnership, he must allocate the basis of his interest among the items of property received in a prescribed sequence.

If a distribution is in complete liquidation, the basis of the interest in the partnership interest, less any money received, is allocated among the items of property received. Thus, tax is postponed until free funds are available to pay it. When distributed property is later sold by a partner or former partner, the gain is a capital gain if the property is a capital asset in his hands (par. 2920).

The tax law recognizes that partnerships may continue with new partners, at least for purposes of federal income taxation, and hence provides rules for taxation of the gain or loss on the sale or transfer of a partnership interest (par. 2921). The difference between the amount received and the basis of partnership interest is a capital gain or loss, with the usual exceptions for the amounts received for an interest in receivables and appreciated inventory. And the transferee, of course, applies the usual rules to determine his basis, which ordinarily would be cost or, in the case of an inherited interest, the value placed on the interest for estate tax purposes (par. 2922).

Perhaps the most difficult aspect of partnership taxation to understand at first acquaintance is a provision which gives a partnership the right to elect to adjust the basis of its property when there has been a distribution of partnership property or a transfer of an interest in the partnership (par. 2923). The election once made must be applied for both purposes and in all transactions until it is revoked with the consent of the Commissioner of Internal Revenue. The effect of the election is to permit the basis of the property held by the partnership to correspond to or reflect certain transactions that have had an effect on the basis of the partner's interests in the firm.

The simplest example to explain is the adjustment when a new partner buys the interest of a former partner for more than the latter's share of the basis of all partnership property (par. 2923(b)). The full amount of the new partner's investment thus is not reflected in the basis of the partnership property, and subsequent depreciation, for example, will be less than it would be if the property itself had been purchased by the new partner and contributed to the partnership. To permit the simpler procedure of buying an interest in a continuing partnership, instead of having an old partnership liquidated and a new one formed, with all the tax complications to the continuing partners, the tax law permits the basis adjustment to reach the same result indirectly. The adjustment applies only to the transferee partner's interest in the basis; only he has paid for something in excess of the partnership's basis. The election, if made, applies both ways, and if a transferee partner has a basis less than his proportionate share of the partnership's basis in property, his share in the latter must be decreased.

The logic for the adjustment on certain distributions of property is less obvious but nonetheless valid (par. 2923(a)). It will be recalled that a partner receiving property generally takes the partnership's basis for it as his own, but that the total cannot exceed his own basis for his partnership interest. Thus, if the partnership basis for property distributed exceeds a partner's basis for his interest in the partnership, the difference is lost when the property is distributed. No one gets a loss, and no one has a right to hold on to that segment of basis. This is where the optional adjustment to basis comes in. The partnership may increase the basis for its other assets by this difference or gap. But if it does so for any lost basis, it must be consistent and decrease basis for any excess of basis which a distributee partner has over the partnership's basis in the property distributed.

The third occasion for adjustment of basis is even less obvious. If a gain is realized by a partner on a distribution, the basis of partnership property must be increased by those partnerships electing the option. Remember that a gain is recognized only if the money received exceeds a partner's basis for his partnership interest. Since his basis reflects retained income, including realized gains, a distribution in excess of basis would seem to be likely to occur only if there is unrealized appreciation in other assets; otherwise, the distribution would seem to be unreasonably generous from the standpoint of the other partners.

When the distributee partner realizes a gain on the distribution and pays a tax on it, it would seem appropriate that someone should get the benefit of a higher basis. The distributee partner cannot get the benefit of higher basis because he received money and the basis of money cannot be written up. Thus, an increase in the basis of partnership assets, whose appreciation has been reflected in the taxable gain to one partner, seems a reasonable adjustment to permit combined bases to reflect realized gains. If a partner with a one-third interest in a partnership with $11,000 cash and property with a basis of $19,000 but a market value of $22,000 withdraws his interest, he would be entitled to one-third of the total value or $11,000, which he receives in cash. If the basis of his partnership interest is $10,000, he has a realized gain of $1,000. In the absence of the adjustment option, no one could get the benefit through basis of this payment of tax. The optional adjustment permits the basis of property of the partnership to be written up to $20,000. It is left to the partners to reflect these possible adjustments in their own relations through the partnership agreement.

Finally, rules are needed to cover payments to retiring partners or heirs of deceased partners (par. 2924). Generally, the payments are treated as distributions in complete liquidation of an interest. Money received reduces the basis of the partnership interest. Any excess of money over basis is capital gain. Any remaining basis is allocated to such other property as is received, and if no other property is received, the excess of basis over money received is a capital loss.

A distinction must be maintained between payments in liquidation of an interest and amounts which are classified as shares of partnership income or guaranteed payments (par. 2924(b)–(c)). The latter, of course, are taxable as income to the recipient and hence are not imputable to the remaining partners. By contrast, liquidation payments do not affect the income of the remaining partners. Thus, there would be a tax benefit to remaining partners to throw as much of a payment as possible to a retired partner into the classification of a share in income, a shift which would be resisted by the recipient. Since the income brackets of the individuals concerned are not necessarily the same, the tax advantage of one group may overcome the reluctance of the other and the classification of payments must be justified by the facts, including the partnership agreement.

Family Partnerships

The chance to use a partnership with children and grandchildren to divide a large income of one person into two or more separate incomes, each subject to a new start on the progressive individual income tax rate schedule, is obviously attractive. Since the separate rate schedule was adopted for joint returns in 1948, the prior attraction for a partnership with one's spouse no longer exists. In the absence of specific statutory provisions, there was a good deal of litigation in attempts to develop distinctions between genuine and sham partnerships, especially those with infants or inactive adult children. Present provisions in the law distinguish between partnerships in which capital is a material factor in producing income and those in which personal services are the principal source of income (par. 2903). In the latter, the chance for abuse is especially great and the requirements for actual participation, and for shares of income related to the value of services, need to be strict.

When capital is a material factor in producing income, the genuine character of a family partnership is recognized even if the partnership interest was received as a gift from a parent, so long as the gift is complete and not a sham, and so long as the allocation of income is in line with the relative contributions of services and of capital of the various partners. The existing rules appear to be adequate to prevent abuse while allowing room for the use of family partnerships on a fairly generous basis.

TAXATION OF CORPORATIONS

Most corporations are taxable as separate legal entities, regardless of what they do with their income and regardless of the tax status of their stockholders. The corporation income tax is at two rates: the lower or normal tax applying to all annual income, and a surtax applying to all income in excess of $25,000 annually. In a practical sense, one can say that a lower rate of tax is applied to the first $25,000 of income, with the full rate to all income above that level.

The two levels of taxation do not represent a partial application to corporations of the principle of progressive taxation. Rather, the special difficulties of small corporations in raising capital in the financial markets and their great dependence on retained earnings have been recognized by the lower rate of tax on the first segment of earnings. Though there have been numerous proposals for a broad application of progressive rates to corporations, they have always been rejected on the ground that legal entities do not themselves have any sense of sacrifice analogous to those of individuals, and that small corporations are often owned by wealthy individuals while much of the stock of the largest and most profitable corporations is held in small blocks by low-income investors.

In this introductory statement, certain special provisions should be noted to give reasonably full perspective on the range of taxes applicable to corporations. If multiple surtax exemptions are used by a group of corporations subject to a single control, an extra six percentage points are added to the surtax.

Only 15 per cent of intercorporate dividends are included in the taxable dividend of a recipient corporation, and an election is available whereby a controlled group of corporations need pay no tax on intercorporate dividends if it elects to be treated as a single corporation in various other ways. A group of affiliated corporations may also elect to file a consolidated income tax return, thereby eliminating the meaning of intercorporate dividends within the group and permitting losses of some to offset the profits of others.

To prevent abuses through the use of a corporation to accumulate income at lower rates than those applicable to high-bracket individuals, penalty taxes are applied to certain unreasonable accumulations of surplus and to certain personal holding companies. All of the provisions are discussed in some detail subsequently.

The corporation income tax is applied not only to business organizations with corporate charters, but also to businesses which have so many of the corporate characteristics that tax avoidance would be encouraged if they were exempt from the corporate tax (par. 3101). Thus various associations and even some partnerships may be taxed as corporations, depending on the extent to which they have such attributes as centralized management, limited liability, transferable interests, and continued existence. Neither the statute nor the regulations provide a single criterion or a formula for a weighted average of relevant factors. Each situation must be appraised by itself, but litigation over the years has provided standards under which normal organizations can be established with confidence as to their tax status.

Not all taxpayers want a strict rule to determine the tax status of noncorporate business associations. Members of some partnerships and associations would like to have the status of employees in order to benefit from pension plans set up by their organizations. One partnership of professional men claimed status as a corporation because of certain provisions of the partnership agreement and won their case.[1] Since partnerships or associations of professional men typically have very little capital with most or all of the income attributable to personal services, income can usually be withdrawn without danger of a double tax at the corporate level and there would be danger of a penalty tax on an unreasonable accumulation of earnings if current income was not withdrawn. The section of the regulations defining the characteristics which

1 *U.S. v. Kintner*, 216 F. 2d 418, 107 Fed. Supp. 976.

make an association taxable as a corporation, extending over six double-column pages, is thus regarded as too strict by those taxpayers who want to avoid the double level of taxation on earnings, and as not strict enough by those who wish to qualify their businesses as corporations to establish pension plans to include themselves (reg. 301.7701–2).

Definition of Income

Corporate taxable income generally follows ordinary accounting concepts. The rules regarding deductible business expenses and accounting methods are covered in a separate chapter, as are the tax provisions relating to depreciation and depletion. Certain income and expense items may arise only in connection with corporations or have a peculiar status for them.

Organization expenses may be amortized over five years. Logically, the benefits of being organized last as long as a corporation endures and the law originally denied amortization. In 1954 the option to write off organization expense was given simply as a convenience to permit tax records to correspond to business records; it is common practice to want to present a simpler balance sheet by writing off organization expenses which are usually of trivial pecuniary significance anyway (par. 3109).

To minimize the multiple taxation of income passing through successive corporations, a credit is allowed for 85 per cent of dividends received from another domestic corporation subject to income taxation. This means that only 15 per cent of dividends are subject to the second and subsequent levels of corporate taxation. Even this tax is a relic of a punitive attitude toward holding companies which developed in the 1930's. Prior to that time there was no tax on intercorporate dividends. For dividends paid from subsidiary to parent corporations, the law was belatedly changed in 1964 to permit once again no taxation if the parent corporation elects to forego certain other tax advantages which may arise from the existence of more than one corporation (par. 3108(c)). At the same time, a penalty tax of 2 per cent on income shown on consolidated income statements for tax purposes was dropped. The law does not now penalize the use of subsidiaries either by an intercorporate dividend tax or by a higher rate of tax if consolidated income statements are filed. In fact, multiple corporations may have substantial tax advantages and the law has had to be tightened to prevent abuses, as described in the next section of this chapter.

A corporation realizes neither income nor loss in buying or selling its own stock (par. 3128). Bond premium and discount are subject to amortization (par. 3129). An historical vestige of the pre-income tax period is found in the differential treatment of premium on bonds issued before and after March 1, 1913. Premium prior to that date, along with appreciation on property and various other favorable events, are not subject to a backward reach of the tax gatherer.

Multiple Corporations

The fact of a lower rate of tax on the first $25,000 of a corporation's income gives a distinct tax advantage to the use of multiple corporations. At a 22 per cent normal tax and 26 per cent surtax, the advantage is $6,500 annually per corporation, which is sufficient to leave a substantial benefit after legal and accounting expenses. The Treasury for many years has unsuccessfully sought legislation which would deny the multiple exemption for both parents and subsidiaries and for corporations controlled by the same group of stockholders. The parent-subsidiary definition is easy, but the definition of a similiar group of stockholders is more difficult but feasible. Discussions about multiple corporations for a single business activity have been obfuscated by references to small and growing business, and the concern about the latter has prevented tight legislation against continued use of many corporations for integrated activities.

At first glance, the law appears to prevent the use of multiple exemptions by providing that only one exemption may be used in the case of controlled corporations, control meaning 80 per cent stock ownership in a subsidiary or by a single family with rather elaborate constructive ownership rules (par. 3122). But a group may elect to take separate surtax exemptions by paying an additional 6 per cent tax on the first $25,000 of taxable income.

The 6 per cent penalty represents the first step in the reduction in the normal corporate tax, from 30 per cent to 24 per cent, made in 1964 when the denial of multiple exemptions was adopted. Prior to that time, for several years the normal tax had been 30 per cent and the surtax 22 per cent for a total of 52 per cent. The reduction in the corporate tax was made in the normal tax, first to 24 per cent and then to 22 per cent, with the surtax increased to 26 per cent, to give disproportionate relief to small business. At the previous 30 per cent and 22 per cent rates, each extra surtax exemption was worth $5,500 annually; with the juxtaposition and change in the surtax rate to 26 per cent, it became worth $6,500. The 6 per cent penalty tax, equal to $1,500, reduces the net gain to $5,000, or only slightly less than it was previously. In the absence of a penalty tax, the inducement would have been increased by the reduction in the normal tax.

The Treasury has attacked the use of multiple corporations to carry on a single business, as when different corporations are established for each small group of houses in a construction project or for different departments in a medium-sized, vertically integrated manufacturing company. The attacks have been only moderately successful. The courts have recognized a variety of business purposes even in these situations, and the use of multiple corporations for separate retail establishments is fairly easy to justify on business grounds.

The rules are somewhat more strict if an existing corporation, or a group of five or fewer people in control of a corporation, transfer property to a new corporation. In such situations, the transferee corporation does not get the additional surtax exemption unless it proves that the tax advantage was not "a major purpose" of the transfer (par. 3121, sec. 1551).

Two other provisions of the law may be applied to multiple corporations. Section 482 gives the Treasury authority to distribute, apportion, or allocate income, deductions, credits, and allowances among a group of organizations, trades or businesses which are owned or controlled directly or indirectly by the same interests where this is necessary to prevent evasion of taxes or reflect income (par. 3124). This section has significance far beyond multiple corporations and is discussed later in connection with foreign operations. But it can be useful to counter attempts to divide income in vertically integrated business.

Section 269 disallows various deductions and credits, if a corporation is acquired with the principal purpose of getting tax benefits (par. 3127). This has turned out to be a relatively weak provision because of the phrase "the principal purpose," in contrast to "a major purpose" in section 1551. It is primarily relevant, when applicable at all, in connection with loss carryovers and is discussed in a later chapter in that connection. It need merely be noted here as a minor deterrent to the use of multiple corporations.

In conclusion, note should be made again of the fact that there is no tax on intercorporate dividends from subsidiary to parent corporations owning 80 per cent or more of the stock and no penalty tax on filing a consolidated return. Prior to 1964, the advantage of the multiple surtax exemption had to be balanced against the intercorporate dividend tax or the 2 per cent penalty tax on consolidated income statements. For large ventures, the disadvantages were usually far greater, and the tax on consolidated returns was regarded as a penalty tax on large business which frequently had to use several corporations to meet the requirements of various state laws.

TAX-OPTION CORPORATIONS

The tax law permits certain corporations to elect to be taxed as partnerships. As originally proposed, a proprietorship or partnership could elect to be taxed as a corporation. When these provisions were under consideration in the Congress in 1954, they were informally referred to as the "vice-versa" proposals: [2] the purpose was to permit the owners of business firms to achieve tax neutrality regardless of the form of organization, which is often determined by extraneous circumstances.

Of the two options, the one for a partnership to be taxed as a corporation was adopted first in 1954. This was really the less significant of the two. It gave no relief to small business and was originally suggested primarily to give symmetry. It was important for partnerships which were required to be organized as such even though the income attributable to each partner was large and it might be desired to retain income to build up the firm's capital. But with the authorization for stock exchange firms to incorporate, the principal intended beneficiaries no longer needed relief and the provision was used by relatively few firms. It was repealed effective April 14, 1966, with permission for partnerships which had elected the option to continue under it through 1968.

The option of a corporation to be taxed as a partnership was not adopted until 1958. The relevant provisions of the law are contained in subchapter S of the law, sections 1371–78, and corporations exercising the option are commonly referred to as subchapter S corporations.

The tax advantages arise principally from one of two circumstances. The income attributable to the individual owners may be so small, and their other income sufficiently small, to permit the applicable individual tax rates to be less than the corporate rate. The advantage of exercising the option in such cases is clear and virtually unqualified, so long as it is agreed that the company will move out from under the option when the full corporate status becomes preferable. (This will not necessarily occur at the same time for all members; the high-bracket investor will find the corporate tax preferable sooner than the lower-bracket owner-manager.)

---

[2] Even more informally, they were spoken of as the Christine Jorgensen proposals. Instructors will remember the reason for the designation and students can discover it by routine research with an off-beat conclusion.

Subchapter S corporations seems even more attractive for new ventures which are expected to operate at a loss for the first few years, a fairly common expectation in many industries. The tax advantage arises from the opportunity to impute current operating losses, and any investment credits, directly to the stockholders, as is done in true partnerships. The higher the tax bracket of the investor, the greater the tax saving from the imputed loss. In effect, the subchapter S status permits a high-bracket investor to recover a major part of his investment by saving taxes on his other income. The advantage is not ignored in soliciting financing for new ventures.

Corporations must meet strict objective tests to qualify (par. 3135). There can be only one class of stock and not more than ten stockholders, none of whom can be aliens or trusts, and all of whom must agree to elect the option. Necessary rules are provided regarding the taxation of actual distributions and specifying the adjustments which must be made to both the corporation's earnings and profits and the stockholder's basis for his stock to avoid double taxation or no taxation (pars. 3136–37). Regulations covering subchapter S extend over eighteen double-column pages.

When the option was granted, there was concern in both the Treasury and the Congress lest the provision be brought into disrepute by whipsawing to get the best of both partnership and corporate status or by other unforeseen maneuvers. To minimize this risk, the law states that the option, once terminated, cannot be exercised again for five years (par. 3139). The limitation on the number of shareholders was adopted to secure experience with relatively simple situations; it has apparently turned out to be unnecessarily strict and constitutes a barrier to the financing of some ventures or the inclusion of some investors in ventures which are financed.

It was feared that the necessary paper work might discourage investors from participating in subchapter S corporations, but an experienced accounting firm for the company provides each investor with simple instructions for a very few entries on his individual tax return, with supporting papers which might be called for an audit. Anyone who has once participated in a well-managed venture will realize that his worry about complications in his individual tax returns are groundless. The legislative intent to encourage investment in new ventures which are either small or have prospects of large initial losses should be realized to an increasing extent as the tax advantages of subchapter S corporations are more widely appreciated. Statutory amendments to remove some of the existing limitations would be helpful.

Another form of tax relief for original investors in new and small corporations is given by Section 1244, noted in Chapter 15. The section permits ordinary loss rather than capital loss deductions to specified investors in certain corporations. Where there is a risk of ultimate loss rather than a probability of early operating losses, its relief may be about as attractive as and much simpler to achieve than that provided by a subchapter S corporation (par. 1625).

9

The Organization

and Capital Structures

of Corporations

No income tax is imposed when one or more people transfer property to a corporation which they control in exchange for stock or securities of the corporation. This is true regardless of the fact that the property transferred may have a value much greater than its basis to them with the result that the corporate stock or securities received in exchange will also have a value much greater than the tax basis of the property turned in to the corporation (par. 1405). The purpose of this part of the law (section 351) is to permit individuals and partnerships to incorporate their businesses when that becomes appropriate or necessary without any tax barriers. In the absence of section 351, the general rule taxing gains realized on exchanges of properties under section 61 would make it necessary to find the cash to pay an income or capital gains tax at the very moment when a business venture is, by the fact of its incorporation, at the stage when it is probably seeking to raise funds from outside investors.

The purpose of the provision for tax-free incorporation is, however, to postpone and not to forgive taxes. Two results clearly follow. The stock or securities received take the same basis as the property transferred, and the corporation takes as its basis for the property it receives the basis which the property had to the person exchanging for stock or securities (par. 1513). Thus, there is no step-up in basis. Any appreciation in the value of property will presumably be reflected in the value of stock or securities and eventually taxed when they are sold. And the corporaton is limited in its basis for depreciation or in computing gain or loss on sale of the property to whatever basis the property had in the hands of the individual who exchanged it for stock or securities.

The tax-free incorporation is purely a relief provision; if the results are not desired, the corporation can be set up with a nominal amount of stock issued for cash and arrangements then made to buy any appreciated property on a taxable basis from the individual owners who in turn invest the proceeds of the sale in the corporation. If the advantage to the corporation of a higher basis is greater than the burden to the individual of the immediate tax, which may be true if he is in a low tax bracket or has losses to offset his gain, it is not necessary to come under section 351.

The tax-free exchange provision also is available for transfer of property to an established corporation. The only requirement is that the person or persons transferring property be in control of the corporation after the transfer, with control being defined as ownership of 80 per cent of the voting stock and 80 per cent of all other stock. Thus, an individual or partnership could exchange their business assets for stock in an existing corporation, even if they had no previous interest in it, if they acquired the requisite 80 per cent stock ownership in the process.

If the stock and securities received in exchange are not in proportion to the current fair market value of the property exchanged, the transaction is still nontaxable insofar as proportionate values are concerned. But those who receive stock or securities greater than justified by the value of the property they turned in will be deemed to have received compensation, taxable as current income, or gifts, subject to gift tax on the donor. The temptation to abuse is considerable in family situations where the members of the younger generation may turn in property of minor value and receive a high fraction of the stock, while the older generation provides the bulk of the assets. Prior to 1954, a disproportionate distribution of stock disqualified the tax-free character of the whole transaction. This result, however, was thought to be too harsh in view of the chances for honest differences of opinion on values which could lead to a result that an incorporation made in good faith might later be held to have involved a taxable exchange of property for stock. Accordingly, it was decided in 1954 by the Congress that the present rule could be adopted on the assumption that there would be adequate audits to assure that income or gift tax is not being avoided through distributions of stock which are disproportionate to the value of property given for it. One might presume that evidence of an attempt to abuse a relief provision at the very inception of a corporation would assure especially attentive audits of future transactions.

The law with respect to transfers of property to a controlled corporation is especially favorable because the general rule that a liability assumed by the transferee is treated as other property, and hence taxable as gain to the extent of a gain, is not applied so long as the assumption of the liability or the acquisition of the property did not have the avoidance of income tax as a principal purpose or did not have a bona fide business purpose (par. 1405(a)). Business property may ordinarily be bought subject to a mortgage, and a going business will ordinarily have outstanding liabilities which will naturally be assumed by a successor corporation; to treat an assumption of such liabilities as a realized gain would nullify much of the purpose of the section authorizing tax-free incorporation. Nevertheless, the temptation exists to borrow against property, and thereby recover much of the investment in it, just before transferring it to a corporation. Since the tax basis of property is not affected by a liability against it, the transferee corporation would continue to have the full basis even though the former owner had reduced his own investment to a nominal amount. It is for this reason that the absence of a principal purpose of tax avoidance and the presence of a bona fide business purpose are necessary to permit the assumption of liabilities without recognition of gain.

As an extreme example, the holder of appreciated property may have recovered more than his investment through borrowing against it, though the property still has a tax basis for depreciation and calculation of gain or loss. It has seemed unduly generous to ignore the assumption of liabilities in situations of this sort and, accordingly, any excess of liability assumed over basis is treated as realized gain, regardless of purpose or intent (par. 1405(b)). If one assumes that lenders are rational, the existence of such an excess of liability presumptively indicates either additional borrowing subsequent to purchase or depreciation running ahead of decline in fair market value. The law has been designed to guard against abuse while maintaining the general objective that normal transfers of property in connection with the incorporation of a business should not be significantly impeded.

Capital Structures of New Corporations

In widely owned corporations, the principal tax influence on capital structures comes from the deductibility of interest and the nondeductibility of dividends on preferred stock in computing corporate taxable income. This differential treatment encourages debt financing and discourages preferred stock financing. In closely controlled corporations, in addition to the differential treatment of interest and preferred dividends, a number of other tax factors may be significant, depending on the expectation of the owners. A highly leveraged common stock may be desirable to put in trust for future generations, thereby keeping the growth in value of the equity out of the estates of the principal investors. Or it may be desirable to put a large part of the original investment in the form of debt in order to receive corporate earnings in the form of nontaxable repayments of debt instead of taxable dividends. Complex capital structures may have many tax advantages in closely controlled corporations. Some of the benefits can be secured only if senior securities, that is, debt and preferred stock, are used at the time of original financing; a later recapitalization may be taxable or new stock received subject to a dormant tax penalty.

Advantages of Debt

Whenever one mentions taxes and corporate financing, the first thing one thinks of is the advantage of debt because of the deductibility of interest (pars. 1901–03). The advantage over stock financing is clear and decisive, so decisive in fact that there have been many attempts to create securities which would qualify as debt for tax purposes while retaining many of the attributes of equity. Though income debentures, on which interest is paid only if earned, can qualify as debt securities, some truly strange hybrids have come to light in the litigation on securities issued to original investors along with stock in closely controlled corporations. Participating debentures, which would siphon off a large part of the income before interest and taxes in the form of "interest," and at the expense of taxes, have been held to be equity. Also, the courts have upheld the Treasury in disallowing interest deductions even when the debt securities had all the attributes of debt, such as unconditional fixed interest, definite maturity, and absence of voting rights, on the grounds that a capital structure may be so thin on the side of equity as to make the debt itself a part of the equity. "Thin capitalizations" are attempted typically when an investor group takes both debt and stock; since the debt is held by the same group, they are not likely to throw their company into bankruptcy. If the debt is held by quite unrelated investors, the charge of thin capitalization is less likely to be effective.

The courts have refrained from setting any uniform acceptable ratio for debt to equity, observing that what is appropriate depends on the stability and certainty of income and other factors which any investment analyst takes into account in his own appraisal of securities. Real estate companies with properties leased for long terms can justify higher ratios than manufacturing ventures. Ratios of 3 or 4 to 1 appear to be as high as most advisers will consider except in very unusual circumstances and some are skeptical if the debt exceeds the equity.

The penalty for a decision that what was intended to be in debt is in fact stock goes far beyond a mere disallowance of a deduction for the so-called interest. Repayment of principal may be held to be a dividend, taxable as such to the holder.

It is often stated that the deductibility of interest makes the net after-tax cost of debt only about half of the specified rate, with a corporate tax of about 50 per cent. In a sense this is true, but one must be cautious to avoid drawing false inferences about necessary rates of return. When funds are borrowed by a corporation at 5 per cent, they must be used to earn at least 5 per cent before taxes if the income per share is not to be reduced. If funds are borrowed as a precautionary measure, or in anticipation of an increase in interest costs, it is correct to say that the net cost of the interest is only about half of the gross cost, so long as the company has enough income to be subject to the full rate of corporate taxation.

Other expenses, such as wages and the cost of materials, are also deductible, but one does not think that an increase in them is only half as important as it seems to be because of deductibility. A dollar more of wages must be recovered by a dollar more from the customers if net income is to be maintained. And so it is with interest. Any increase in interest must be fully recouped if net income is not to be reduced. If not recouped, the impact on net is only about half of the short-fall, so long as there is a net, and this is significant, but it does not mean that a recoupment of half the increase in gross interest will maintain the net income. The concept of a tax shield through deductions of expenses and ordinary losses is important in analysis and planning, but its significance must not be overextended as it sometimes is in moments of carelessness.

Though the deductibility of interest is the most familiar tax advantage of debt, it is by no means the most important. In closely controlled corporations in which the investors expect to retain most or all of the income for expansion, a principal tax objective may be to keep most of the expected appreciation out of the estates of the principal investors. Senior securities in the capital structure, either debt or preferred stock, offer a simple and obvious method. By keeping the investment in the common stock as small as is acceptable without making a too-thin capitalization, the younger generations can get a higher fraction of the total equity, and hence a higher fraction of the appreciation, with their existing capital, or current gifts to them of common stock can be kept to a minimum. If a total investment of $100,000 with a prospect of doubling in value can take the form of $50,000 debentures, $30,000 preferred and $20,000 common, only the $20,000 has to be available in the hands of younger generations, or transferred to them or to trusts for them, to enable the entire appreciation to build up directly for them and not be included in the estates of the older generation who provide $80,000 of the total investment. By a proper arrangement of voting rights, perhaps facilitated by a judicious selection of par values with one vote per share, virtually any desired distribution of voting control can be created without reference to the relative stated values of total preferred and common stock outstanding.

The third advantage of debt financing is the opportunity to recover part of an original investment without tax, even if it is in effect a distribution of earnings. As will be noted later, any distribution to common stockholders, even if it takes the form of a redemption of stock, is likely to be taxed as a dividend except under specified conditions which would be difficult for a successful growing company to meet. But the courts recognize that an individual may have a dual status as stockholder and creditor, so long as the debt is a genuine one, and earnings can be used to retire debt.

The three tax advantages of debt financing are not mutually consistent. Obviously the retirement of debt precludes the opportunity for subsequent distributions of deductible interest; a choice must be made between a tax-free recovery of part of an investment and continued "half-price" distributions of part of the future earnings. The retirement of debt, however, is not inconsistent with the use of debt to create a high leverage common stock to receive all the benefit of growth. In fact, the use of earnings to retire debt can create growth in the common stock equity even if the corporation as such, as measured by total assets, is not growing. In some instances, a family group may find a business with assured stable income very attractive in estate planning. Growth in the equity can be created simply by establishing the company with the maximum acceptable debt which is retired with the earnings.

Use of Preferred Stock in Capital Structures

The nondeductibility of preferred stock dividends imposes a major tax burden on its use in capital structures. The higher the corporate tax rate, the higher the necessary earnings before tax to cover a preferred stock dividend requirement. At a 48 per cent tax rate, funds raised by a preferred stock issue must earn almost double the stated dividend to avoid a reduction in earnings on common stock.

In casual discussions, one often hears the comment that debt financing is favored and preferred stock financing is penalized by the tax law. Either statement is correct, depending on the point of view taken, but the two together are not correct from the same point of view. If they were, at a 50 per cent tax rate the net cost of debt would be only one-quarter that of preferred stock financing, and this is not true.

For most purposes, it seems more accurate to think of the corporation income tax as penalizing preferred stock financing and being neutral with regard to debt financing. This concept is different from the familiar proposition that taxes reduce the net cost of borrowing, but as already indicated this proposition can be misleading. When one thinks of the rate of return from the use of corporate funds, one usually thinks at least in the first instances of a rate of return before tax. A comparison is then made with the cost of funds which must be covered before there is any benefit to existing common shareholders. It is in such a comparison that the tax law is neutral with respect to debt financing and penalizes preferred stock financing. Consider also a change in the corporate tax rate on an existing corporation with all income and expense items unchanged. The extent of debt financing has no effect on the net income available for common. But the extent of preferred stock financing has a pronounced effect because the preferred dividends must be paid out of after-tax income. The tax compounds the leverage of the preferred stock, and a large tax increase, from perhaps 15 to 50 per cent, could wipe out the earnings on the common stock.

In the public utility industry, substantial preferred stock financing is typical and in many instances is actually required by state utility commissions. To avoid confiscatory impacts on common stockholders when corporate tax rates were being raised from a little over 10 per cent to wartime levels, a special relief provision was adopted to allow a deduction for part of the dividends paid (par. 3110(a)). Companies in other industries which also had unusually large preferred stock issues in their capital structures received no similar relief.

To the extent that preferred stock is held by other corporations the tax disadvantage of nondeductibility of dividends to the issuing corporation is largely or even completely offset by their complete or virtual tax exemption to corporate shareholders. All dividends received from other domestic corporations are given an 85 per cent credit, meaning that only 15 per cent of the dividends are included in taxable income (par. 3108(a)). And a corporation may elect to have any dividends received from an affiliated corporation, defined as one in which at least 80 per cent of all classes of stock is owned, wholly tax-exempt (par. 3108(c)). The consequence of the election is a single corporation surtax exemption and a single $100,000 exemption for the tax on accumulated earnings and for the annual estimated tax.

If there were enough corporate investors in preferred stock to absorb the total outstanding, the prices would rise to a point to offset the disadvantage of nondeductibility by issuers, just as the yield on tax-exempt bonds would not fail to reflect their tax advantage to the highest-bracket investors if there were only enough outstanding to meet the limited investment demand from this small group. But in both cases the amounts outstanding are far more than can be absorbed by those investors who stand to gain most from the favored tax treatment; the marginal buyers gain little or nothing and the tax advantages of the intramarginal investors are not reflected in reduced costs to the issuers.

However, in financing a subsidiary the tax exemption of the dividend to the parent exactly offsets the nondeductibility to the subsidiary, if both corporations are subject to the full tax rate. If financed wholly by a parent corporation, the choice might be for preferred stock to keep the balance sheet clean. But if the subsidiary is a joint venture with individuals, a conflict of desires arises because the preferred dividend is taxable to the individual investors who will argue that the form of senior financing is not a matter of indifference since income distributed to them on preferred stock is subject to a double tax. The fair solution is not self-evident, nor is it even clear after careful analysis.[1]

[1] Consider, as a simplified example, a subsidiary corporation which is expected to have earnings before interest and taxes of $300, with both the parent and subsidiary subject to a corporation tax of 50 per cent. Assume that the parent corporation plans to leave $100 as retained earnings and withdraw $50 net after taxes. This can be accomplished equally well by a tax-exempt preferred stock dividend of $50 after a corporate tax on the subsidiary of $150, or by $100 interest subject to a $50 tax on the parent, after a corporate tax of $100 on the subsidiary. Total taxes, net to the parent corporation, and retained earnings are the same in each case. But if an individual investor, also assumed to be subject to a 50 per cent marginal tax rate, has a 10 per cent interest in the subsidiary, his $5 share of the preferred dividend is cut in half by his individual tax. Total net dividends are reduced to $47.50, total taxes are increased to $152.50, with retained earnings kept at $100. The individual investor would argue that this is a high price for him to pay for a "clean balance sheet." To give him the same net return after tax on his senior securities as the corporate investor receives, the dividend rate would have to be doubled, but this would cut the retained earnings in half and also give the corporate investor twice as much withdrawal as it considered appropriate. And even then the individual investor would be at a disadvantage compared to his situation with debt financing; his $5 net dividend and $5 equitable interest in retained earnings is less than the $5 net interest and $10 equitable interest in returned earnings which he would have under debt financing. Or if a $2.50 net income on senior securities is taken as a norm, he could have this and a $12.50 equitable interest in retained earnings under debt financing. A reconciliation of the interests of the two investors is not available by a change in dividend or interest rates.

Though the tax law makes preferred stock financing unattractive in a widely owned corporation, it is still used when debt limits are approached and common stock financing is considered undesirable. The nondeductibility of dividends may be thought of as making preferred stock financing about twice as expensive as it would be otherwise. Given the relative standing of debentures and preferred stock in priorities, preferred stock dividends are usually higher than interest on debt and hence preferred stock financing is ordinarily more than twice as expensive as debt. But it may still be preferable to a new common stock issue if the after-tax rate of return on the use of new funds is confidently expected to be well above the preferred dividend rate.

In closely controlled corporations, preferred may be preferable to debt, in spite of its tax disadvantages, in establishing a highly leveraged common stock and in distributing voting control. Though preferred stock does not have the tax advantages of debt, it can be used along with common to give more leverage on common than would be possible with debt alone. While 90 debt and 10 common would be unacceptable, 60 debt, 30 preferred, and 10 common might be appropriate. But it must be remembered that in addition to the nondeductibility of dividends on preferred stock, there may be a further tax disadvantage in that redemption of the preferred stock is more likely to be treated as a distribution of earnings and taxed as a dividend than are funds received on retirement of debt (par. 1710). The danger is by no means so great as a redemption of common stock, but if the same investor group holds both classes of stock, the redemption may be challenged.

Though senior securities, whether debt or preferred stock, have certain advantages, these are available only when the debt or stock is issued in exchange for a new investment in the company. Debt or preferred shares issued to common stockholders in a recapitalization are either currently taxable as a dividend, in the case of debt, or have the latent tax disadvantage of having the proceeds taxed as ordinary income at the time of sale or redemption, in the case of preferred stock. These tax rules are discussed in later chapters.

IO

Corporate
Distribution to Stockholders

The tax law concerning corporate distributions to stockholders is exceedingly complex. In the ordinary course of events distributions may be expected to consist of corporate profits and as such be taxable to stockholders as ordinary dividend income. However, there are many bona fide business situations in which distributions constitute a return of capital.

The tax law contains specific provisions covering distributions of capital, but their existence offers a temptation to taxpayers to try to arrange ordinary distributions of profits in forms which will qualify for capital gains treatment. The history of the law in this area reflects a continuing attempt to prevent abuses by taxpayers without penalizing normal transactions.

GENERAL RULE

Any distribution of money or other property from a corporation to its stockholders is presumed to be a distribution of its earnings and profits, to the extent thereof, and taxable as a dividend, unless it meets the conditions for one of the specified exemptions covering stock dividends, stock rights, liquidating dividends, or stock redemptions. This general rule given in section 316 of the Code, though not always stated sufficiently emphatically, should never be forgotten (par. 1701). Regardless of state laws or the way a distribution may be charged on a company's own books, the rule of section 316 and the concepts developed under it are controlling for federal tax purposes.

The need for this general rule is apparent if one considers for a moment the abuse which would be possible if a company's own recording of a distribution were accepted for tax purposes, because such a treatment would permit a company to call and retire periodically a small part of its stock, and when necessary split the remaining stock to maintain convenient units for ownership and additional retirements. Thus it would be possible to distribute earnings systematically under the guise of stock redemptions.

In the application of the general rule, problems arise concerning the definition of earnings and profits within a single year and the effects of successive profits, losses, and distributions over a series of years. The following paragraphs describe the principal specific rules in these areas.

Earnings and Profits

In spite of its critical importance in determining the tax status of corporate distributions, the phrase "earnings and profits" is never defined in either the Code or the regulations. Various provisions of both deal with the effect on earnings of profits of certain specified transactions, but a general definition has never been given. As a result, the concept has been refined by litigation (par. 1708).

The earnings and profits of a year are substantially similar to the taxable income of the year, but with modifications to take account of the fact that items not entering into the calculation of taxable income may properly affect distributable earnings and profits. For example, charitable contributions by a corporation in excess of the 5 per cent allowable deduction will reduce earnings and profits available for distribution to stockholders and that fact is recognized. Similarly, an excess of capital losses over capital gains reduces earnings and profits though it does not reduce taxable income. On the other hand, tax-exempt interest on municipal bonds, while not included in the taxable income of corporations, nonetheless constitutes earnings and profits. Such interest loses its identity on receipt by a corporation and when distributed to stockholders is taxable as an ordinary dividend.

It should be noted that many items affecting book surplus do not enter into earnings and profits. Write-ups and write-downs of assets against surplus, and capitalizations of surplus through stock dividends or creations of surplus through write-downs of capital, do not influence, absorb, or create earnings and profits available for taxable distributions to stockholders. After a few years of operations, it is highly unlikely that a corporation's surplus account will correspond to its earnings and profits as defined for tax purposes, and a company may have substantial earnings and profits in spite of a deficit in its book surplus, or negative earnings and profits in spite of a substantial book surplus.

The rule that all distributions are presumed to be from earnings and profits to the extent thereof has, as its corollary, a rule that if there are no earnings and profits a distribution is deemed to be a return of capital up to the basis of stock for each individual stockholder, with any excess treated as ordinary gain or capital gain, depending on the status of the stock in the hands of the holder. It thus follows that if a corporation can get itself in a position where it has no earnings and profits but does have disposable funds, it can make tax-free or capital gains distribution to its stockholders.

Distributions of money or other property ordinarily reduce corporate earnings and profits (par. 3117(a)). Special rules have been found necessary to prevent maneuvers by which corporations put themselves in a position to have excess funds with no earnings and profits. They may be noted, not so much for their own sake because they are seldom applicable, but because a brief review of them should help one to understand the basic concept of earnings and profits (pars. 3115, 3117).

The problems arise when property other than money is distributed to stockholders. Generally, stockholders are taxed on the fair market value of the property as a dividend and take that value as their basis (par. 1706). The corporation ordinarily is not presumed to realize any gain or loss on the distribution, and its earnings and profits are decreased by its basis for the property distributed (par. 3117(a)). Note that when the value of the property exceeds its basis to the corporation, the amount the stockholder includes in his income (fair market value) exceeds the amount of reduction in earnings and profits (basis of the property to the corporation). Note further that there is no untaxed step-up in basis. The stockholder has included in his income the fair market value of the property he has received; by doing so, he has paid for the right to use this value as his basis, as it were. Or, if there are no earnings and profits and the payment is applied against the stockholder's basis of his stock, he again has "paid for" the use of fair market value as his subsequent basis of the property received by reducing the basis of his stock by that amount.

The only gap in the interrelationships is at the level of the distributing corporation. One might argue that it should have its earnings and profits reduced by the fair market value of the property, that is, by the amount on which the stockholder is taxed. But this would give a tax advantage to distributions of property instead of cash. If the corporation sold the property and then distributed cash, which might be considered the normal way of conducting a business, it would realize a gain and increase its earnings and profits. The limitation in the reduction in earnings and profits to the corporation's basis of property distributed may be thought of as offsetting, in the long run, the immediate tax advantage of putting stockholders in possession of property on which the corporation has not realized a gain, though there is a gain to be had for the taking.

But the Congress has decided that there are limits to the nonrecognition of gain by corporations. A few distributions are treated as though the corporation had sold the property at the time of distribution. This rule applies to distributions of lifo inventory (to the extent of the differences between the lifo inventory and the inventory value under any method other than lifo), property subject to a recapture of depreciation under sections 1245 and 1250, and property subject to a liability which is in excess of the basis of the property to the extent of the excess (par. 3115(b)–(d)). The reason for this last provision will indicate the logic of the presumptive realization of gain. Consider, for example, a corporation with earnings and profits of $100,000 owning real estate which had cost $100,000 but had appreciated to $1 million. The corporation might borrow $500,000 by mortgaging the real estate. On distribution of the real estate to stockholders the corporation would be deemed to have realized a gain of $400,000 and be taxed accordingly. In the absence of this rule, it would be possible for the corporation to realize on appreciated property indirectly by borrowing against it, then wipe out its earnings and profits by distributing the property and have the excess proceeds of the realization to distribute tax-free. To the extent that a liability exceeds basis, indicating a great deal of appreciation in value, the law provides that there should be a tax on the corporation to the extent of the excess, along with a consequent increase in earnings and profits which makes distributions of the gain taxable as a dividend to the stockholders.

In other situations the law merely provides that the earnings and profits of a corporation are deemed to be increased by the fact of a distribution, though no taxable gain is deemed to be realized by the corporation (par. 3117(b)–(c)). Section 312 of the statute deals with property distributed subject to a liability and appreciated inventory. As a general rule, when property is distributed, earnings and profits are decreased by the adjusted basis of the property. However, when the property is distributed subject to a liability, earnings and profits are decreased only by the basis reduced by the liability. This provision is necessary to prevent a complete wiping out of earnings and profits (with a qualification of subsequent distributions as tax-free) through the purchase of a valuable property which is then mortgaged for a large amount. Consider, for example, a corporation with earnings of $1 million which buys a piece of real estate for $1 million against which it later borrows $750,000. The basis of the property is still $1 million, though its fair market value in the hands of stockholders receiving it is only $250,000, which is the amount of the dividend taxable to them on a distribution. If the earnings of the corporation could be reduced by $1 million, earnings would be wiped out completely, and later distributions, perhaps even of the borrowed money, could be made tax-free.

The same treatment requiring an increase in earnings and profits covers distributions of appreciated inventory (defined to include receivables from the sale of inventory) to prevent abuses by paying dividends in kind, with the inventory property subsequently sold by or on behalf of the stockholders who received it (sections 312(b) and 311(b)). If there were no special rules, it would be possible in extreme cases to create and use corporations to make profitable inventory assets which would be distributed to stockholders and taxed as capital gains, to the extent that their fair market value exceeds the basis of stock, and then sold by the stockholders at the same fair market value with no additional tax. Under this practice, both the corporate tax and the ordinary income tax on stockholders would be avoided. Additional rules concerning collapsible corporations are contained in section 341, discussed in the last section of this chapter.

The difference in the treatment of lifo inventory and appreciated inventory is notable. Distribution of the former means that the corporation as such realizes a gain and pays a tax. This is consistent with the idea that the lifo treatment of inventory is a concession in the tax law to avoid cyclical fluctuations in taxable income as prices of inventory items fluctuate cyclically or to avoid imposing a tax on inventory profits which arise from a secular or inflationary price rise but, by definition, do not provide disposable funds with which to pay a tax. When a corporation disposes of lifo inventory property, it no longer needs the protection of the tax concession and is reasonably taxed on the gain (to the extent of the difference between the lifo value and the value under any other method), which may have been developing over many years.

By contrast, the appreciated inventory treatment, by merely increasing earnings and profits, assures that the stockholder will have the market value of the property taxed to him as a dividend, even though the corporation is not taxed. The intent here is not to secure a double level of taxation, at the corporation and the stockholder, but merely to prevent ordinary income from being converted into capital gains, as it would be if the corporation "ran out of" earnings and profits. The difference between the corporation's basis of inventory and its fair market value may be deemed to arise in the normal course of business, in the absence of lifo, and hence there is no special benefit of a tax concession which should equitably be recouped. It is considered sufficient to have this gain taxed at one level as ordinary income. The recoupment of excess depreciation falls into the same concept as the gain from lifo inventory; the fact that there is an amount to recapture indicates that tax deductions for depreciation turn out to have been unduly generous.

EFFECT OF SUCCESSIVE PROFITS, LOSSES, AND DISTRIBUTIONS ON EARNINGS AND PROFITS. A distribution is considered for tax purposes to be from earnings and profits if it is covered by the earnings and profits of the current year or by earnings and profits since March 1, 1913, the date of reference in the first income tax act after the adoption of the Sixteenth Amendment authorizing income taxation for the federal government (par. 1708).

A distribution is thus treated as from earnings and profits so long as it is covered either by current earnings and profits without reference to the existence or absence of a net balance in earnings and profits since the formation of the company, or by earnings and profits accumulated since 1913 without reference to current earnings and profits. The provision giving priority to the current year's earnings and profits was an important relief feature of the law under the undistributed profits tax adopted in 1936, since under the latter law corporations were given credit against their undistributed profits tax only for distributions which were taxable as dividends to the recipients. Without this additional provision, corporations could have been in the position of distributing all of their current earnings and still be subject to the penalty tax on undistributed earnings if the distributions were not taxable to stockholders because of an accumulated deficiency in earnings and profits. The rule has been continued in the law in spite of the elimination of the undistributed profits tax. It serves now to prevent an abuse that would otherwise exist by using corporate shells with large past deficits as vehicles to distribute current earnings tax-free.

After earnings and profits of the current year, distributions are presumed to be made from earnings and profits accumulated since March 1, 1913. In most instances, the accumulated earnings and profits since March 1, 1913, are measured by the net of profits and losses since that date. However, to the extent that pre-1913 earnings are available to absorb post-1913 losses (after such losses wipe out earnings accumulated between March 1, 1913, and the year of loss), the post-1913 losses do not have to be made good by subsequent earnings. Also, distributions in excess of earnings do not create or add to accumulated losses.

STOCK DIVIDENDS

Distributions in the form of stock dividends have been subject to a succession of distinctly different treatments under the tax law. A review of the changes on this subject gives an appreciation of the evolutionary character of the tax law and also provides a basis for understanding the arguments that may be advanced for further modification of the law if stock dividends are used more extensively.

The first modern individual income tax law in 1913 made no specific reference to stock dividends, but they were deemed to be taxable as ordinary dividends. Stock dividends were specifically taxed by the Revenue Acts of 1916 and 1918. In 1920, the Supreme Court held in *Eisner v. Macomber* (252 U.S. 189) that a stock dividend did not constitute income within the meaning of the Sixteenth Amendment and hence was not taxable. This decision recognized the fact that a stock dividend merely divided an existing equity interest into more units.

The case before the court involved a dividend paid in common stock on common stock, but the opinion did not specifically note that fact, and the decision was generally interpreted to apply to all stock dividends. The law was amended in accordance with this interpretation. Stock dividends were stated to be nontaxable, and the tax basis of the original stock purchase was required to be allocated between the original stock and the new stock received as a dividend in accordance with the relative fair market values when the dividend stock was received.

The rule established in 1920 continued until 1936 when the Supreme Court gave its decision in *Koshland v. Helvering* (298 U.S. 441) holding that it was not proper to require the allocation of basis to a dividend on common stock paid in preferred stock of an issue already outstanding. The distinction was drawn between a stock dividend in this form, which gave a new set of rights, and a dividend in common on common, which merely redivided existing interests into smaller units. The *Eisner v. Macomber* decision was thus not overruled but merely confined in its application to factual situations similar to those to which the decision applied.

After the *Koshland* decision, the Congress changed the law to make taxable such stock dividends as could be constitutionally taxed and left it to the courts to work out the lines of distinction. The concept underlying the *Koshland* decision was continued and the only stock dividends ruled to be nontaxable were those which merely subdivided existing equity rights into new forms without giving any rights which took precedence over those previously held. It was held that a dividend on common stock paid in preferred stock, when no preferred stock was outstanding prior to the dividend issue, was nontaxable since the preferred stock in this case did not really give the common stockholders any sort of claim prior to what they had before; they still held the residual equity interest even though it was divided pro rata into two successive segments. By contrast, if some of the preferred stock was already outstanding, common stockholders receiving preferred stock as a dividend would share in and dilute the prior interests of the preferred stockholders.

Preferred Stock Bail-Outs

In the years just before 1954, taxpayers took advantage of the tax-free status of certain preferred stock dividends to withdraw earnings from a company on a capital gains basis through what came to be known as a "preferred stock bail-out." The procedure involved three steps: the issuance of a nontaxable preferred stock dividend (when none of the preferred stock was previously outstanding), the sale of the preferred stock to a third party or parties, and the subsequent retirement of the stock by the corporation. The net effect of the three steps was to have the corporation pay out money and the common stockholders to receive money while still holding their common stock. If the payments were made directly it would have clearly been a taxable dividend; if the stock had been issued to and redeemed from the common stockholders, the proceeds would probably have been taxable as ordinary income under the provision of the law applying to a redemption of stock which had the effect of distributing earnings, as discussed in the next part of this chapter. The use of the intermediate third party served to remove the set of transactions from this provision and form triumphed over substance.

In the tax revision of 1954, the Congress acted, on the advice of the Treasury, to eliminate the preferred stock bail-out. It was done indirectly by providing that the proceeds from the sale of stock received as a dividend on stock, except common stock received on common stock, would be taxed as ordinary income to the extent of earnings and profits at the time of distribution of the stock dividend (par. 1710(c), sec. 306). At the same time, all dividends paid in stock on stock were made nontaxable (par. 1703, sec. 305). The effect of these new provisions is to continue the rule established in *Eisner v. Macomber* insofar as dividends in common stock on common stock are concerned. Such stock dividends are in all respects similar to stock splits, except that they involve a capitalization of surplus, which is not a significant distinction for most financial and investment purposes. All other stock dividends are also nontaxable on issue, except when they are offered as an option to a cash dividend or as discharge of preferred dividends for the current or preceding year.

The taxation as ordinary income of the proceeds of sale of preferred stock received as a tax-free stock dividend is a severe penalty against bail-outs. Because there are some bona fide reasons for issuing noncommon stock dividends other than tax avoidance, section 306(b) gives several exceptions to the rule of taxation of proceeds of sale as ordinary income. When both common stock and preferred stock are sold, thus terminating a stockholder's entire interest in a company, the capital gains provisions apply to the entire proceeds. In such cases, since no common stock is retained, the essence of the bail-out abuse does not exist. Also, if the redemption occurs under conditions that qualify for the special rules applicable to redemptions in liquidation, the capital gains provisions will apply.

The section 306 taint is removed if preferred stock is transferred to others who do not have to use the basis of the original holder as a substituted basis (reg. 1.306–3(e)). This is a roundabout way of saying that the taint is removed by death. It gives an exception for preferred stock created before the death of the owner of a business provided he keeps it until he dies. There is thus an opportunity to use preferred stock dividends once in a generation. There is finally a general exception covering situations where it is established to the satisfaction of the Secretary of the Treasury or his delegate that the transaction was "not in pursuance of a plan having as one of its principal purposes the avoidance of the federal income tax" (section 306(b)(4)). The same restrictions and exemptions apply to preferred stock received in exchange for common stock in a tax-free reorganization.

Debt obligations of a corporation are taxed on receipt by stockholders as property. There is thus no opportunity to "bail-out" earnings by issuing and subsequently paying off debt.

Stock Rights and Fractional Shares

Stock rights are treated in the same manner as stock dividends (par. 1704, sec. 305). An important simplifying relief provision was adopted in 1954 under which it is not necessary to allocate basis if the fair market value of the rights is less than 15 per cent of the fair market value of the old stock (par. 1704(a), sec. 307(b)). Thus these rights may take a zero basis for purposes of computing capital gain on sale, and the entire cost of the original stock retained as its basis. Under the previous rule, basis had to be allocated as of the date of issuance of the rights, with gain or loss calculated against this allocated basis. The old rule, while theoretically correct, imposed ridiculously complex calculations on large numbers of stockholders for trivial refinements in tax computations. It was probably not applied correctly in the case of most stockholders, and the new rule legitimatizes a commonsense practice; there is no net effect on total taxes if the entire stockholding is ultimately sold, and the use of a zero basis for the rights means that when rights are sold taxpayers have the option of paying a higher immediate tax for the sake of convenience in tax calculations.

Unfortunately, there is no comparable treatment for fractional shares received in connection with stock dividends. If a fractional share is sold, basis must be allocated to it. Even if a stockholder for the sake of convenience chooses to overpay his tax on the assumption of zero basis for a fractional share, he has not escaped an ultimate annoyance. When he finally sells some or all of his original holding of stock, along with whole-share dividends, the original basis must be adjusted down for the amounts, probably infinitesimal, which should have been allocated to the fractional shares previously sold. As a result, the most convenient thing to do is to purchase a fractional share to round-up to a full share, and hope that one will not forget to record this purchase price as part of the basis for that particular share. To avoid the annoyance of having to keep track of different bases for single shares, some investors have an invariable policy of selling all shares at the same time. If the original purchase, whole-share dividends, fractional-share dividends, and fractional-share purchases are sold simultaneously, one can put all costs of purchase into a single pool. The fact that fractional shares arise for most investors in the second and succeeding stock dividends after an original purchase makes the absence of a zero basis option for fractional shares probably the principal harassment in the tax law for ordinary investors who keep their own records.

Impact of Tax Law on Use of Stock Dividends

The reciprocal impact of the tax law and business practices in the area of stock dividends has already been referred to briefly. Dividends in common on common stock are fairly frequent in widely owned companies. Though some stockholders object to them on the grounds that they merely complicate an investor's accounts by making odd-lot holdings and in some cases require the purchase or sale of a fractional share, with consequent capital gain or loss tax calculation if the fractional share is sold, they serve to provide something which is ostensibly more significant than uncapitalized surplus. When a large stock dividend is issued, it is comparable to a stock split, and the decline in market price is frequently less than in proportion to the dilution inherent in the equity per share. Small stock dividends may be used as a means of increasing total cash dividends without increasing the dividend rate—and with an unchanged cash dividend rate, the market price per share is likely to be unaffected, giving an increase in aggregate market value for each and all stockholders. None of these business or investment purposes is impeded by the tax treatment of common stock dividends.

Small recurring stock dividends may also be useful to permit stockholders to realize part or all of their equitable interest in retained corporate earnings without ostensibly reducing their original capital investments as represented by any given number of shares of stock. The sale of a part of an original investment to secure funds for living expenses is an overt act regarded as living on one's capital and is avoided by conservative investors, even though retained earnings may so increase the equity interest and value of the remaining shares that the net investment is maintained or increased. But a standing order to sell all or part of an annual stock dividend based on current earnings will leave the original investment of 10, 100, or 1,000 shares untouched and provide a cash receipt part of which is not taxed because it is regarded in the tax law as a recovery of capital and the rest of which is taxable as a capital gain. The availability of cash in this favorable tax form, in lieu of an ordinary cash dividend, may come to be regarded as a respectable source of spendable "income," even though it is theoretically equivalent to an annual sale of a few shares of an original investment in a company which is retaining enough earnings to maintain or increase the total equity represented by the reduced number of shares. Possible developments in investor and management attitudes toward small recurring stock dividends present one of the most interesting subjects for consideration in the field of corporate finance and investment analysis. From the standpoint of the tax law, it is also interesting to consider how the Supreme Court would decide a stock dividend case if the dividend was a small annual one related to earnings and commonly sold by most stockholders.

Dividends paid in preferred stock have been uncommon in widely owned companies. There have been a few instances in the past, though the reasons have not been altogether clear. The purpose has apparently been to give something to stockholders at a time when neither cash nor additional common stock was deemed suitable. The tax rule applying to such dividends has apparently stopped their use because of the tax status of the proceeds of the sale, not to mention the possible uncertainty as to whether one of the exceptions might be applicable. However, no significant business or financial purpose appears to be thwarted by section 306.

In closely controlled corporations, the reasons previously described for common stock dividends on common stock do not apply since, by definition, there is no market price to be considered or maximized. Stock dividends, or stock splits, are likely to be used just before a public offering of stock in order to get marketable units; such dividends are of course not in any way penalized by the tax law.

Many special sitautions exist in closely controlled corporations for issuing preferred stock dividends on common stock. It may be desired to have different classes of stock for different prospective heirs, as, for example, preferred stock for a widow or daughters and common stock for sons. It is also not uncommon for existing owners to want to create common stock with relatively low value by putting most of the equity interest into a new preferred stock issue, which in turn makes the common stock within the reach of a new management group. The owners of a company may also wish to split their existing common stock holdings into common and preferred with the expectation of selling, or having available for sale, the preferred stock to meet estate taxes or to provide diversification in an estate, without diluting the common stock control in a family business.

All of the foregoing legitimate business reasons for issuing preferred stock as dividends on common stock are impeded to varying degrees by the provisions of section 306 on the sale of preferred stock received as a dividend. The exceptions referred to previously were intended to relieve the tax barriers to the extent possible. The area is one in which it is difficult to strike a balance between prevention of abuse and unnecessary tax penalties on ordinary transactions which have no objectives of tax avoidance.

DISTRIBUTIONS IN REDEMPTION OF STOCK

Ostensibly a redemption of stock implies a contraction of a corporation and hence may be thought of as a return of capital. But, as already noted, if the tax law permitted all redemptions of stock to be considered as tax-free returns of capital, the temptation to distribute earnings through stock redemptions would be very great and methods to make periodic redemptions could be readily established, especially in closely controlled corporations. The tax law accordingly contains many provisions specifically directed to stock redemptions. They will be considered here in successive sections dealing with redemptions in continuing corporations including partial liquidations and in complete liquidations. A final section covers the special tax rules for collapsible corporations.

Redemptions Without Liquidation: General Rules—Section 302

The structure of the law regarding stock redemptions is rather peculiar (par. 1710). Section 302(a) states positively that a redemption of stock shall be treated as a payment in exchange for the stock, that is, subject to capital gains treatment, if conditions specified in subsection (b) apply. But (b)(1) immediately states negatively that subsection (a) shall apply only if the redemption is not essentially equivalent to a dividend. And the Code stops at that point, giving no further indication as to when a redemption is essentially equivalent to a dividend. Section 302(b) goes on to give objective tests, including a substantially disproportionate redemption of stock in (b)(2) or a redemption of all of the stock owned by a shareholder in (b)(3), which will give assurance that the redemption will not be considered as essentially equivalent to a dividend and hence the proceeds will be entitled to capital gains treatment.

Redemptions specified in the objective tests can be and often are relevant to stock redemptions in closely controlled corporations when a group of stockholders, perhaps one branch of a family or one generation, wishes to withdraw from a business which has or can get sufficient funds to buy them out. But the main burden for decision on the tax status of a redemption is thrown back onto the negative statement in (b)(1) by a statement in (b)(5) that a failure to meet the requirements of (b)(2) or (b)(3) shall not be taken into account in determining whether a redemption is essentially equivalent to a dividend. In other words, the specified conditions of disproportionate or complete redemption give assured escape routes, but their availability is not to be taken as indicating that any other routes are less available.

When one considers the history of the law regarding stock redemptions, the present sequence of statements is not so illogical as it appears to be. Prior to 1954, section 115(g)(1) of the 1939 Code made the positive statement that redemptions should be considered as dividends to the extent that they were distributions "essentially equivalent to dividends." This phrase thus became a basis for litigation and over the years it was given meaning and substance by court decisions. Among the circumstances found by the courts to make redemptions other than essentially equivalent to dividends were substantially disproportionate redemptions, redemptions which completely terminated a stockholder's interest, and redemptions associated with contractions of a corporation's activities. The first two of these circumstances were given positive assurance of favorable tax treatment, as noted, in sections 302(b)(2) and (3), and the third was also given statutory sanction with objective tests in section 346 concerning partial liquidations, discussed subsequently. Presumably the other conditions which the courts had found significant under the prior law are still relevant under the existing law; certainly that presumption is indicated as the intent of Congress by section 302(b)(5) which, as noted, states the nonexclusive character of the specified redemptions.

The report of the Senate Finance Committee in 1954 noted that the test to be applied for (b)(1) was in general that currently enforced under existing law. Unfortunately, the regulations give no guidance as to what other redemptions may be regarded as not "essentially equivalent to dividend." Section 1.302-2(b) merely states that it depends on the facts and circumstances of each case. Among the relevant facts are the "net effects," the extent of past dividends and existing earned surplus, the source of the initiative for the redemption, the extent of contraction of a business, and the validity of a business purpose and the weight to be ascribed to it. But the full range of opinions and situations can only be appreciated by reading from the cases in the area (see Prentice-Hall, *Federal Taxes*, pars. 17,376–80).

A substantially disproportionate redemption of stock, which automatically qualified as an exchange and hence is entitled to capital gains treatment, is precisely defined in the Code. A stockholder whose stock is redeemed after the redemption must own less than 50 per cent of the voting stock and less than 80 per cent of the percentage of voting stock which he previously held in the corporation.

The regulations furnish the following example of disproportionate redemption. Corporation M has outstanding 400 shares of common stock of which A, B, C, and D each own 100 shares or 25 per cent. Corporation M redeems 55 shares from A, 25 shares from B, and 20 shares from C. For the redemption to be disproportionate as to any holder, such shareholder must own after the redemption less than 20 per cent (80 per cent of 25 per cent) of the 300 shares of stock then outstanding. After the redemptions, A owns 45 shares (15 per cent), B owns 75 shares (25 per cent), and C owns 80 shares (26⅔ per cent). The distribution is disproportionate only with respect to A (reg. 1.302-3(b)).

In the above example no computation of the 50 per cent amount had to be undertaken since no shareholder involved in the redemption held that amount. Had A held 300 shares, B 35, C 35, and D 30 shares, A would be required to redeem 201 shares in order to qualify for non-dividend treatment. Although 80 per cent of 75 per cent is only 60 per cent, and therefore one might say that A need redeem only 151 shares (60 per cent $\times$ 250 = 150; 150 − 1 = 149, which is less than 80 per cent $\times$ 75 per cent, and the maximum amount which A can hold after the redemption), it still allows a 50 per cent or more control. However, by redeeming 201 shares A relinquishes control and also meets the less-than-50 per cent requirement.

Although the computation may at times be quite complex, the statutory formula does allow prediction of the consequences of the disproportionate redemptions in most cases. As a protection against shareholder agreements which would bypass the objectives of the Code by alternating such redemptions among different shareholders, a specific provision in section 302(b)(2)(D) states that a redemption will not be treated as disproportionate if it is made pursuant to a plan the purpose or effect of which is a series of redemptions which result in the aggregate in a distribution which is not substantially disproportionate.

The second provision allowing assured capital treatment on a redemption, the complete termination of a shareholder's interest in the corporation, is largely a codification of previous decisions under the prior law. In such cases the object is to sever all relations with the company and only incidentally to withdraw retained earnings. The act of redemption is much more akin to a sale than any of the other redemptions outlined.

Safeguards have been inserted which qualify both disproportionate and complete redemptions. They attempt to prevent abuse of these liberalized provisions in closely held corporations where, although a family member redeems his stock, he is nevertheless in control because of his close relationship to the other stockholders (par. 1709). Section 302(c) makes section 318 applicable to redemptions and section 318 provides that an individual shall be considered as owning the stock which his spouse, children, grandchildren, or parents own. Thus, if A owns 20 shares, his wife 10 shares, his son 10, and his parents 20 shares of the 60 shares of voting stock of the AB Corporation, A cannot receive capital treatment in a substantially disproportionate redemption since no matter how many shares he redeems he will still be treated as owning any shares held by these people. In addition, other subparagraphs of section 318 attribute to A shares held in partnerships, trusts, estates, and in controlled corporations. Furthermore, shares in these latter categories can be reattributed to A if a family member is considered to own them.[1]

These rules are also applied when a shareholder completely terminates his interest. They will not be applied, however, if the shareholder in no way associates himself with the enterprise, other than as a creditor, for the ten years following the redemption. But they will be applied even then if there was a transaction in the preceding ten years with the tax avoidance purpose of bypassing these attribution rules. Furthermore, the rules relating to attribution of ownership of shares held by trusts, estates, partnerships, and corporations will always be applied regardless of the shareholder's continued association or disassociation from the business. Even if a shareholder fails to meet the complete termination or substantially disproportionate redemption tests, he can always argue that the redemption was not essentially equivalent to a dividend. The failure to meet the specific conditions does not impede qualification for capital gains treatment under the general rule.

Redemptions in Partial Liquidations—Section 346

Section 346 provides statutory rules for capital gains treatment in cases of corporate contraction (par. 1707(b)). It looks principally to the effect of the redemption on the corporate level, whereas section 302 views the transaction from the shareholder level. If, from the corporate viewpoint, there has been a "contraction" of the business, followed by a redemption of stock, capital gains treatment to the shareholder will be found. A typical case would be one in which a fire curtailed business operations, and the insurance proceeds were distributed in redemption.

Partial liquidations were recognized as one of the circumstances which kept a distribution from being essentially equivalent to a dividend under the 1939 Code, and section 346(a) continues to use the concept developed in court decisions by first stating as a general rule that a distribution is to be treated as in partial liquidation if it is not essentially equivalent to a dividend, as long as it is pursuant to a plan and occurs

---

[1] An illustration of the complexity these rules entail may be gained from this illustration. XY Corporation has 100 shares outstanding: 30 are owned by X, 10 each by Y and his two sons, A and B, and 40 in a trust for the benefit of Y and his sons. If A sought to redeem his shares, he would be attributed with ownership of 53⅓ shares: his own 10; ⅓ of the 40 shares owned by the trust itself; all of his father's 10 shares; ⅓ of the trust's 40 shares attributed to his father; ⅓ of his brother's ten shares attributed through the trust; and another 3⅓ of his brothers' ten shares attributable through the trusts to the father. If A were to redeem all his 10 shares he would still not have a substantially disproportionate redemption since he would not meet the 80 per cent test, although he would meet the 50 per cent test.

within the taxable year in which the plan is adopted or the following taxable year. A distribution which is one of a series in redemption of all of the stock of a corporation pursuant to a plan also qualifies under the general rule as a partial liquidation.

In addition to the general rule of 346(a), a positive rule is given in 346(b), which will permit a redemption to qualify as a partial liquidation, with capital gains treatment. Two requirements must be met: (1) an active business must be distributed to stockholders, by direct distribution of its assets or the proceeds of its sale; and (2) an active business must be continued by the enterprise. Both of these businesses must have been actively conducted throughout the preceding five-year period by someone, and cannot have been acquired by the corporation in a taxable transaction. The purpose of this objective test is to provide a basis for some certainty in a difficult area.

The principal problem in applying this subsection involves the definition of "actively conducted trade or business." It is defined by the regulations under the related issue of corporate separations, as follows:

> A trade or business consists of a specific existing group of activities being carried on for the purpose of earning income or profit from only such group of activities, and the activities included in such group must include every operation which forms a part of, or a step in, the process of earning income or profit from such group. Such group of activities ordinarily must include the collection of income and the payment of expenses. It does not include—(1) the holding for investment of stock, securities, land, or other property, including casual sales thereof (whether or not the proceeds of such sales are reinvested), (2) the ownership and operation of land or buildings all or substantially all of which are used and occupied by the owner in the operation of a trade or business, or (3) a group of activities which, while a part of a business operated for profit, are not themselves independently producing income even though such activities would produce income with the addition of other activities or with large increases in activities previously incidental or substantial (reg. 1.355-1(c)).

The purpose of the concept and definition of actively conducted trade or business is to prevent the withdrawal of earnings at the capital gains rates as partial liquidations when the property liquidated represents only a temporary investment of corporate funds in an incidental business function which was made for the purpose of preparing the way for an artificial "partial liquidation." The numbered exceptions cover the types of transactions which were deemed to be especially subject to abuse.

There are definite advantages to the shareholders when they can come within the definition of a partial liquidation under section 346 rather than the general rule under section 302. (1) The attribution rules of section 318 are inapplicable, thus allowing redemptions at capital gains rates much more easily in closely held corporations. (2) The limitations in 302 as to substantially disproportionate redemptions and complete termination do not apply, and pro rata distributions are allowed. (3) Section 306 stock, that is, stock other than common stock, issued as a dividend, can be redeemed under section 346 at capital gains rates, but receives ordinary dividend treatment in all other redemptions except those which are in complete termination of a shareholder's interest as defined in section 302(b)(3) and (c). (4) The corporation can distribute lifo inventory and property subject to liability without the recognition of gain to the corporation under section 346, but there would be gain to the corporation on such distributions under section 302 in many cases (section 311 applies only to section 302 whereas section 336 applies in section 346 cases).

When a redemption is treated as an exchange of stock, the money and fair market value of any other property received are treated as a recovery of capital up to the basis of the stock in the hands of each shareholder and the excess of value received is taxed as capital gain.

The basis of property received under section 302 and 346, when subject to capital gain or loss treatment, is its fair market value. And it is the fair market value of the property over the basis of the stock which measures the amount of gain or loss. In this manner a shareholder will not be taxed twice upon the same gain. For example, in a distribution meeting the requirements of section 302(a), a shareholder received property having a fair market value of $100,000 in redemption of his stock which had a basis of $40,000. He will recognize a $60,000 capital gain, which may be either long- or short-term, depending on how long he held the stock. The basis of the property in his hands is $100,000.

If the distribution were equivalent to a dividend, then although the property is taxed fully, there is no reduction in the basis of the shareholder's remaining stock. For example, assume that an individual purchased all of the stock of a corporation for $100,000. Later the corporation redeemed half of the stock for property worth $150,000, and it is determined that this amount constituted a dividend. The remaining stock of the corporation has a basis of $100,000, the property received is taxed in full as a dividend, and it has a basis of $150,000 in the hands of the stockholder.

The general rule that a distribution is a dividend only to the extent of the earnings and profits of the corporation applies to redemptions which are found to be essentially equivalent to a dividend. If the value of the money and property received exceeds the earnings and profits of the corporation, the excess is applied first to reduce the basis of stock to the extent of the basis to each stockholder, with the balance treated as capital gain.

Some question was raised in the earlier cases as to whether capital gain should result where the corporation kept the shares as treasury stock instead of cancelling them, since the redemption might not then be permanent in nature. Section 317(b) now provides that retention of the shares in the treasury will not disqualify an otherwise proper redemption, and section 1032 provides that no gain or loss will be recognized to a corporation when it deals in treasury stock.

Other Redemptions of Stock in Continuing Corporations— Sections 303 and 304

Two additional provisions of the Code deal with special cases of stock redemptions. The first, section 303, allows redemption at capital gains rather than dividend rates when necessary to pay estate taxes and expenses of administration of estates, provided that the stock of the corporation which is included in the decedent's estate exceeds 35 per cent of the gross estate or 50 per cent of the net estate (par. 1710(b)). Section 303, originally added to the law in 1951 and liberalized in 1954, thus relieves some of the pressure for forced sales of family corporations in order to meet the estate tax arising on the death of a principal shareholder.

The Senate Finance Committee explained the purpose of the provision as follows:

> It has been brought to the attention of your committee that the problem of financing the estate tax is acute in the case of estates consisting largely of shares in a family corporation. The market for such shares is usually very limited, and it is frequently difficult, if not impossible, to dispose of a minority interest. If, therefore, the estate tax cannot be financed through the sale of other assets in the estate, the executors will be forced to dispose of the family business. In many cases the result will be absorption of a family enterprise by larger competitors, thus tending to accentuate the degree of concentration of industry in this country. S. Rep. No. 2375, 81st Cong., 2d Sess. 54 (1951).

Section 303 is a particularly important one for the owner of a family company in planning his estate. It permits earnings to be withdrawn once a generation to the extent of the estate tax imposed on the owner. It is, of course, not necessary for a corporation to have funds in hand at the time of the death of the owner of stock to be redeemed. Funds may be secured by borrowing, the sale of assets, or any other source.

Section 304 is a restrictive provision designed to prevent avoidance of the limitations established in the redemption rules where two or more corporations are controlled by the same interests (par. 1710(a)). A 1949 case held that the forerunner of section 302 was so limited as to apply only to the redemption by a corporation of its own stock and not to the purchase by a wholly owned subsidiary of the parent's stock from the parent's stockholders, even though, if the parent had directly re-deemed its stock, the redemption would have been essentially equivalent to a dividend. A provision of the Revenue Act of 1950 was enacted to cover this situation, and in 1954 it was extended to cases of brother-sister corporations. In its operation, section 304 treats as redemptions what appear to be sales of stock to related corporations. Further limita-tions in the section define a controlled corporation for purposes of these provisions (50 per cent), and state which corporation is deemed to have made the distribution.

Redemptions in Complete Corporate Liquidations—Section 331

Prior to the Revenue Act of 1918, all corporate distributions, in-cluding those in the form of liquidating dividends, were taxed to stock-holders as ordinary income. After 1918, except for two brief periods, gains to stockholders on liquidation were treated as sales or exchange of stock, and as such were subject to capital gains treatment.

Section 331 forthrightly provides that as a general rule "amounts distributed in complete liquidation of a corporation shall be treated as in full payment in exchange for the stock" (par. 1707(a)). Thus, any excess in the value of money and other property received over the basis of the stock to each stockholder is treated as capital gain. To prevent any double taxation of the gain when the property is later sold by the former stockholders, section 334 states that the basis of property received will be its fair market value at the time of distribution, which is the same figure as is used in calculating gain on the distribution (par. 1706). And sec-tion 336 provides that a liquidating corporation itself does not recog-nize a gain or loss on the distribution of property unless it distributes certain "installment obligations" which are similar to accounts receivable arising from installment sales and as such represent unrealized income (par. 3116). The corporation also may have ordinary income when it distributes depreciated property subject to the recapture provisions of sections 1245 and 1250.

A particularly important provision was adopted in 1954 to remove uncertainty and give relief from double taxation when a corporation sold some or all of its assets prior to or during a liquidation. Under general provisions of the law, the corporation would be taxed on any gains it had on such sales, and the proceeds, when distributed to stockholders, would be taxed again if the values received exceed the basis of stock. To avoid this double tax, liquidations were often made in kind, with the stockholders then individually or collectively selling the assets. Since the basis of the assets to the stockholders was fair market value, there was no second tax on the sale of the assets; in fact, the price received often determined the fair market value used in measuring the gain on liquidation. But a liquidation in kind with subsequent sale was at best cumbersome and at times not feasible. Also there was much uncertainty and litigation as to whether the sale had actually been made by the corporation or the stockholders.

Section 337 states that gain or loss will not be recognized to a corporation which sells or exchanges any of its property and distributes its assets within a twelve-month period beginning on the date of adoption of a plan of liquidation (par. 3116(a)). This sequence of events arises in connection with purchases and sales of businesses and an analysis of section 337 is postponed to the chapter which deals with that subject. The section is mentioned here to show the full range of statutory provisions on complete liquidations.

The general rule of section 331 giving capital gains treatment for stock redemptions in liquidation is simple enough in application for straightforward liquidations. But a liquidation may be contrived as a mere subterfuge for withdrawing the earnings of a corporation as capital gains instead of dividends, or a liquidation followed by a reincorporation may attempt to raise the basis of its property to secure larger depreciation deductions. The regulations and successive court decisions have had to deal with liquidations extending over prolonged periods and with liquidations followed by reincorporations or a continuation of a business as a partnership.

Liquidation has been consistently held to be a matter of fact. The absence of a resolution by the stockholders to dissolve a corporation does not prevent a distribution from qualifying as a distribution in liquidation. Even more significantly, the adoption of a resolution will not of itself make subsequent distributions liquidating dividends if in fact the corporation is not in the process of liquidation. The temptation to declare a corporation in process of liquidation in order to make distributions of subsequent earnings and profits liquidating dividends is considerable, and in one case a court upheld a liquidation of a company with coal and timber lands extending over twenty years. But typically the courts have been fairly strict in preventing abuse of the liquidation status as a device to distribute earnings from a continuing business.

The other possible abuse may arise when a corporation has excess funds which it wishes to distribute or fully depreciated property which has present value and continuing use. A liquidation would give the stockholders the excess funds at capital gains rates and establish a new basis for property subject to depreciation, all for the price of a capital gains tax. The assets needed in the business can then be transferred without tax to a newly formed corporation which will take the higher basis and be entitled to depreciation on it. Since a capital gains tax must be paid before the benefits of the higher depreciation are realized, a present-value calculation is necessary to determine whether the higher basis is really worthwhile, but the withdrawal of accumulated earnings not needed in the business is an unqualified advantage.

To guard against liquidations and reincorporations the regulations provide that the effects of such a set of transactions, regardless of the sequence of events, may have the effect of a distribution of a dividend, or of a tax-free reorganization in which no increase in basis is recognized (par. 1707(d), section 1.331–1(c)). An attempt had been made to develop statutory language to cover such situations as part of the 1954 Code, but the Congress felt that sufficient powers already were available to the Treasury to prevent abuses.

A separate section of the Code, (332), covers the tax consequences of the liquidation of a subsidiary into a parent corporation. Since this involves another form of corporate reorganization, broadly defined, the distinctive rules for these liquidations are postponed to the chapter on reorganization. In brief, no gain is recognized and the corporation usually takes the property received at the basis it had in the hands of the subsidiary. This is precisely the reverse of the tax rules generally applicable to individual shareholders. It is based on the concept that such a transaction creates no real change in equity interests or investments.

One-Month Complete Liquidations—Section 333

A completely different tax treatment of liquidations is made available for companies whose assets have appreciated greatly, but which do not have large accumulated earnings and profits. Real estate or lumber companies would be the typical examples. Section 333 provides that if all the property is transferred within one month of the adoption of a plan of liquidations, all stockholders who elect to do so may postpone recognition of gain by taking as their basis for the property received in liquidation the basis of the property in the hands of the corporation being liquidated (par. 3317). The owners of at least 80 per cent of the stock must elect to come under this section to make it applicable. But as a condition for nonrecognition of gain, the electing individual stockholders must report as a dividend their appropriate share of earnings and profits since 1913 or the money received and fair market value of securities purchased after 1953, whichever is the greater. Corporate shareholders report this amount as capital gain, which gives a greater tax liability in view of the low tax on intercorporate dividends.

The purpose of section 333 is to give a group of investors an opportunity to liquidate a corporate venture without a major tax barrier so long as current earnings have either been relatively small or been distributed up to the time of liquidation. The tax treatment is similar to that of withdrawal from a partnership insofar as appreciated assets are concerned. In a section 333 liquidation, all earnings and profits are subject to double taxation, at the corporate and stockholder level; in this respect, the use of the corporation turns out to be less favorable than a partnership where there is only one tax on income and realized gains. But section 333 offers the only way for individual stockholders to receive property from a corporation and avoid taxation of any of the gain which has been developed by a corporation, either through its activities or through passive holding of property. In the situations for which it is appropriate, it can give tremendous relief.

Collapsible Corporations—Section 341

In the absence of some rule to prevent such action, a closely controlled corporation might be used to make a product, such as a motion picture film or a building, and be liquidated before the product was sold. Under the general rules of liquidation, the stockholders would realize a capital gain up to the fair market value of the property which would become the basis in their individual hands. The property would then be sold with little or no further gain, the fair market value at the time of liquidation being approximately the price at which the property could be sold. Thus, what would have been regular operating income to a continuing corporation, or ordinary income to a partnership, would be converted into capital gain by the use of a succession of corporations each one of which was liquidated just before the product was sold. The procedure would be feasible only when one product of large value was made; for a flow of products of small unit value, the expense of incorporation and liquidation would be excessive. And the product would have to have a sufficiently certain price on final sale to give it a fair market value at the time of liquidation to absorb most of the profit.

Section 341 of the Code is designed to prevent such abuses by what are called collapsible corporations (par. 1620). The law on the subject, section 341, is both detailed and complicated, running to more than eight pages in a loose-leaf service, and with over twenty-eight pages of explanatory material and case references (P.-H., *Federal Taxes*, pars. 9281–86E). The law specifies that the gain on redemption of stock in a corporation is to be taxed as ordinary income instead of capital gain if the corporation is formed or used principally to manufacture, produce or buy certain types of property with a view to having the stockholders realize gain before the corporation has realized a substantial part of the taxable income from the property. The proscribed property is that which is held primarily for sale to customers or unrealized receivables or fees. A corporation is presumed to be collapsible if the fair market value of such assets is more than half of the fair market value of its total assets (with specified exceptions) and 120 per cent or more of the adjusted basis of such assets.

The rules regarding collapsible corporations are applicable only to stockholders who own directly or indirectly 5 per cent or more of the stock and not even to them unless 70 per cent of the gain in a year is attributable to the specified property and is realized within three years after its manufacture, construction or purchase. There are additional exceptions based on the relation of unrealized appreciation to net worth.

To prevent indirect realization of gain, the proceeds of a sale of stock in a collapsible corporation are taxed as ordinary income, just as is the property received in redemption of stock. An amendment in 1964 authorized an exceedingly complicated procedure by which stockholders could get capital gains treatment on the sale of stock if the corporation consents to have gain recognized to it on the disposition by it of the specified assets. The tax on the stockholder can thus be kept to the capital gains level by having the corporation pick up as corporate income the gain which it would have received if it sold the property in the ordinary course of business even though it in fact disposes of the property in some other manner; in effect the double level of taxation must be incurred to let the stockholder get the benefit of the capital gains rate. Under the general rule for dispositions of stock in collapsible corporations, there is only one level of taxation, to the stockholder, but this is at ordinary income rates.

The collapsible corporation rules have never been regarded as thoroughly satisfactory. Something of the sort is needed in the tax law for the reasons indicated, but any specific provisions may trap people who fall under its rules by inadvertence while letting others escape who manage to keep outside the established tests.

By 1954, prior legislation had pretty well blocked the use of collapsible corporations, and collapsible partnerships were becoming fashionable just as personal holding companies, discussed in a later chapter, had been in fashion a generation previously (pars. 3400–10). The exceptions concerning partnership distributions of inventory items and unrealized receivables adopted in that year were designed to nip in the bud the use of collapsible partnerships (pars. 2918(b)). The first extensive abuse of corporations was to insulate investment income from personal income tax by having it received by, taxed to, and held by personal holding companies. A generation later, corporations were used to convert ordinary income, which would have been taxable as such either to a corporation or to individuals depending on the form of business chosen, into capital gains at the individual level. In retrospect, one is surprised at the long periods before devious routes were discovered through the law. Also, in retrospect, the action of Congress to block the routes has been reasonably prompt, though for those in the Treasury who are responsible to point out and urge specific changes the blocking action has at times seemed unduly deliberate.

II

Tax Factors

in the Acquisition, Use,

and Disposition of Land

and Depreciable Property in Business

Tax factors abound in virtually all types of business decisions concerning the acquisition, retention, disposition, and replacement of machinery, equipment, and buildings. In many respects the tax law conforms closely to familiar business and accounting practice. In others, the provisions of the tax law are distinctive and may even seem strange. In no respect is the difference between tax and business concepts more dramatic than in the tax definition of capital assets which specifically excludes land and depreciable property used in a trade or business (par. 1601). Some of the provisions of the tax law modify business decisions and complicate, even to the point of confusion, ordinary accounting practices.

This chapter will cover, in succession, the tax treatment of depreciation, the determination of cost or other tax basis of land and depreciable property, and the determination and tax treatment of gains and losses on the sale or other disposition of land and depreciable property. A final section covers the tax treatment of rents paid for leased property and the rules applicable to sales and leasebacks. Although it might seem more logical to consider tax basis, which is the amount subject to depreciation, prior to depreciation itself, the sequence used here seems preferable because it goes from the more to the less familiar.

DEPRECIATION

The tax law concerning depreciation itself conforms fairly well to business practice with respect to both the methods of depreciation and the allowable time periods or estimated service lives.

METHODS: The tax law authorizes the use of straight line depreciation, declining balance depreciation at double the straight line rates, sum of the years-digits depreciation, or any other method which does not give faster depreciation than the declining balance method (par. 2006–09). The tax law also permits depreciation to be related to units of production or use. Furthermore, it is possible to shift from declining balance to straight line depreciation to secure a complete write-off of cost or other basis which does not occur under the declining balance method. Though the use of some of these methods is limited to certain types of property, the tax law on the whole is very broad in its authorization of methods of depreciation. No method used or proposed to be used to any appreciable extent in business is not allowed for tax purposes.

Until 1954, straight line depreciation was virtually the standard method used for both tax and business purposes in the United States (par. 2006). A few companies took faster depreciation when they operated extra shifts, and a very few used declining balance depreciation at 150 per cent of the straight line rate applied to all depreciable assets (par. 2007(b)). But straight line depreciation was almost universal.

Prior to 1954, the tax law was frequently criticized as being much too restrictive on depreciation. In the general revision of the Code that year, declining balance depreciation at double the straight line rate was authorized for all new tangible depreciable property, that is, for buildings, machinery, and equipment, but not for such items as patents and copyrights (par. 2007). To prevent complete write-off in the first year, property had to have a life of at least three years to qualify. In the course of legislative consideration, the sum of the years-digits method of depreciation was suggested as an alternative method which, like declining balance, gave larger depreciation in the earlier years of use but, unlike the declining balance method, gave a full write-off. Though little used or widely discussed prior to 1954, the sum of the years-digits method was also authorized in the Code to permit wide latitude to business in its depreciation practices and to minimize discrepancies between tax and business accounting (par. 2008).

Any other method which gave no faster depreciation than that allowable under the declining balance method for the first two-thirds of useful life was also authorized. A procedure by which a total life was divided into thirds, with the middle third taking one-third of the total basis in equal annual amounts and the first third of the life receiving three times as much as the last third, was, for example, used by some companies. (Property with a cost of $15,000 and a fifteen-year life would, under this method, be depreciated at $1,500 a year from the first through the fifth year, at $1,000 a year from the sixth through the tenth year, and at $500 a year for the last five years.)

Under declining balance depreciation, a constant percentage is applied to the remaining balance of original cost. For property costing $1,000 with a ten-year life, the depreciation rate under the double rate declining balance method would be 20 per cent and the depreciation in successive years would be $200, $160 (equal to 20 per cent of $800), $128 (20 per cent of $640), $102.40 (20 per cent of $512), and so on. The sum of the years-digits depreciation is determined by adding together the number of years in the estimated life and using that as a constant denominator in a fraction, the numerator of which is the successive years of life in reverse order. For property with a five-year life, the denominator is $1 + 2 + 3 + 4 + 5 = 15$, and depreciation in successive years would be 5/15, 4/15, 3/15, 2/15, and 1/15 of original cost. The Internal Revenue Service has provided tables for the use of the sum of the years-digits method for groups of assets in a single account. Tax services and accounting manuals give analyses of the relative amounts of depreciation in successive years under the different methods for properties with various service lives (par. 2009).

The reasons advanced in 1954 for permitting larger depreciation deductions in the earlier years of use were numerous. Basically, there seemed to be nothing sacrosanct about the conventional straight line depreciation, which had, perhaps, become predominant merely because of its greater simplicity. Faster depreciation recognized the greater utility and faster decline in value in the earlier years of property which is subject to obsolescence through changes in technology or style. Maintenance costs are usually higher in later years; with larger depreciation in earlier years, the combined cost of holding depreciable property and keeping it usable could be more nearly uniform over its entire life.

Faster depreciation permitted a faster recovery of the investment in depreciable property. This in turn facilitated the financing of new investments in buildings, machinery, and equipment and earlier replacement of existing property. The more rapid recovery of an investment also has a favorable psychological influence since there is a greater willingness to commit funds for shorter periods in which events can be predicted with less uncertainty. Finally, the faster depreciation and quicker recovery of an investment makes it more possible to tap outside sources of financing. Term bank loans may, for example, be appropriate when a substantial part of an investment can be recovered within five years.

The foregoing references to faster recovery of an investment are based solely on the fact of lower income taxes against any given level of before-tax income. The result is larger net incomes and net cash flows in the early years of use of depreciable property. At any given level of operations and prices, that is the only direct and immediate consequence of faster tax depreciation. In later years of the life of depreciable property, depreciation would be less and income taxes more than if straight line depreciation had been used. Continued purchases and depreciation of new property will, typically, at least offset this effect of lower depreciation in later years. With increasing total investment in depreciable property for both individual firms and the entire economy, the advantage of faster depreciation will expand over the years.

If faster tax depreciation leads to faster depreciation on a company's own books, the analysis of the effects becomes much more complicated because the greater depreciation expense may lead to changes in prices of products and hence changes in the scale of business activity. The range of possible consequences is discussed briefly after the analysis of allowable estimates of service lines, a subject which also raises problems regarding discrepancies between tax and book depreciation.

A special deduction of 20 per cent of the first $10,000 of investment in tangible personal property, such as machines and equipment, with a life of at least six years, was authorized in the tax law in 1958 (par. 2010). This allowance is of particular important to small business concerns; though available to all taxpayers except trusts, it is of negligible importance to large companies. The allowance is an annual one for each taxpayer and can be applied to any item or combination of items of purchased property. The deduction is, however, treated as depreciation and applied against the basis of the property which is then subject to regular depreciation, including first-year depreciation at the regular rate against the reduced basis.

During World War II and the period of and for some years after the Korean conflict, the tax law authorized special five-year amortization for some or all of the cost of facilities necessary for defense production, certified as such by a designated federal office responsible for defense planning. The purpose of the legislation was to encourage private construction and acquisition of defense facilities to obviate government ownership of the sort which occurred during World War I and which led to so many postwar problems in dismantling and disposition. The rapid amortization was especially significant because it permitted so much of the cost to be deducted against income subject to the high excess-profits taxes effective during war periods. Happily, both an excess-profits tax and five-year amortization are now of only historical importance and hopefully they will remain so.

ESTIMATES OF USEFUL LIFE OF DEPRECIABLE PROPERTY: Estimates of useful service lives of depreciable property have been a major and continuing source of disagreement between taxpayers and the government. New guidelines and rules were established in 1962, by Revenue Procedure 62–21, after several years of preparation (par. 2014(a)). They should greatly reduce controversy over depreciation deductions; their promulgation was a major event in the development of the tax law.

The history of policies concerning estimates of useful life falls into three main periods. Prior to 1935, the administration of the law was relatively liberal, at least in comparison with that between 1935 and 1962, though more stringent than in most other countries. In 1935, a proposal was made in Congress to reduce all depreciation allowances by 25 per cent as an emergency device to collect more revenue during the depression. In recognition of the fact that this action would have been quite arbitrary and would discourage replacement of property and hence prolong the depression, the Treasury suggested that it could secure an equivalent amount of revenue by administrative tightening. T.D. 4422, issued in that year, required taxpayers to justify their current depreciation deductions by allocating a general depreciation reserve among items or categories of property and taking no more depreciation than that necessary to write off the remaining net basis over the remaining life of the separate items or categories. This Treasury Decision emphasized the importance of depreciation to the tax agents in the field; very strict attention to depreciation started at that time and continued at least until 1962.

Two seemingly unrelated features of the tax law reinforced, and to a considerable extent may have justified, strict review of depreciation deductions. Profit on the sale of depreciated property was treated as a capital gain with the advantage of the lower tax rate. This treatment was contrary to that in other countries where on sale of depreciated property a balancing charge, equal to the difference between depreciated cost and sale price, up to the original purchase price, is brought into current income directly or, in some instances, used to reduce the tax basis of newly acquired depreciable property. In either case, the advantage in other countries of fast depreciation which turns out to be excessive is purely a time advantage; the rule in this country put a real premium on excessive depreciation because, in addition to the time factor, a taxpayer secured a cash advantage equal to the difference in tax rates, in the case of corporations 27 percentage points with tax rates of 52 per cent and 25 per cent. The law was amended in 1962, as will be noted below, to treat as ordinary income the gain on sale of depreciated tangible personal property up to the original purchase price. An amendment of this sort was essential to prevent liberalization of depreciation from becoming an invitation to shenanigans.

The second aspect of the tax law which discouraged liberal depreciation was an early decision of the Board of Tax Appeals, now the Tax Court. In Goodell-Pratt (3 B.T.A. 30) the Board allowed a taxpayer who had previously deducted certain research expenses to restore them to his books as a capital outlay for purposes of determining the excess profits tax base in World War I. Though not strictly applicable to depreciation, a statement in the opinion that "we believe that from the standpoint of good accounting no right ever rested in any business enterprise to treat certain expenditures according to either of two diametrically opposed theories" implied that part of the cost of fully depreciated property which turned out to be still useful might be written off again—and again. At least that was the fear of some of the senior administrative tax officials, and this fear conditioned the administrative policies under their direction. Later legislation, now embodied in section 1311–14, and subsequent litigation have applied the general legal doctrine of estoppel to the tax law to a considerable extent, thus limiting the circumstances under which double deductions may be claimed or double inclusions of income asserted.

In the guidelines issued in July 1962, service lives are authorized for four broad groups of property with several subgroups in each. Group one applies to assets used by business in general, including office furniture, fixtures, machines, and equipment (10 years), transportation equipment (automobiles 3 years, light trucks 4 years, and heavy trucks 6 years), and buildings (40 to 60 years). Group two covers nonmanufacturing activities, except utilities. Group three applies to manufacturing with generally a single class and life for each manufacturing industry, with the class including production machinery and equipment, special purpose structures and other property not specifically included in other guideline classes. The authorized service lives range from 6 years for oil and gas drilling and field services, 8 years for aerospace and electronic equipment manufacturing, to 18 years for ferrous metal, sugar, and vegetable oils and 20 years for cement manufacturing. "Other manufacturing," not included in the twenty-nine named industries, is given a life of 12 years. Group four covers transportation, communications, and public utilities.

The 1962 guidelines were vastly simpler than the predecessor Bulletin F of the Internal Revenue Service, which included many hundreds of suggested lives with detailed listings for different sorts of depreciable property in each industry. It was expected by the Treasury that three or four guideline classes would cover all depreciable assets of most tax-payers. The possibilities for simplification and reduction of controversy are tremendous.

However, a major limitation is imposed in the use of the guidelines. A new "reserve ratio test" is established which has no parallel in the tax law of other countries (par. 2014(b)). Under this test, if the depreciation reserve rises to a point which indicates that retirements of property are not consistent with the guideline life being used for depreciation, subject to a fairly generous margin of tolerance, the depreciation allowed for tax purposes will be reduced until the reserve ratio comes within the allowed margin.

A great deal of ingenuity was applied in developing the reserve ratio concept. Tables are given for the allowed ranges in the reserve ratios for different rates of growth in capital investment and for various methods of depreciation. For the first three years after issuance of the guidelines, the authorized lives could be used regardless of the reserve ratio. Depreciation, in fact, could be taken on all property currently on the books during this three-year transition, even though it has been fully depreciated previously. This was possible because the depreciation rate indicated by the guideline is, to repeat, applied to all property in the class for three years regardless of either segregated or aggregated depreciation reserves. If, however, the reserve is excessive at the end of three years, allowable depreciation for subsequent years must be reduced to an amount such that the depreciation reserve approaches the permissible maximum by at least one percentage point per year. So long as progress is made at this rate, no further limitation is imposed until the end of one life cycle established by the applicable guideline.

Thus, if the guideline life is ten years, depreciation could be taken for three years on all property currently on the books at a 10 per cent rate straight line or 20 per cent declining balance regardless of the size of the depreciation reserve. It may also be taken for another seven years at the same rate, if the reserve ratio does not exceed the margin of tolerance, which is about 20 per cent greater than that which would exist if retirements were actually made on a ten-year cycle; with a ten-year life, no growth, and straight line depreciation the maximum acceptable ratio is 58 per cent. If the ratio exceeds the maximum, depreciation must be such that the reserve ratio drops by one percentage point each year. It might at the end of ten years still be very high; if, for instance, it was 85 per cent at the end of three years, it might still be 78 per cent, after a reduction of one percentage point a year. At that time, the depreciation allowable in the future will be adjusted, drastically if necessary, to conform to the actual life cycle of depreciable property.

In 1965, when it appeared that the reserve ratio test would significantly reduce depreciation deductions at the end of the three-year grace period, the Treasury gave a new and different grace period by adding 15 percentage points to the upper limits of the allowable reserve ratios in that year. This is a transitional allowance, however, and must be reduced to zero by the end of the guideline life for each group of depreciable property. Five percentage points of the transitional allowance must be reduced over the first half of the guideline life and the remainder over the last half. The adoption of this transition allowance relieved the pressure for most taxpayers and reduced the objections to the reserve ratio test which had become vigorous and general. Since the expiration of the transitional allowance will not occur simultaneously for all taxpayers, or even for all classes of property for any one taxpayer, there may not be as concentrated objections to the reserve ratio test in the future as developed in 1965.

A calculation of the allowable reserve ratio will seem a formidable task to a small businessman, especially when account is taken of the growth factors. The relevant tables which do not take much space to show in a sample form cover sixty-four pages in a loose-leaf form (par. 2014). The reserve ratio may be calculated under either a tabular form or a guideline form, the latter being particularly helpful for certain patterns of acquisition or retirements of assets within a guideline class or for a new taxpayer. A full appreciation of the complexities of the reserve ratio test can best be secured by scanning the description of it extending over 143 pages in the 1968 loose-leaf Prentice-Hall *Federal Taxes* (15,073–216).

Taxpayers are authorized to use lives shorter than those set by the guidelines when the facts, as indicated by the reserve ratio test or otherwise, indicate that a shorter life is appropriate. Taxpayers may also continue under their established depreciation practices without adopting the new guidelines. It seems probable, however, that the reserve ratio test will in some modified form be applied to all situations in the future.

A reserve ratio, since it is a ratio, may, of course, be lowered by actions which operate on either the numerator or the denominator, that is, not only by reducing the annual depreciation charge but also by retiring assets or by acquiring new assets. Retirement of assets, with an equal reduction in both the assets and the reserve, improves the ratio, as does an increase in the denominator alone through new acquisitions.

One of the alleged advantages of the reserve ratio test is that it will increase capital investment as companies take appropriate action to keep the reserve ratio from reducing their depreciation deductions. Critics of the reserve ratio test doubt that a company would either prematurely scrap property which is economically useful or purchase additional property not otherwise needed simply to obviate a reduction in allowable depreciation for tax purposes. Rather, the critics contend, the existence of the reserve ratio test with its impending forced reduction of depreciation will discourage the adoption of the guidelines and the shorter life estimates which they offer. Continuing analysis will be necessary to determine which of these two influences of the reserve ratio test becomes the dominant one.

Since the statutory allowance for depreciation simply provides a deduction for "a reasonable allowance for the exhaustion, wear and tear (including a reasonable allowance for obsolescence)," the Treasury contends that something like the reserve ratio test is necessary to assure reasonableness. This position may well be correct. An authorization of lives substantially shorter than actual lives might be considered unreasonable. But if the reserve ratio test does discourage the use of specified lives, which though relatively short in comparison to those previously given in Bulletin F are still somewhat longer than those authorized in many European countries which do not use a reserve ratio test, then it would seem necessary to provide by statute for something like the guidelines but without the reserve ratio test. The restricted depreciation allowances under our tax law have long been a handicap to U.S. business in meeting the competition of new plants and equipment abroad. Only by such additional legislation could U.S. business be made fully competitive internationally from the standpoint of tax depreciation allowances.

SALVAGE VALUE: Salvage value refers to the sales price of depreciated property, whether as scrap or as a six-month-old automobile in good condition. Anticipated salvage value is generally required to be taken into account when establishing the annual depreciation charge in the first instance and only the anticipated net depreciation written off over the anticipated service life. Thus, an item of equipment costing $1,000 with an estimated scrap value of $50 and life of ten years theoretically should be depreciated at $95 annually under straight line depreciation. A $2,500 automobile with an anticipated sale price of $1,300 after two years should be depreciated at $600 annually straight line.

Two important exceptions are made in the law to the general requirement that anticipated salvage value be taken into account in fixing depreciation. Salvage value may be ignored when the declining balance method of depreciation is used (par. 2007). This is permitted because property is never fully written off under that method and the scrap value is likely to be less than the remaining book value at any time. A problem arises when depreciated property is sold not as scrap but as good secondhand property, as in the cars of self-drive rental companies. The courts have upheld the Treasury in its position that property cannot be depreciated below its anticipated salvage value in any case, a rule which prevents excess depreciation though it does not preclude too rapid depreciation to that level.

The leading court cases involved car rental companies and settled two separate issues.[1] First, the limitation of depreciation to estimated salvage value was to be based on the salvage value anticipated in light of the practice of the particular taxpayer, not on physical scrap. Thus, a car rental company which always maintained current model cars was limited to the sales price of year-old cars and could not write off more depreciation than that decrease in value; for example, it could not write off 50 per cent of cost in the first year under double-rate declining value depreciation with a four-year life and a zero value as junk at the end of four years if in fact the market price of one-year-old cars was two-thirds of purchase price. This limitation is significant when applied to companies with many similar assets where it is possible to establish a pattern of disposition. It is not of much use in limiting excess depreciation where the taxpayer is a company with only one hotel or one ship, since it is not easy to establish a pattern of disposition and replacement for a company with only one item of property in a major class.

The second and closely related issue upheld the Treasury position that the useful life was the life anticipated by the taxpayer, not the physical life or even the average useful life for average taxpayers. Actually any other rule would be a harsh one for almost all taxpayers, but in this particular case the rental car company wanted to establish a right to take declining balance depreciation by asserting a four-year life (to qualify for the declining balance method), though its own practice was to dispose of cars in less than two years. If the company had won its case, it would have established a rule which would have drastically reduced depreciation allowances for business generally, and seriously retarded plant modernization and economic growth.

The second exception to the rule that salvage value must be taken into account in establishing depreciation was added to the law in 1962. Under an amendment, anticipated salvage value on depreciable personal property with a life of three or more years may be reduced by 10 per cent of cost (par. 2000). This means that it can be ignored if it consists

---

[1] *Massey Motors, v. U.S.*, 80 S. Ct. 1411; *The Hertz Corporation v. U.S.*, 80 S. Ct. 1420.

only of scrap value since this is usually less than 10 per cent of original cost. This was a most desirable change in the interest of simplicity; it prevents quibbling over small amounts which develop more resentment than revenue. Since the same bill taxes as ordinary income any gain up to original purchase price on the sale of depreciated tangible personal property, there was no longer any fear of tax manipulation by playing the tax rates against each other. The salvage value limitation is still important where substantial secondhand values are anticipated; it is not appropriate when only scrap value is involved. Prior to the amendment, a negligible scrap value might have to be assigned to a filing cabinet, with depreciation designed to recover perhaps $58 instead of a $60 cost.

BASIS FOR DEPRECIATION: In general, the concept of basis of property for tax depreciation is the same as that used to record the cost of depreciable property on a company's books for its own purposes (pars. 2003, 1501–03). To be sure, there is a disposition by taxpayers to claim as immediate current expenses for tax purposes certain installation charges or similar items which might be capitalized for book purposes. By contrast, in tax audits there is a disposition to force the capitalization of controversial items, to prevent immediate tax reductions. But these are usually minor items, and a policy consistently applied by a company is likely to be accepted for tax purposes and, to avoid complications in records, what is allowed for tax purposes is adopted for book purposes.

Similarly, there is a basis for conflict on the fuzzy line of demarcation between repairs and improvements (par. 1825). To reduce current taxes, a company is inclined to claim that an outlay is a current expense though it might be disposed to consider it as an improvement subject to depreciation in order to increase current book income. In the tax audit, borderline items are likely to be disallowed as current expenses and capitalized in order to increase current taxes. Here again, reasonable rules consistently applied are usually accepted for both tax and book purposes and the two tend to conform to each other.

There is perhaps some unintended discrimination against small business in the demarcation between maintenance and improvements. A large company with its own maintenance crew is not likely to be required to capitalize some of the work of its painters because a particular paint job will last two or three years, while a small company hiring an outside painting contractor might be required by an overly meticulous field agent to capitalize the cost of each paint job and write it off over the appropriate number of years. This problem, to the extent that it has existed, may be expected to be reduced under the broader categories of the new depreciation guidelines.

Though the tax law conforms fairly closely to business practice on the determination of the cost of buildings, machinery, and equipment which are purchased or constructed, several special tax rules exist for depreciable property acquired in other ways, such as mergers, by gift or bequest, or in exchanges of one item of property for another. These rules, and the reasons for them, may be noted here briefly; most of them are discussed in more detail in other chapters to which they are more closely related.

DEPRECIABLE PROPERTY ACQUIRED THROUGH MERGERS: The tax law permits certain mergers to be made without the immediate imposition of the taxes which ordinarily would apply when property is sold or exchanged. Since the purpose is to give a postponement rather than a forgiveness of tax, the logical corollary is to carry forward the basis of property previously held, thereby assuring ultimate taxation when the property received in exchange is depreciated and finally sold. Depreciable property acquired by a corporation in a tax-free merger carries its previous basis, which is used both for computing gain or loss on a subsequent taxable sale and for subsequent depreciation (par. 3308). There is, thus, no step-up in basis through a nontaxable merger.

For the same reason, when a proprietorship or partnership is incorporated, the gain is not recognized if certain conditions are met (par. 1405). This is an important relief provision in the law to prevent a drain of cash on the owners of a business at the very time when it is expanding. But again, the intent is to postpone not to forgive the tax. The new corporation takes as its basis of all assets, including depreciable assets, the basis of the preceding proprietorship or partnership at the moment of incorporation (par. 1513).

One further special rule on basis is available when one company buys 80 per cent of the stock of another company within a year and then within two years adopts a plan to merge its new acquisition into itself. In such a case, the acquiring company may use its cost of the purchased stock as the basis for the assets which it ultimately receives, with an allocation of the total purchase price over the assets in proportion to their fair market values, and with any excess attributed to purchased good will, a nondepreciable asset (par. 3316). This special rule is in contrast to the usual tax treatment of the merger of a subsidiary into a parent corporation, which is itself nontaxable, with the parent continuing to use for itself the basis of the individual items of property in the hands of the subsidiary.

DEPRECIABLE PROPERTY ACQUIRED BY GIFT OR BEQUEST: The usual rules of basis of property acquired by gift and bequest apply to depreciable property. Thus, depreciable property acquired by gift carries forward the basis of the donor (par. 1511). The donee receives no step-up in basis. If the market value at date of gift is less than the basis to the donor, the basis is reduced to fair market value for purposes of computing subsequent loss, though not for subsequent depreciation or for computing gain. By contrast, property acquired by bequest takes the fair market value at date of death, or one year later if the estate is valued at that date for estate tax purposes, as the basis to the new owner, regardless of the cost or basis to the decedent (par. 1507).

A special rule applies to depreciable property contributed to a corporation by a nonstockholder (par. 3130(a)). The basis in this case is zero. This situation arises when a public body or local business group contributes property to a company as an inducement to it to establish itself in a particular locality. Though the contribution is not regarded as income, it was felt by 1954 that contributed assets should not receive the additional tax benefit of depreciation and the law was so amended. To prevent subterfuge if the contribution is in the form of cash, property acquired with the cash has a zero tax basis, or if the cash is not used to buy identifiable property then the basis of other property must be reduced.

INVESTMENT CREDIT

The investment credit adopted in 1962 is hard to classify. It is not a form of depreciation; to many critics it has no proper place in the tax law at all. For want of a better place, the discussion of the investment credit is included here along with the discussion of depreciation (par. 2019).

The investment credit gives a 7 per cent credit against income tax for qualified purchases of depreciable tangible personal property other than livestock. For certain public utilities the credit is 3 per cent. The credit is on a sliding scale related to the life of the depreciable property. If the life is less than 4 years, no credit is allowed; one-third of the full credit is allowed if the life is 4 or 5 years; two-thirds if the life is 6 or 7 years, and the full credit for property with a life of 8 years or more.

The credit cannot exceed $25,000 plus one-half of the income tax liability in excess of $25,000. Thus, a company with a small income can completely wipe out its tax liability by an investment credit; for larger companies, the credit can be only slightly above one-quarter of the tax. Provision is made for carry-backs of 3 years and carry-forwards of 7 years, comparable to the regular loss carry-back and carry-forward. Provision is also made for a recapture of the credit. If, for example, a full credit is taken on the assumption that property would have an

8-year life but is in fact sold in the seventh year, in the year of disposition one-third of the credit (the difference between the full credit and the two-thirds which should have been taken) is added back to the tax due.

Over the objection of the Treasury, the Senate before accepting the investment credit in 1962 provided that the basis of property subject to the credit should be reduced by the amount of the credit. This prevented the credit from being fully effective in reducing the purchase price. The advocates of the amendment felt that it simply kept the credit from being an unqualified handout from the Treasury, as it was regarded by many of its opponents both in and out of the business community. The effect of the reduction of basis by the credit meant that to that extent subsequent depreciation, and the tax saving arising therefrom, would be reduced. Thus a tax credit of $1,000 would, without the required reduction in basis, mean a saving in taxes of that amount for a company which has sufficient tax to make use of the credit. With the $1,000 required to be applied as a reduction in basis, however, subsequent depreciation was reduced by that amount and, at a 52 per cent tax rate, subsequent taxes were increased by $520. There was then an immediate tax reduction of $1,000, partially offset by later higher taxes of $520, or a net tax reduction of $480, ignoring present value advantages of the original full tax reduction.

It should be emphasized that the reduction in basis only partially offset the effect of the credit. The credit was against the tax, involving a net pecuniary benefit dollar for dollar. The adjustment to basis merely reduced a subsequent deduction which had a pecuniary significance equal to the marginal applicable tax rate.

In 1964, the requirement for reduction in basis by the amount of the credit was removed, thus simplifying the calculations and also making the credit an unqualified Treasury subsidy for qualifying investments. By 1966, temporary suspension of the investment credit had become a favorite proposal as part of a package of anti-inflationary tax increases. Most business groups, which had been unenthusiastic about the investment credit in 1962, objected to any removal or suspension of it by 1966. They argued further that with the long lead time involved in major capital investments, an on-and-off investment credit could not be effective for cyclical purposes and would simply add uncertainty, always an unfavorable factor, to long-range planning. Some argued that simultaneous removal of the investment credit and the reserve ratio test would be useful and timely in 1966.

The Treasury has held, over objections of taxpayers, that the investment credit is mandatory. When small items of property are involved, the extra records and calculations which are necessary if property with an anticipated life of eight years is in fact sold in seven, much more than offset, in the opinions of many taxpayer groups, the benefit of the original investment credit. The insistence of the Treasury that "shall be allowed" should be interpreted as meaning "must be taken" has added complication to tax and business records and increased the resentment of business taxpayers.

At the recommendation of the administration, the investment credit was suspended, with certain exceptions, for the period from October 10, 1966, through 1967. Among the exceptions to suspension were the first $20,000 of property acquired during the period (a relief to small business), property acquired under a binding contract made prior to that date, air and water pollution control facilities, and property acquired to replace property destroyed by a casualty.

The suspension was intended to slow down what was regarded as excessive business capital investments. At the time, there was much uncertainty regarding the actual effect of the suspension on major capital programs with long lead times. Some observers thought that the impact would be concentrated on items with relatively short lives which could be prolonged, such as trucks. Even those who thought that the suspension would not have a large effect on major programs recognized that it might slow down orders and contracts in the latter part of 1967 in view of the expectation of its availability in 1968. For this reason, it was argued that the only way to avoid an upsetting bunching of orders would be to restore the credit suddenly sometime in the middle of 1967. This was, in fact, done, effective March 10, 1967.

The effects of the investment credit on investment, and the reasons for such effects as do occur, will be debated for some time. Whether one chooses to regard the investment credit as a reduction in tax on income or in the cost of capital equipment, the return on an investment is increased. To the extent that investment decisions are significantly influenced by small changes in return, the investment credit can be important. Others, including the author, who believe that the spread between expected returns on most industrial investments and costs of funds is so great that a small change in either will not be important, may agree nonetheless that the credit has a significant effect by increasing internal cash flows.

Or, one may feel that the principal impact arose from the simple fact that a recommendation of the investment credit demonstrated that the new administration in 1961 had rejected the argument that aggregate demand was the critical factor for economic activity and growth. The mere fact that that administration recognized that investment did not depend entirely on aggregate demand, thereby rejecting the programs of many of its supporters, gave a basis for confidence and improved the investment climate. The method adopted and even its pecuniary importance were, so it can be argued, less significant than the indirect effects.

DIFFERENCES BETWEEN TAX AND BOOK ACCOUNTING FOR DEPRECIATION AND THE INVESTMENT CREDIT

Differences between tax and book accounting for depreciation have greatly complicated both record keeping and the analysis of business financial statements since World War II. There is no uniformity in practice. There is not even uniformity among professional accountants as to what policies should be adopted. The difficulty of analysis and the downright confusion which has developed have led some critics to the conclusion that tax depreciation should not be permitted to exceed the depreciation taken on a company's own books, a common requirement in the continental European countries.

In addition to differences in estimates of useful life, differences between tax and book accounting for depreciable property have arisen from three specific features of the tax law. First, in chronology, was the authorization for five-year amortization of certain defense facilities during World War II. If the property covered by the certificate of necessity had a fairly good prospect for continued use in postwar and overstate-was reasonable to avoid understatements of postwar costs and overstatements of postwar income by continuing to take depreciation for book purposes over the probable actual life rather than the five-year period authorized for tax purposes. Under such circumstances, it was reasonable to consider the immediate reduction in taxes from the accelerated amortization of depreciable property as a short-term phenomenon which would be offset by higher taxes after the exhaustion of the depreciation basis. Income could be more accurately stated over the entire period of prospective use if this shift in timing was recognized as such. This was accomplished by setting up a "reserve for future taxes" through a charge to income during the years of accelerated amortization, in an amount equal to the difference between the taxes actually paid and the tax that would have been paid if tax depreciation had been limited to that taken on the books. This charge to income, to establish the reserve, kept net income from being overstated. In the later years, that part of the tax arising from the previous exhaustion of the tax basis for tax depreciation was charged to the reserve, thereby letting the net income reflect only the tax which would have been due if there had been no accelerated amortization in the first place.

This adjustment was intended to smooth the impact of an acceleration of a regular deduction which was to be available for a limited period. There was little controversy over the validity of the concept, though some real difficulty in projecting the extent of postwar use of property subject to the rapid amortization.

In the years following the authorization of double-rate declining balance depreciation in 1954, a good many companies took the faster depreciation for tax purposes while continuing to use straight line depreciation for book purposes. There were many reasons given for the failure to adopt declining balance depreciation for book purposes; in fact, the real reason was probably in most instances a simple desire not to reduce reported income. The use of the same faster depreciation for book purposes would have reduced income before taxes and, at the 52 per cent corporate tax rate then in effect, the saving in tax would have offset only slightly more than half of the reduction in income before tax. It became recommended practice by the American Institute of Certified Public Accountants to set up a reserve for future taxes by charging income in the early years of use for an additional amount as though only straight line depreciation had been taken for tax purposes, with this amount credited to the reserve for future taxes. In later years, when tax depreciation fell below book depreciation on particular items of property, an appropriate part of the higher tax due would be charged against the reserve rather than current income, thus regularizing the tax charge and the net income after tax. But this procedure, though formally recommended by the accounting profession, was by no means universally accepted either by those within the profession or by those concerned with financial statements outside the profession.

The objection to the use of a reserve for future taxes because of a permanent difference in the method of accounting for depreciation for tax and book purposes was based on the belief that the so-called reserve would never be needed or used except in the unlikely event that future investments in depreciable property, in terms of total dollars, declined. The reserve at any one time and for the indefinite future, it was argued, was really an element of net worth and should be shown as such by being left in surplus, as it would be if the reserve had never been created in the first place.

Contrary to the situation under temporary wartime acceleration of depreciation, the differential between declining balance and straight line depreciation is presumably permanent. The saving in taxes in the early years of use is real; the higher taxes in the later years of use of specific items of property will be offset by simultaneous savings in what will be the early years of use of newly acquired property so long as the total dollar investment in depreciable property is maintained; and this process continues ad infinitum.

Thus, in the first years of differences in accounting method, there is a net tax saving through faster depreciation for tax purposes. Later there comes a time when tax depreciation falls short of book depreciation on particular items of property and, for a one-asset company such as a transportation company with one ship or a real estate company with one building, a reserve for future taxes would turn out to be appropriate. But so long as new investments in depreciable property give new items subject to faster depreciation in their early years sufficient to offset the smaller depreciation in later years from old property, there will be a stabilized situation, after the years of tax saving and the increase in net worth. If gross investments in depreciable property increase and the distribution of useful lives does not lengthen, there will be a continuing annual saving in taxes and increase in net worth, though at a declining rate. Only when the investment fails to be maintained will the potential increase in taxes from the decreased annual depreciation become real. This contingency seems so unlikely for the bulk of industry that the whole concept of the reserve for future taxes seemed to its critics to be an example of theoretical perfection at the expense of both complication and confusion to the unsophisticated.

In retrospect, some of those involved in the authorization of faster depreciation in 1954 believe that it might have been better to have included a requirement that tax depreciation could not exceed the depreciation taken on a company's own books. Such a condition was considered in 1954. It was rejected largely because of the difficulties which had arisen under a somewhat similar provision regarding the use of last-in first-out inventory accounting. Lifo inventory accounting for tax purposes is not permitted unless the taxpayer establishes to the satisfaction of the Commissioner that no other method has been used "for credit purposes" or for the purpose of reports to shareholders, partners, or other beneficiaries (sec. 472(c)). In its first years, this limitation was quite strictly applied and discouraged the adoption of lifo accounting. Later, the interpretation was somewhat relaxed with, for example, a specific authorization in the regulations to use market instead of cost which may be necessary to avoid overstating assets for credit purposes (reg. 1.472–2(e)).

In 1954, there was a strong desire to avoid imposing any new restraint on business practices through the tax law, and even the simple requirement that tax depreciation could not run ahead of book depreciation as used in reports to stockholders and public agencies seemed at the time unduly onerous. If the extent of use of reserves for future taxes when tax and book depreciation differed had been anticipated in 1954, it is likely that the decision would have been in favor of a requirement that tax depreciation could not exceed current or previous book depreciation. A little restraint on business practice would have been better than a lot of complication in business reports.

The investment credit established in 1962 has raised a new and somewhat different complication in accounting reports. The investment credit very simply and very directly reduces the income tax in the years in which qualified investments are made. The tax reduction increases net income after tax and, when the year's income account is closed, it increases surplus on the balance sheet. Or so it was thought. But the investment credit may also be regarded as an indirect way of reducing the cost of depreciable property; the tax return is merely a convenient mechanism to avoid direct payments by the government. Much of the legislative history of the credit supports the view that the purpose was not so much a reduction of tax as a reduction of cost of depreciable property.

Consistent with the objective of regularizing taxes and income, the American Institute of Certified Public Accountants first proposed that the investment credit should be used to reduce the cost of property to which it applied. Thus, depreciation for book purposes would be less, and net income more, in each year of use of the property, including the first year. An unfortunate result of this procedure, however, is that total taxes are overstated since the credit is applied to reduce cost of property acquired rather than tax in the year of acquisition, and in years of subsequent use there is no reason to modify the taxes actually paid. This result is consistent with the concept that the investment credit really has nothing to do with taxes, and that the tax return is merely a convenient way to subsidize qualified capital investment or, as the critics of the credit put it, to give an undesired and undesirable handout to business. In the final statement on accounting principles an equally appropriate alternative was recognized under which the investment credit is treated as deferred income to be amortized over the productive life of the acquired property. Income would thus be increased in each year of use by a charge to the deferred income account rather than by lower book depreciation. Under this procedure also, total taxes actually paid would be overstated.

Accounting reports to the public, in the judgment of many, should be comprehensible as well as theoretically correct and it is a matter of judgment whether theoretical perfection justifies virtual incomprehensibility. This problem of balance arises even more seriously from many proposals to "improve" the tax law and tax forms.

In spite of objections both within and outside the profession, the Accounting Principles Board of the American Institute established a rule at the end of 1967 requiring "normalization" of taxes in many respects, including situations in which tax and book depreciation are substantially different. Normalization is also required by the use of deferred debits to reflect future tax reduction from loss carry-overs. Because of strong opposition from the Treasury, which argued that the taxes actually due on a year's income was the best measure of tax liability for the year and that any requirement for spreading would reduce the incentive effect and thus thwart the purpose of the law, no action was taken at that time regarding accounting for the investment credit.

A general requirement that tax depreciation could not exceed depreciation taken for book purposes, and without any reserve for future taxes, would help to clear the way for the eventual conversion of the investment credit into an allowance for additional first-year depreciation, similar to that now available to the extent of 20 per cent of the first $10,000 annual investment in tangible personal property. This change would remove the element of subsidy implicit in the investment credit. It would concentrate attention on the write-off of the actual cost of depreciable property, with wide latitude for the exercise of judgment. It would greatly simplify both tax and business accounting records.

GAINS AND LOSSES ON SALES OF DEPRECIATED PROPERTY

Two problems arise under this heading: how are gains and losses to be measured, and how are gains to be taxed and losses allowed as deductions?

The measurement of the gain or loss is simple if there is a single asset. The net tax basis, which is usually the cost less the depreciation taken to date, is deducted from the proceeds of sale of the property; a positive figure measures a gain, a negative figure a loss (par. 2017). There are, to be sure, minor problems such as the allocation of the cost of removal between maintenance and net proceeds. If regular employees in a maintenance crew dismantle a piece of equipment, the easiest thing is to treat their wages as current expense rather than as a charge against the sales proceeds of the property disposed of. If losses and gains were always fully and immediately deductible or taxable, it would make no difference how this charge was handled. But if the deduction of losses is limited or postponed, or if gains are taxable at a lower rate, there is a tax advantage in charging as current expense items which more appropriately should be regarded as costs of disposition of depreciated assets. But these are relatively minor problems, and reasonable policies consistently applied are usually acceptable for tax as well as business purposes.

The measurement of gain or loss is much less clear if a group of similar items are being depreciated, one of which is disposed of prematurely. At first glance, it would appear reasonable to compute gain or loss on this one item; with early retirement there would presumably be a loss. But with a group of items there will typically be both early retirements and late retirements. There would be a dispersion of actual lives in use around the average; on those items used longer than the average, depreciation would continue to run and total depreciation would exceed actual cost. Thus, when the depreciation is based on average life, loss is not allowed on ordinary premature retirements because the deficient depreciation on those specific items is presumably offset by the excess depreciation on items which are used beyond the average life. If over the years the premature and delayed retirements do not offset each other, the average life will be proven to be incorrect and the basic depreciation rate should be adjusted.

The tax law conforms to the foregoing analysis (par. 2017(3) (a)–(b)). If depreciation is based on the average life of a group of depreciable items of property, a premature retirement is not regarded as a special event calling for any calculation of loss or gain. The depreciation reserve is charged and the asset account is credited for the full original cost, even though there will not have been sufficient depreciation on that specific term to cover its cost. But other items which are used beyond their expected life are left in the asset account and the regular depreciation rate applied to the total balance in the asset account giving an offsetting excess depreciation.

The foregoing treatment of loss on disposition covers normal retirements, that is, dispositions for which there are no distinctive or unusual reasons. In cases of abnormal retirement due, for example, to casualty or extraordinary obsolescence, a loss will be recognized equal to the difference between depreciated basis and the amount realized (par. 2018(3)). Depreciated basis is the original basis less depreciation to date.

If depreciation for a group of items is based on the longest life in a normal dispersion around the average life, rather than on the average life itself, loss may be taken on each retirement at any age short of that used to fix the depreciation rate. This is· reasonable because there will be few if any items kept in the asset account beyond the period used to fix the depreciation rate; there will be little if any excess depreciation to offset the inadequate depreciation on the earlier retirements.

With the gain or loss on sale of depreciable property measured and the time for inclusion determined, the final issue is whether the gain or loss should be included as ordinary items in computing taxable income or given capital gains treatment. On this aspect of the problem, the law has been changed several times and may well be changed again. The law gives ordinary loss treatment to losses, as measured and recognized above. Net gains, that is gains in excess of losses in any year, are treated as capital gains except gains on depreciated tangible personal property which are to be included in ordinary income up to the tax basis of the property before depreciation. Thus, to the extent that gains on this limited class of property arise from what turns out to be excess depreciation, which was previously deducted in computing regular taxable income, there is a balancing charge included in taxable income in the year of disposition. The advantage of faster depreciation arises from the time factor alone. If one assumes no change in the tax rate over the period of use and disposition, there is no tax benefit other than in timing, from an excess deduction which first reduces income but is later balanced by an offsetting increase in income.

The recapture of excess depreciation was adopted in 1962 for tangible personal property (par. 1613(a)). The Treasury recommended in 1961 that the proposed new provision should apply to all forms of depreciable property but the Congress did not accept the recommendation. In 1963, the Treasury made a new proposal for limited recapture as ordinary income of excess depreciation on real estate on a sliding scale for sales within a relatively short period after original purchase. A limited recapture for real estate was adopted in 1964 (par. 1613(b)). The present law is the result of successive changes, each one of which was a rational move to meet an immediate situation. A brief review will give historical perspective and some rationale for the existing provisions.

Depreciable property was originally included in the tax definition of capital assets. In 1934, in order to maintain revenues, deductions for capital losses were limited and allowed only as offsets to capital gains. This created a perverse economic effect since it was better from the tax standpoint to hold and depreciate unwanted or uneconomical machinery than to scrap it and replace it with more efficient equipment. During the depression of the 1930's, losses rather than gains prevailed and it was especially undesirable to have anything in the tax law which discouraged outlays on capital equipment. The immediate problem was solved in 1938 by excluding depreciable property from the definition of capital assets. Thus, losses on the sale of depreciable property were ordinary losses, deductible in full. To be sure, gains would be taxable in full, but there were not many gains at the time.

Within two years, however, the problem was reversed. The demands for war production during World War II made even old machine tools valuable, and it was in the national interest that idle equipment be sold to whatever new user needed it. But with an excess-profits tax at 85 per cent and the gain treated as ordinary income, virtually the entire proceeds of sale of fully depreciated property would go in taxes. If there were any possible chance of use, it was better to hoard idle machinery than to sell it. Even if no prospect for use existed, it was reasonable to hold for sale after the war when the excess-profits tax would have expired. In 1942, accordingly, the law was amended again to permit net gains on the sale of depreciable property to be treated as capital gains, though depreciable property was still not included in the definition of capital assets, thereby permitting net losses to be deductible in full. This situation continued until 1962. The legislation adopted then, treating gains up to original purchase price as ordinary income, provided a basis for more liberal depreciation allowances with no danger of abuse for those categories of property to which the new law applied. Similar legislation for all depreciable property would seem to be in prospect.

PURCHASE OR LEASE OF DEPRECIABLE PROPERTY

The tax law is intended to be neutral as regards purchase or lease of capital equipment. Both the statute and administrative policy as stated in regulations and rulings are designed to give neither preference nor penalty to the rapidly growing practice of securing depreciable property by leases. Administrative practice, however, may not always conform to policy, and leases may still give appreciable tax advantages.

When the practice of leasing received its first big impetus after World War II, it was promoted to a large extent on the basis of the tax advantages then available. The advantage came from so-called leases, which were like installment purchases but with the payments hopefully deductible as rent. In an installment purchase the buyer takes ordinary depreciation over the useful service life; the timing and form of the purchase payments are quite irrelevant. But if equipment with a prospective useful life of fifteen years is leased for seven years at a "rent" which pretty well covers the purchase price plus interest, and the lease is then subject to renewal for several more years at a nominal rent with a final option to purchase at a nominal price, it is like an installment purchase as regards payments to secure the property but with a great tax advantage if the payments are deductible as rent, since they come much sooner than the allowable depreciation.

A digression into accounting theory and financial practice is necessary to set the tax consequences of leasing in perspective. It should be emphasized that the advantage of a lease is the possible earlier tax deduction of any given amounts; it is not, most emphatically, the earlier payments of any given amount. A payment involves a drain on cash, which is not good, and the cash outlay is only partially offset by the deductibility of the payment, if it is deductible. This is self-evident with a moment's thought, but at times the protagonists of leasing have seemed to urge that lease payments should be accelerated in order to give quicker deductions. So long as the tax rate is under 100 per cent, a simultaneous acceleration of payment and deduction increases the short-term cash outflow and is unattractive to the lessee. If the tax deduction can be accelerated without accelerating the cash payment for the property, there is a clear gain. A little acceleration of payment may be acceptable if it carries with it a big acceleration of the deduction; the balance depends on the amounts involved and the interest factor used in present value calculations.

A few specific examples may help to clarify the point in the foregoing paragraph. If one has a choice between financing equipment by a fifteen-year mortgage with fifteen-year depreciation, and lease payments spread over 10 years, the latter would not be preferable even if the lease payments were deductible. However, a lease arrangement with deductible payments over 10 years is preferable to an installment purchase with installments over 10 years and depreciation over 15 years. A lease arrangement with deductible payments over 10 years might be preferable to an installment purchase with payments over 12 years but depreciation over 18, depending on the interest factor used in determining the present value of future payments and deductions.

Some accountants urge that long-run lease commitments should be included in financial statements as a form of debt. Leasing in fact is often an alternative to borrowing to buy capital equipment. One of its alleged advantages has been that it gives a better balance sheet with lower debt ratios. The many proposals that lease obligations be shown in financial statements are thus intended to prevent the use of what may be regarded as subterfuge and to assure that fundamentally similar situations shall not be presented as dissimilar. But the understandable argument that a lease commitment and a debt are analogous in concept does not mean that they are in fact interchangeable.

Property will be leased to companies which cannot borrow from the money market for similar periods, and managements will incur lease obligations though they would be uncomfortable with debt. This may be a reflection on management and on the money markets and the fluidity of funds therein, but whatever the explanation it is a fact and will probably remain so for some years. It is not true that lease commitments and debts displace each other dollar for dollar in the actual financial operations of business. Perhaps this should be true and perhaps it sometime will be true, but it is not true now.

The argument that debt and lease commitments are similar seems sometimes carried to the point of assuming that companies will always make full use of their combined lease-debt capacity. If so, the cash drain for payments is the same regardless of the form of obligation, assuming annual adjustments to make full use of available outside financing. The final step in the argument is that whatever form of financing gives the more rapid tax deduction on any property acquired is preferable, and this may be a lease arrangement. But this entire analysis rests on the doubtful proposition that debt and lease obligations are interchangeable.

In the early days of leasing, the Treasury was apparently too disposed to concentrate on the form rather than the substance of a lease agreement. Rent was deductible, and whatever was called rent presumably was rent. Abuses soon became apparent, however. So-called rental payments covered the ordinary purchase price in a relatively short period and the lessee had the right to renew the lease or purchase the property for a nominal amount. A succession of court cases gradually led to the development of a list of factors, any one of which made a lease suspect. In the last analysis, each case must be settled in the light of all the facts and circumstances. The danger of relying on objective tests is shown by a five-year lease of sprinkler equipment installed in ceilings. There was no option to purchase or to renew. The lessor had the right to remove the pipes and had only to restore the ceilings to their preinstallation condition. But with the cost of removal and restoration exceeding the value of secondhand pipe, it is clear that a lease was in fact a purchase; if recognized as a lease for tax purposes, fifteen- or twenty-year depreciation could be accelerated to five years.

In 1955, a Treasury ruling listed seven conditions which would be taken as indicating a purchase agreement in the absence of evidence of a true rental (par. 1826(e)). These include provisions that (1) part of the payments apply specifically to an equity to be acquired by the lessee; (2) the lessee will acquire title on payment of a certain amount of rent which must be paid in any case; (3) the total amount payable in a short period is very large compared to the total which was required to secure title; (4) payments materially exceed current fair rental value; (5) property may be purchased under option that is (a) nominal in relation to value when option may be exercised or, (b) relatively small compared to total payments; (6) part of payments is designated as interest or may be readily recognized as such; or (7) total rent plus option price approximates the price at which property could have been bought plus interest and carrying charges.

The adoption of declining balance and other methods of faster depreciation in 1954 is claimed to have substantially reduced the alleged tax advantages of leasing. One criterion for distinguishing between leases and purchases not specifically included in the list above is a comparison between lease payments and depreciation which would be allowed if the depreciable property had been purchased. If there is no significant acceleration, there is no significant tax advantage and an otherwise suspect transaction need not be questioned. The authorization of faster depreciation in effect legitimatized certain leases with sliding scales of payments. It also justified an upward revision in the extent of acceptable concentration of lease payments in the early years of a lease. Presumably, the new depreciation guidelines in 1962, with their shorter lives, had a similar effect of validating for tax purposes some leases which might previously have been treated as purchases. If there is little or no tax advantage in claiming deductions for rents because depreciation is now authorized over shorter service lives, there is less reason to question the validity of a lease.

In spite of the foregoing statements and examples of a policy which is intended neither to favor nor to penalize leases as compared with purchases of capital equipment, it appears that there may be a tendency in administrative practice to accept rents as rents when the amounts involved are small even though there is a forward shift in tax deductions.

SALES AND LEASEBACKS: A special form of lease which at one time had great tax advantages is the sale and leaseback. The extreme benefits occurred during World War II when a loss on the sale of depreciable property could be deducted in full and applied against the excess-profits tax. The property was then leased back with subsequent rental payments being deductible. The present value of the future rent payments could be a small price to pay for the high present value of an immediate deduction, especially when the current deduction could be taken against income subject to what was recognized as a temporarily high tax rate.

To be sure, a loss was not better than a gain; even at excess-profits tax rates, a taxed gain is better than a deductible loss. However, there was temptation for collusion, overt or even unintended. Since a sale and leaseback is a single composite transaction, and since the appropriate rent is related to the price paid by the purchaser, there was a temptation to have a lower purchase price (and large deductible loss) combined with lower future rents, thus bringing the deduction forward in time.

Sales and leasebacks can also have tax advantages in case of gains. A present gain taxable as a capital gain may be acceptable if the subsequent lease payments amount to no more than depreciation and interest, as would typically be the case. The situation here is more favorable than the usual sale and repurchase to establish a higher tax basis for depreciation because in such cases the total investment is not reduced; rather it is increased by the amount of capital gains tax payable. In the sale and leaseback, by contrast, there is an immediate cash inflow, the sales price less the tax on the gain, followed by subsequent deductible cash outlays.

The sale and leaseback is not solely or even primarily a device to save taxes. The immediate improvement in cash position is a major advantage. Note that the possibility of improvement denies the validity of the argument that a lease commitment and debt are in fact identical. The continued use of sales and leasebacks is itself evidence of the lack of identity in practice between lease obligations and debt.

In the early years of use of sale of leasebacks, some overly simplified ideas were advanced. A comparison of the turnover of an investment in capital equipment and inventory was sometimes made, with the conclusion that a merchandising company could not afford to have funds tied up in a building or equipment. This view ignored, among other things, the diversity of funds available for financing different forms of assets, as for example mortgage loans for buildings which would not be available to finance inventories or for general corporate purposes.

The key provision in the tax law which restrains sales and leasebacks was inserted for quite different purposes. Section 1031 states that among nonrecognized gains and losses are those arising from exchanges of property held for productive use or investment for other property of like kind (par. 1406). (Securities are specifically excepted.) By regulation, the Treasury has held that real estate and a leasehold in real estate running for thirty years or more are "property of like kind." This interpretation has been upheld by the courts, with one exception which has apparently not been regarded as a useful precedent for those who want to engage in sales and leasebacks. This provision was put in to give relief to business when properties are exchanged, with no new funds available to pay a tax on a gain. But it is mandatory and also works to prevent tax recognition of loss on a transaction which the taxpayer may wish to have recognized.

Thus, if one desires tax advantages in a sale and leaseback, the lease must be for less than thirty years, including renewal options. This limitation is a major impediment when a building or other property has a probable life of considerably more than thirty years, because it means that the original owner cannot protect itself beyond thirty years and will have to pay whatever the going value is after thirty years, in spite of the fact that the initial lease of less than thirty years may have covered the entire investment of the purchaser-lessor plus interest. Present value calculations may and frequently do justify the sale and leaseback contract even with the thirty-year restriction. With a substantial discount rate based on a high rate of return on funds in a business, the present value of rents paid after thirty years may be negligible and much more than offset by the profits to be made from the interim use of funds received from the sale of a building.

But regardless of present value calculations, it seems likely that a management would be chagrined and embarrassed by stockholders' questions, if it had to pay a high rent at the time of renewal of a lease on property it had once owned and then sold and leased for a first period at a rent which permitted the purchaser to recoup his entire investment with interest. In substance, the situation might be no different from that in which a company had rented a building at what turned out to be successively higher rents, instead of buying it in the first place; but this analogy might be small comfort in any discussion in which any of the participants did not think in terms of present value.

One part of the tax on unrelated business income of tax-exempt organizations is specifically directed at sales and leasebacks. The law provides that there shall be included as taxable income that fraction of the net rental income which debt incurred to purchase or improve the property bears to its adjusted basis (par. 3440). This provision of the law was adopted after a few tax-exempt organizations had been especially active in purchasing property for leaseback; the fact that the rental income was tax-exempt enabled them to amortize debt very rapidly and to offer especially favorable purchase terms. This appeared to be one of several misuses of their tax-exempt status and was restricted along with other more obvious commercial activities by what are now Sections 511–515, adopted in their original form in 1950 (par. 3435–39). The restriction is not confined to leasebacks; the tax applies equally to rent from property from whomsoever it is acquired, or even to property constructed directly by the tax-exempt organization, so long as a debt is related to the property. The debt need not even be a debt of the tax-exempt organization; if property is acquired subject to a mortgage, the mortgage debt is taken into account in calculating unrelated business income even though the mortgage was not assumed by the organization.

Rental property, however acquired, can be especially valuable to those few colleges and universities who by their charters have exemption from state and local property taxes for some investment real estate as well as their educational plant. With property taxes as high as they are, the property tax saving may be equal to a normal return on the market value of a taxable property or, regarded another way, exemption from property taxes may double the value of the exempt property. But such charters are few and presumably no new ones will ever be granted with this provision; the exemple is cited as an extreme case of tax influences on valuation.

IMPROVEMENTS BY LESSEE: A lessee is permitted to take depreciation over the period of the lease on buildings and improvements which he erects on leased land (par. 2002). The owner of the land is not deemed to receive income either at the time the improvement is made or when the lease expires (par. 1318). Since it is neither included in landowner's income nor made by him with his own funds, the cost or value of an improvement made by a lessee does not influence the owner's basis for his property. An exception to the foregoing general treatment arises if the lessee makes an improvement instead of paying rent, in which case the fair market value of the improvement is considered income to the owner of the land at the time the improvement is made.

Prior to 1958, it became possible under a series of court decisions for lessees to write off the cost of improvements over the life of an original lease, ignoring renewal options unless it could be shown that the renewal would be made. The fact that it clearly would be foolish not to renew the lease was not deemed adequate evidence. It was becoming fairly common practice for lessees to erect buildings on land under a ten-year lease, with renewal options for a succession of additional five- or ten-year periods covering the full life of the building. Under the court interpretation of the existing law, the lessee could usually write off the cost of the building over the first ten years.

The law was amended in 1958 to require that the renewal periods must be taken into account in determining the period for depreciation of improvements if the initial or unexpired term of the lease is less than 60 per cent of the estimated life of the improvements, unless the lessee establishes that it is improbable that the lease will be renewed (par. 2002). If the lessor and lessee are related persons, as defined in the law, the cost of improvements must be written off over their useful life even in the absence of an option to renew the lease.

12

Tax-Free
Corporate Reorganizations—
Mergers and Divisions
of Existing Corporations

The tax concept of corporate reorganizations, as given in section 368, is in many respects much broader than that usually applied in financial discussions or in popular usage; in some respects it is narrower (par. 3303). Reorganizations which qualify under the tax law can be made generally without recognition of gain or loss to the holders of stock and securities or to the corporations involved. In the transactions qualifying for nonrecognition, there must be continuity of both an investment and business activity (reg. 1.368–1(a)). The tax basis of property previously owned is applied to property received or transferred to a new owner, as may be appropriate, to avoid any tax-free step-up in basis, thus giving postponement but not forgiveness of tax.

In the ordinary course of events, no free funds arise from a reorganization which could be used to pay a tax if one were imposed under the general rules that gains are recognized on exchanges of property as well as on sale. To the extent that free funds do become available in an otherwise nontaxable reorganization, gains are recognized and a tax is imposed.

The reoganization provisions of the tax law are among the most complicated parts of the entire Code, and they are often criticized for this reason. But it must be remembered that they are there to give tax relief and permit rearrangements within and between corporations which otherwise would be burdened and often prevented by current taxation under a simpler law.

202

A mere change of corporate charter from one state to another or a recapitalization involving a change from par to no par stock is the clearest example of an event on which it would seem unreasonable and inequitable to impose a tax simply because the market value of the new stock certificate was higher than the price which had been paid for the old stock certificate many years previously. Such reorganizations are covered by the last two of six types specified in section 368. But the section also gives nonrecognition to combinations of two or more corporations (mergers in the popular use of the word) provided that they occur in any of three specified ways and to a splitting of one corporation into two or more separate corporations (called divisive reorganizations) provided that this is done in a specified manner.

A particularly significant consequence of the nonrecognition of gains in mergers is the inducement for owners of closely controlled corporations to accept offers for mergers instead of selling to a group of new owners who would run the company as a separate entity. An outright sale of a company is always a taxable transaction, as will be explained in the next chapter, and when most of the value represents unrealized gains, a taxable sale would yield only about three-fourths as much as an offer for a tax-free merger, provided the stock of the acquiring company was regarded as an acceptable investment for continued holding. Or, to put the arithmetic in another way, the price in an offer for purchase must be almost a third greater than the value of stock in an offer of merger to give the same after-tax values to the former owners.

A brief survey of the sections of the Code dealing with reorganizations is helpful before discussing the details and the various judicial doctrines which have grown out of it. Although the law is at times quite complex, it should be recognized that it must cover concisely the very large number of ways in which mergers and other reorganizations may occur.

Section 368 is the starting point in any analysis of a reorganization. It outlines six transactions which can qualify for nonrecognition, that is, for postponement of a tax (par. 3303). In order to qualify as a reorganization, only these six methods can be adopted. The first, (A), is the statutory merger or consolidation. In many ways it is the simplest in its operations, but requires the presence of a state statute under which the merger or consolidation may be made. The (B) and (C) types are frequently referred to as "practical mergers," since they are designed to give the same tax consequences as a statutory merger when alternative methods are chosen, either owing to the absence of a state provision for merger or consolidation or to the exigencies of the particular situation. The (D), (E), and (F) types of reorganizations are concerned with corporate divisions, recapitalizations, and mere changes in the form of the business.

If a transaction fits into the definitions of section 368, the actual tax consequences to the corporations and their shareholders are governed by other sections of the Code. Section 354 states that neither gain nor loss will be recognized to investors who exchange their stock or securities for other stock or securities in a reorganization (par. 3304(a)). Section 356 provides for recognition of gain where cash or property other than stock or securities is received by shareholders in a reorganization (pars. 3305–06). And section 358 provides for a substitution of the basis of the stock previously held by a shareholder as the basis of the new stock acquired in the reorganization; it is in this way that the tax recognition of gain or loss is postponed until a later transaction, instead of being permanently foregone (par. 3307).

Sections 357, 361, and 362 apply to the corporations involved in the reorganization. Generally, no gain is recognized to the selling or transferor corporation when it transfers its property to the purchasing or acquiring corporation in exchange for stock in the latter (par. 3304(b), sec. 361(a)). If the selling corporation receives other property in addition to stock or securities of the purchasing corporation, there will still be no gain recognized to the selling corporation if it distributes the other property to its shareholders. Furthermore, the selling corporation will have no gain when its liabilities are assumed by the purchasing corporation (par. 3309, sec. 357(a)). Section 362(b) provides for a carryover of basis to the purchasing corporation, that is, the basis to it of the property it acquired in the reorganization will be the same as if it were in the hands of the selling corporation (par. 3308). In addition, section 1032 denies any gain or loss to the purchasing corporation when it uses its stock, either treasury or newly issued, to finance the acquisition (pars. 3304(c), 1408).

These general principles are described in some detail in the following sections. The first will discuss the definition of a reorganization and the other two will cover in some detail the effects on the corporations and stockholders respectively. A discussion of carryovers of losses and other tax attributes is given in the following chapter.

Definition of a Reorganization

A REORGANIZATIONS. The A-type combination of businesses refers to a merger or consolidation carried out under the corporation laws of the United States or a state. These laws usually require the shareholders of each corporation to vote on the proposed combination, after a formal plan of reorganization or merger has been submitted to them by the board of directors. Many state statutes provide that dissenting stockholders have a right to appraisal of their holdings and redemption of their stock, and that more than half or two-thirds of the shareholders must approve the proposal. Some corporation laws restrict the types of consideration which can be received or given to either stock, securities, or assets, although in most states it is possible to have any combination of these exchanged.

In an A reorganization, there is usually a great deal of flexibility in the way one corporation can acquire another. The acquiring corporation can exchange its stock directly with the stockholders of the acquired corporation, or give them some stock or securities plus cash or other assets, or it can make a similar exchange directly with the acquired corporation for its assets, with the acquired corporation then either liquidating or continuing as a holding company with its assets then consisting of whatever it received from the acquiring company. Such flexibility is not possible in B and C reorganizations.

B Reorganizations. Both the B and C reorganizations are available when state law does not permit statutory merger, or when the method permitted is unwieldly from the participants' viewpoint. In many cases the results of all three types will be the same, but complete uniformity does not exist in the statute. In addition, certain restrictions have been placed upon the consideration moving from the acquiring corporation in exchange for the stock or assets of the merged corporation.

The B type involves an exchange of stock on the shareholder level; the acquiring company exchanges its stock for the stock of the selling corporation held by the selling corporation's stockholders. Following this exchange, the acquiring company must have "control" of the acquired company, which is defined as "ownership of stock possessing at least 80 per cent of the total combined voting power of all classes of stock entitled to vote and at least 80 per cent of the total number of shares of all other classes of stock of the corporation."

The statutory wording of the B reorganizations is important. For example, the acquiring corporation can transfer only its voting stock in exchange for the stock or assets which it acquires. No such limitation appears in an A reorganization, although it is also necessary to a major extent in the C reorganization. The principal controversies developed by this phrase have centered about the words "solely" and "voting stock."

The use of bonds or cash or the assumption of liabilities have been held to nullify this type of reorganization. Furthermore, the entire plan of reorganization must involve the use of voting stock. That is, the acquiring company cannot buy some stock for cash and then obtain the controlling shares through an exchange of stock. Nor can it first obtain control by using its voting stock as consideration and then purchase the remaining shares for cash if it is all a part of the same transaction.

This strict use of the word "solely" raised a very special problem where a corporation had purchased some shares for cash many years previously and later decided to enter a reorganization. It was argued by the Internal Revenue Service that the term "solely" related to every acquisition of stock by the acquiring company and not only to the acquisition under the plan of reorganization which might give it a controlling interest. However, Congress stepped in in 1954 and allowed these "creeping acquisitions," with the parenthetical clause in section 368(a)(1)(B).

Conflict also has developed over the phrase "if immediately after the acquisition, the acquiring corporation has control of such other corporation." Where the acquiring corporation has previously agreed to sell or dispose of some of the shares it has acquired on the exchange, and this agreement would diminish its control, the courts have tended to view the transaction as one not within the reorganization concept. Although it has control for a short time after the acquisition, especially "immediately" thereafter, the courts have considered brief control insufficient if some of the acquired stock is to be sold in the near future. They call the acquired stock "fettered" stock, distinguishing between those cases where the acquiring corporation merely has possession and where it has ownership unfettered by another transfer agreement. When the transaction is looked at as a whole, the result of a fettering agreement is often the same as if the acquiring corporation obtained stock plus cash in exchange for its stock, rather than having a true stock for stock exchange.

C Reorganizations. The C reorganization contemplates an exchange on the corporate level rather than the shareholder level as in the B reorganization. The acquiring corporation exchanges its voting stock for substantially all the assets of the selling corporation, which may then liquidate or remain as a holding company with the stock. This form is useful where the acquiring corporation wishes to obtain the assets but does not wish to retain the corporate shell of the selling corporation because of a fear of hidden liabilities or for other reasons. Similar results can be achieved under the B reorganization if the selling corporation is liquidated tax-free into the new parent under section 332, discussed in a later section of this chapter. However, this is a cumbersome procedure as compared to a C reorganization under which the result can be secured directly.

The Code does not define the phrase "substantially all the properties of another corporation," which appears in the C reorganization. The courts have upheld transfers of 85 and 90 per cent as qualifying, however. Even lower percentages may qualify if the purpose of the retention of the assets was to liquidate its liabilities, and not to engage in business or to distribute assets to shareholders.

A major departure from the previous law under C reorganizations was enacted in 1954. The law now allows, in section 368(a)(2)(B), consideration in addition to voting stock to be given for assets. Up to 20 per cent of the consideration can be cash or other property provided that at least 80 per cent of all the selling corporation's assets are acquired for voting stock. This seemingly would allow much greater freedom in the C type of reorganization. However, two restrictions have been placed on this 80 per cent requirement. First, the stock given in these situations must be transferred in exchange for 80 per cent of all the property of the selling corporation and not "substantially all" of its assets. Second, the assumption of the selling company's liabilities, or acceptance of property subject to liabilities, will be considered as if the acquiring company had transferred cash in the amount of the liability assumed in the exchange. Since it is common in a C reorganization for the transferor corporation to retain some assets to pay liabilities, and since the liabilities which are assumed by the purchasing corporation or to which the property is subject are often in excess of 20 per cent, this modification has limited use. Furthermore, there is always the possibility that a liability which is only contingent or unknown at the time of the exchange will become absolute in future years. If this type of liability has been assumed under the plan of reorganization, a future event may wreak havoc on the tax consequences of a past transaction.

Nonstatutory Limitations of Tax-Free Reorganizations

As noted at the start of this chapter, the nonrecognition of gain or loss in reorganizations is an exception to the general tax rule that exchanges of property are taxable events. Over the years, the Internal Revenue Service has taken the position that tax-free reorganization provisions are a privileged area and that it is not sufficient to meet the letter of the law if the purpose and effects of transactions do not come within those for which the Congress intended to give relief. Two limitations have been developed and sustained by the courts—continuity of interest and business purpose. They are both stated in the regulations as applicable to all reorganizations, but in fact each one is likely to be applicable only in particular types of situations.

The continuity of interest concept requires that an equity interest in the acquiring corporation be received and held by the acquired corporation or by its stockholders. Preferred stock has been held to qualify as an equity interest, though normally only common stock is thought of as equity. In the B and C reorganizations where common stock must be given, the continuity of interest requirement is almost automatically met, but it may be a significant constraint in A reorganizations. An excerpt from the regulations gives the flavor as well as some of the substance of the administrative policy.

> The purpose of the reorganization provisions of the Code is to except from the general rule [taxing exchanges of property] certain specifically described exchanges incident to such readjustments of corporate structures made in one of the particular ways specified in the Code, as are required by business exigencies and which effect only a readjustment in continuing interest in property under modified corporate forms. Requisite to a reorganization under the Code are a continuity of the business enterprise under the modified corporate form, and . . . a continuity of interest therein on the part of those persons who, directly or indirectly, were the owner of the enterprise prior to the reorganization. The Code recognizes as a reorganization the amalgamation (occurring in a specified way) of two corporate enterprises under a single corporate structure if there exists among the holders of the stock and securities of either of the old corporations the requisite continuity of interest in the new corporation, but there is not a reorganization if the holders of the stock and securities of the old corporation are merely the holders of short-term notes in the new corporation. In order to exclude transactions not intended to be included, the specifications of the reorganization provisions of the law are precise. Both the terms of the specifications and their underlying assumptions and purposes must be satisfied in order to entitle the taxpayer to the benefit of the exception from the general rule. Accordingly, under the Code, a short-term purchase money note is not a security of a party to a reorganization, an ordinary dividend is to be treated as an ordinary dividend, and a sale is nevertheless to be treated as a sale even though the mechanics of a reorganization have been set up (reg. 1.368–1(b)).

A two-fold test for continuity of interest has been laid down by the courts: (1) That the transferor corporation or its shareholders retain a substantial proprietary stake in the enterprise represented by a material interest in the affairs of the transferee corporation; (2) that such retained interest represent a substantial part of the value of the property transferred to it. (*Southwest Natural Gas Co. v. Commissioner*, 189 F. 2d 332 (5th Cir. 1951)). Test (1) means something other than an interest as an officer or manager, and, as previously mentioned, does not include situations where only a creditor's interest is retained. Test (2) has been held satisfied where the S shareholders received common stock of the surviving company representing 25 per cent of the value of the transferred assets. Perhaps a greater amount would be required if stock other than common were given in the exchange.

The "business purpose" rule is stated in the regulations as follows:

> A plan of reorganization must contemplate the bona fide execution of one of the transactions specifically described as a reorganization in section 368 (a) and for the bona fide consummation of each of the requisite acts under which nonrecognition of gain is claimed. Such transaction and such acts must be an ordinary and necessary incident of the conduct of the enterprise and must provide for a continuation of the enterprise. A scheme, which involves an abrupt departure from normal reorganization procedure in connection with a transaction on which the imposition of a tax is imminent, such as a mere device that puts on the form of a corporate reorganization as a disguise for concealing its real character, and the object and accomplishment of which is the consummation of a preconceived plan having no business or corporate purpose, is not a plan or reorganization (reg. 1.368–1(c)).

The business purpose concept is seldom applied to mergers. It is an important constraint in situations where a company seeks to separate some assets from the rest of its business and distribute them to shareholders at the capital gains rate. In fact, the doctrine originated in just such a case. S corporation owned shares in Sub corporation which it wished to give to its shareholders without the imposition of the tax on dividends. In order to do this, the S shareholders formed P corporation. S then gave its Sub holdings to P in exchange for the P stock, and distributed P stock to the S shareholders. The creation of P followed exactly the definition of a reorganization, and the distribution of the P stock to the S shareholders met the literal terms of the statute at the time the transaction took place. Three days later, P was dissolved and the shareholders paid only the capital gains tax on the liquidating distribution, which consisted solely of Sub stock.

The Supreme Court, however, held that the transaction should not be termed a reorganization. P corporation served no business purpose; except for the tax effects, the Sub stock could just as well have been distributed by S directly to its shareholders. Therefore, the creation and liquidation of P could be wholly ignored, and the transaction treated as if S had distributed the Sub stock as a dividend. (*Gregory v. Helvering*, 293 U.S. 465 (1935)). As the judge in the Circuit Court stated: "A transaction, otherwise within an exemption of the tax law, does not lose its immunity, because it is actuated by a desire to avoid, or if one chooses, to evade, taxation. Anyone may so arrange his affairs that his taxes should be as low as possible; he is not bound to choose that pattern which will best pay the Treasury; there is not even a patriotic duty to increase one's taxes. . . . But underlying presumption is plain that the readjustment shall be undertaken for reasons germane to the conduct of the venture in hand, not as an ephemeral incident, egregious to its prosecution. To dodge the shareholders' taxes is not one of the transactions contemplated as corporate 'reorganizations.' " As regards the plain meaning of the Code, and the fact that it was specific in allowing this type of transaction, he went on to say that "the meaning of a sentence may be more than that of the separate words, as a melody is more than the notes, and no degree of particularity can ever obviate recourse to the setting in which all appear, and which all collectively create." (Judge Learned Hand, in *Helvering v. Gregory*, 68 F. 2d 809 (2d Cir. 1934)).

Corporate mergers and acquisitions, as distinct from divisions, have been held to have valid business purposes in virtually all the cases which have raised the issue. For instance, simplified operations, accounting and income reporting methods have been held to qualify, as well as a desire for a simplified capital structure, discharge of accumulated dividend obligations, and saving of expense and abolition of complexity of organization. There are many other sound business reasons for a merger.

Detailed Analysis of Effects of Nontaxable Reorganizations on Corporations

The general effects of nontaxable reorganizations on the corporations involved and on their stockholders have already been described. This section of the chapter gives a more detailed description of the law for those who wish to become more familiar with it. Various examples are given to illustrate the application of the law; in each case the acquired corporation is referred to as S and the acquiring corporation is referred to as P. (They may be thought of in popular terms as being respectively the selling corporations (S) and the purchasing corporations (P), but since they come under the rules of nontaxable exchanges, they do not typically involve actual sales and purchases.) Successive subsections are devoted to the treatment of corporations and stockholders.

TREATMENT OF CORPORATIONS—NONRECOGNITION. A discussion of tax consequences for corporations will concentrate on A and C reorganizations (statutory mergers or consolidations and an exchange of voting stock for property). Only these types take place in the first instance solely at the corporate level. Some consideration will also be given to the P corporation in the B reorganization.

Section 361 states as a general rule that no gain or loss will be recognized to the corporation in a reorganization transferring property in exchange for stock or securities in another corporation a party to a reorganization (par. 3304(b)). This section of the Code refers only to the corporation that transfers property and receives stock and securities, S, and not to the corporation issuing stock or securities in exchange for property, P.

Assume, for example, that in a C reorganization, corporation P acquires all the assets of corporation S in exchange solely for voting stock of P, and that the assets transferred by S have a basis of $1,000,000 and a fair market value of $1,500,000 and that the stock of P received on the exchange has a fair market value of $1,500,000. Under section 361(a), the transfer by S of its assets in exchange for the P stock is tax-free, and the gain of $500,000 is not recognized or taxed to S. No section of the Code specifically applies to P in the above case. However, where only stock is issued in exchange for property, section 1032 states: "No gain or loss shall be recognized on the receipt of money or other property in exchange for stock (including treasury stock) of such corporation" (par. 3128, 3304(c)). If P had issued securities in addition to stock, it would still have no gain under the general principle that gain or loss is ordinarily not realized by a purchaser when acquiring assets, and is postponed until he disposes of them in a taxable transaction. But if P were to exchange property for the S assets, there would be a taxable exchange unless it could qualify for nonrecognition under the provisions for exchanges of like properties (par. 1406).

If S had received money or other property in addition to stock or securities, section 361(b) would apply (par. 3305). The receipt of such other property or money is considered "boot" on the exchange. S would then be taxable on any gain, but only to the extent of the boot received. However, if, in pursuance of the plan of reorganization, S distributes the boot received to its stockholders, no gain or loss is recognized to S. If the object of the reorganization is to consolidate the interests of two previously separate concerns, the retention of the S corporate shell would only place the S stockholders further from their previous equities in the S assets, and multiply the number of outstanding holding companies. By allowing the corporation to distribute the money and other property to its stockholders without the imposition of a tax at the corporate level, there is no tax penalty on such a distribution and liquidation of the corporation. In the absence of relief, a capital gains tax would otherwise be applicable. As will be seen in the next section, the shareholders can exchange tax-free their stock in S for the P stock which S holds. However, no loss will in any case be recognized in a tax-free reorganization, as this would be an easy method for the creation of losses when interests of the parties have not been substantially altered. Thus, it is a fundamental principle that where the recognition of losses is desired the reorganization routes must be avoided.

The preceding paragraph may be illustrated as follows. Assume in the above example that S received P stock worth $1,100,000, $300,000 cash, and property having a fair market value $100,000. S has a gain of $500,000 but only $400,000 is recognized, since there was only that amount of boot. However, S will not have any recognized gain if it distributes the boot to its shareholders, either in liquidation or otherwise. S need not distribute all the boot, but it will be taxed on any which remains undistributed. Had the P stock been worth only $400,000, S would have had a loss of $200,000. However, this loss would not be recognized.

Although gain or loss is not recognized in a tax-free reorganization, this does not mean that the transaction is tax-exempt and free from all tax consequences. The actual result of a reorganization is to postpone the tax on any gain or the deduction for loss until a more substantial and significant change occurs in the interests of those involved. It is basic to reorganization theory that such a change has not been brought about when only stock or securities are issued in the exchange. The receipt of money or other property does represent the partial elimination of equity interests in the property, and to that extent is a realization of those interests as if a monetary sale had taken place. Such a transfer, therefore, is taxed to the amount of the gain represented by the assets received.

TREATMENT OF CORPORATIONS—BASIS. Furthermore, since the interests have not been substantially altered, the basis of property received in a reorganization must be adjusted to reflect the position of the parties prior to the exchange. This is accomplished through the vehicles of carryover and substituted basis. Thus, if the recipient of the property is but an alter ego of the transferor there has been no disposition of a taxable nature requiring an adjustment of basis. This is known as a carryover of basis (par. 3307). In a reorganization where S transfers property to P and retains a substantial interest in the property there is no change of basis, the S basis being carried over to the property now in P's hands. This principle is expressed in section 362(b): "If property was acquired by a corporation [P above] in connection with a reorganization to which [the reorganization sections] applies, then the basis shall be the same as it would be in the hands of the transferor [S above] . . ." But where part of the interest in the property has been converted into cash, to that extent the result is the same as if S had made a sale rather than an exchange of equivalent items. If this gain is not reflected in the basis of the asset in P's hands, there will be the possibility of the same gain being taxed again when P disposes of the asset in a taxable transaction. Therefore, section 362(b) goes on to state that the basis in P's hands will be the same as it was in S's, increased in the amount of gain recognized to S on the transfer. Since losses are never recognized in reorganizations they are not reflected in P's basis, although there may be an adjustment in S's basis, as will be discussed hereafter.

The transferor of the property, in the above cases S, takes a substituted basis. That is, it applies the basis of the property previously held to the stock or securities received in the exchange. In this manner any potential gain or loss on the property is postponed until a more significant and taxable event occurs. In a tax-free reorganization where S has transferred property for P stock, its interest has not been so altered that a tax is imposed. Rather, it applies to the stock received the basis of the property transferred and postpones recognition of gain or loss until the stock is converted in a taxable transaction.

Section 358(b) expresses this by stating that the basis of the property permitted to be received by S without the recognition of gain or loss shall be the same as that of the property exchanged. In the original example of this part, where S exchanges assets solely for stock, its basis for the P stock would remain that of the assets transferred, $1,000,000. Should S later sell the P stock, the gain or loss would be computed from this figure.

Where S had a recognized gain of $400,000 in the previous example, an additional adjustment in the basis of the stock is necessary. S has then partially sold its interest in the assets, and the gain was immitaely taxed. If S merely substituted its previous basis for the stock, part of its gain or loss on a later sale might not be recognized. For instance, where there was a $200,000 loss, a retention of the former basis would mean that if S made an immediate sale of the P stock for $1,000,000 there would be no tax. However, S received assets of $400,000 on the exchange. Its gain is really $400,000 on the entire transaction. On the other hand, if S sold the stock for $400,000, its loss would be $600,000 if a substituted basis were applied to the stock. However, S received $400,000 in assets on the exchange in addition to the P stock, and has suffered a true loss of only $200,000. Section 358(a)(1)(A) and (B) provide a formula which will result in a proper recognition of gain or loss at a later time.

The transferor, S, takes its original basis and subtracts from it the fair market value of any property and money received on the exchange, and then adds to this figure the amount of gain recognized to it. In many instances this will still equal its original basis, but it does provide an accurate method for determining future gain or loss. Where S received $400,000 in property and cash which was taxed to it, it would compute basis as follows: Original basis of S assets, $1,000,000 minus property and money received, $400,000 plus recognized gain, $400,000 equals basis for P stock of $1,000,000. In the case of loss with P stock worth only $400,000, S would take its original basis, $1,000,000, subtract the amount of property and money received, $400,000, and have a basis for the P stock of $600,000. The loss would be realized when the P stock was sold.

TREATMENT OF CORPORATIONS—ASSUMPTION OF LIABILITIES. Other complications are present where a liability of the transferor, S is assumed by the acquiring corporation, P (par. 3309). This can only occur in the A and C reorganizations, since no liabilities can be assumed by P in an exchange on the stockholder level. In the B case, P in effect retains the status quo of the acquired corporation by keeping it in subsidiary form, and never has received property subject to a liability from S. Section 357 states as a general rule that if the exchange qualifies under the other reorganization sections it will not lose its tax-free status because of the assumption of liabilities of the transferor. Furthermore, contrary to the normal rule, the assumption of S's liabilities by P will not be considered as if S had received money to the extent of the liability assumed. For instance, in a nonreorganization case, S sells property having a $10,000 basis and subject to a liability of $5,000 for $8,000, the purchaser assuming the liability. In the absence of section 357, S would have a $3,000 gain, since the assumption of the liability is generally considered additional consideration moving from the purchaser.

Section 357 was added to the law because Congress felt that recognition of gain was inappropriate here since there were no substantial changes in the interests of the parties, and the contrary rule would impede many justifiable reorganizations. However, if the principal purpose of the exchange is tax avoidance, or if it does not have a bona fide business purpose, then the total amount of liabilities will be considered money received by the transferor, and not merely the liability with which a tax avoidance motive existed. The regulations state that the presence of liabilities in a reorganization "may, in some cases so alter the character of the transaction as to place the transaction outside the purposes and assumptions of the reorganization provisions" (reg. 1.368–2(d)(1)). This may be the case where the transferors have little or no equity in the property transferred on account of a recent large loan against the assets.

Nevertheless, even though liabilities will not destroy the reorganization, they must be taken into account in determining the basis of the stock received, and are for this purpose considered as money received in the exchange (section 358(d)). For example, if the S property had a basis of $1,000,000, but was subject to a liability of $250,000, there would be no gain or loss recognized to S on the receipt of P stock in a C reorganization. However, S's basis for the P stock would be only $750,000, since the liability is treated as money received by S which decreases its basis. P's basis for the property remains $1,000,000.

TREATMENT OF STOCKHOLDERS—NONRECOGNITION ASPECTS. Principles essentially equivalent to those discussed in relation to corporations apply as well to stockholders in a reorganization. It has already been noted that the S corporation can be maintained in being or liquidated in a B or C reorganization, with the corporation being taxed in the former case only if it has received property other than stock or securities of P. Shareholders of S will not be taxed unless there has been a distribution to them or an exchange with respect to the P stock and property now in S's hands. If only a distribution on their stock is made to them, it will have the effects of a dividend. An exchange of their S stock for the P stock, however, receives special nonrecognition treatment (par. 3304(a)).

Section 354(a) provides that an exchange by the shareholders of their S for P stock in a reorganization will be tax-free. Thus, all B reorganizations are tax-free to shareholders under this provision, as well as exchanges by S shareholders of their stock for P stock held by S when it exchanges property in an A or C reorganization. In other words, if the plan of reorganization contemplates an exchange on the shareholder level, whether one takes place on the corporate level or not, the same result may be achieved—the S shareholders become P shareholders with no recognition of gain. A specific comment in the regulations states that stock rights or stock warrants are not within the nonrecognition provisions of this section (reg. 1.354–1(e)).

Securities of a party to a reorganization may also be exchanged tax-free provided that the amount of securities received does not exceed the amount of securities surrendered. This limitation avoids the withdrawal of earnings and profits tax-free, and is akin to the safeguards placed on preferred stock bail-outs. For instance, an S shareholder exchanges his S stock for P stock and securities. He has on the one hand retained an interest in the property and on the other has converted his interest into that of a creditor. This conversion of a proprietary interest into a creditor interest is considered enough of a change to warrant taxation. Nevertheless, this does not mean that there is no tax-free reorganization; it only provides that the excess amount of securities received will be considered taxable boot under section 356(a).

Section 356 outlines the rules to be applied if the shareholder receives other property or money in addition to the items received tax-free. Although loss is never recognized, the gain which is recognized may be either capital gain or ordinary dividend income (par. 3306). The latter consequence will result where the distribution to the shareholder has the "effect of a dividend," which is similar to the phrase, "essentially equivalent to a dividend," found in the stock redemption sections. In any event, the amount of gain recognized is limited to the amount of boot received, and dividend treatment cannot exceed the amount of recognized gain. It should be noted that these qualifications apply only in A and C reorganizations since the presence of boot disqualifies a B reorganization from tax-free status.

The following example of the operation of section 356 is given in the regulations.

> In an exchange to which the provisions of section 356 apply and to which section 354 would apply but for the receipt of property not permitted to be received without the recognition of gain or loss, A, (either an individual or a corporation) received the following in exchange for a share of [S] stock having an adjusted basis to him of $85.

One share of [P] stock worth	$100
Cash	25
Other property (basis $25) fair market value	50
Total fair market value of consideration received	$175
Adjusted basis of stock surrendered in exchange	85
Total gain	$ 90
Gain to be recognized, limited to cash and other property received	75
A's pro rata share of earnings and profits [having effect of a dividend to him]	30
Remainder to be treated as a capital gain from the exchange of property	$ 45

(reg. 1.356–1(c), example 1.)

If no further provision were made, it might be quite easy to secure the equivalent of preferred stock bail-outs at capital gains rates through reorganizations. Corporation S, with a large accumulated surplus, for example, could merge into newly formed corporation P, and exchange common and preferred stock of P for the outstanding S stock. This would be a nontaxable transaction. The former S shareholders could then sell the preferred at capital gains rates while retaining control of the enterprise. This is another variation of the preferred stock bail-out which was discussed previously.

When the law was changed to prevent preferred stock bail-outs in 1954, preferred stock received in a reorganization was classified as section 306 stock along with preferred stock dividends (par. 1710(c), sec. 306(c)(1)(B)). In order for the stock to be section 306 stock, the effect must have been substantially the same as the receipt of a stock dividend. The general limitation in section 306 that the gain taxable as ordinary income is limited to the pro rata share of earnings and profits at the time of distribution of the stock also applies. The example given in the regulations suggests that the Treasury will seek to designate virtually all preferred stock in a reorganization as section 306 stock. The example states:

> Corporation A, having only common stock outstanding, is merged in a statutory merger (qualifying as a reorganization under Section 368(a)) with Corporation B. Pursuant to such merger, the stockholders of Corporation A received both common and preferred stock in Corporation B. The preferred stock received by such shareholders is section 306 stock (reg. 1.306-(d), example (1)).

However, preferred stock received in a reorganization is subject to other provisions in section 306, including the various ways in which the section 306 taint will not arise or can be removed.

TREATMENT OF STOCKHOLDERS—BASIS ASPECTS. The same formula which is used to determine the basis of stock received by corporation S in a reorganization is also used when computing a shareholder's basis in the exchange. There is also added to the shareholder's basis the amount treated as a dividend. Thus, the formula for a shareholder's basis of stock or securities received tax-free in a reorganization is: the basis of his former stock or securities, decreased by the value of property and money received in the exchange, and increased by the amount taxed either as a dividend or capital gain (par. 3307(a), sec. 358(a)). Since the full market value of any property received is considered in determining the taxable gain and is reflected in the basis of the stock or securities, the property takes its full market value as its basis in the stockholder's hands. In other words, an S stockholder takes a substituted basis for the P stock he receives, subject to various adjustments if other property is received in addition or if there is recognized gain.

Divisive Reorganizations

A divisive reorganization produces substantially the same effect as a partial liquidation and is given substantially the same tax treatment (pars. 3310–11, cf. par. 1707(b)). The relevant sections were drafted at the same time as part of the new law in 1954. A divisive reorganization may take any of three forms: a split-up, in which one corporation is split into two or more corporations; a split-off, in which a corporation transfers part of its assets to a new corporation whose stock is then distributed to the shareholders of the original corporation who in turn surrender part of their stock in the original corporation; and a spin-off, which is similar to a split-off except that stock in the original corporation is not surrendered when stock in the newly formed corporation is received. The law on divisive reorganizations is quite liberal in permitting whatever form of rearrangement of assets in corporate form is desired without current taxation, but it is quite strict in preventing abuse.

The entire transaction must not be principally a device to distribute earnings and profits. There must be two or more active businesses and each corporation must have a separate trade or business after the division. But the distribution does not have to be pro rata. Thus, in a closely controlled corporation with two or more trades or businesses, when different groups of stockholders disagree on policy, they can divide the activities and go their separate ways without having to pay a tax on the excess of market value of the stock in a new company over the basis of the stock in the old company. This provision is important in permitting companies to continue as independent entities instead of being merged with larger companies when one member of an older generation of owner-managers dies and survivors or their heirs have different objectives.

Securities may be received in exchange for securities, as well as stock for stock. But if there is an excess of fair market value of principal amount over the principal amount of securities surrendered, the excess is treated as taxable gain, which may be taxed as a dividend. If other property is also received, it is treated as a boot, taxable as a gain and perhaps as a dividend. Thus, so long as the stockholders and security holders continue as such in the divided activities, there is no tax; to the extent that they receive other property, or securities in excess of securities surrendered, a tax will apply.

Consistent with the tax-free exchanges or receipt of new stock, the basis of the original investment is allocated among the various stocks held after the divisive reorganization in proportion to their market values (par. 3311).

Reorganizations Involving Subsidiary Corporations

Subsidiary corporations may be involved in reorganizations in any of three ways. They may be used in acquisitions, with newly acquired companies or properties transferred to subsidiaries instead of to parent corporations. A new subsidiary may be created and property transferred to it from the parent corporation. And existing subsidiaries may be liquidated into parent corporations. The tax law provides rules for tax-free transactions in all three areas, subject to the usual safeguards to avoid any step-up in basis and assure the tax is merely postponed and not foregone.

TRANSFERS TO SUBSIDIARIES OF ACQUIRING CORPORATIONS. Prior to the 1954 Code, a series of cases had held that when assets acquired by a parent company in tax-free reorganizations in exchange for its stock were then transferred to a subsidiary, the continuity of interest was broken since the former stockholders of the acquired company had only an indirect interest in the assets through the stock of the parent. The conclusion seemed rather surprising because indirect ownership of this sort is the inevitable result of a B reorganization, under which an acquiring corporation exchanges its stock for the stock of the acquired corporation which thereby becomes a subsidiary. This limitation on acquisitions of assets and transfers of them to subsidiary corporations was removed by section 368(a)(1)(C), which specifically authorizes a corporation to acquire substantially all the properties of another corporation in exchange solely for voting stock of its parent corporation as distinct from its own stock. Or under section 368(a)(2)(C), a corporation may acquire assets directly and then transfer them to its controlled subsidiary (par. 3303(c)). The statute in both cases prevents any assertion that the continuity of interest is insufficient because of the use of subsidiary corporations.

TRANSFERS TO SUBSIDIARIES. Subsidiaries may be useful when corporations are being liquidated or divided into two or more separate businesses. If some parts of a business are to be continued with other assets liquidated, a new corporation may be a useful vehicle for the continuing business. Or, if a single business is to be divided, separate corporations are almost necessary unless one part can be carried on as a partnership. The tax law in section 368(a)(1)(D) authorizes tax-free transfers to subsidiaries, either existing or new, if two conditions are met (par. 3303(d)). The first requirement is that the transferor corporation or its stockholders or any combination of them must be in control of the subsidiary immediately after the transfer, with control being defined as ownership of at least 80 per cent of voting power and of all other classes of stock. The second requirement is that the stock or securities of the subsidiary are then transferred or distributed to the owners and security holders of the corporation which transferred the property in the first place. The distribution or transfer must be either in accordance with a plan of reorganization in which substantially all the other properties of the transferor are being distributed or in a divisive reorganization as authorized in section 355.

Section 368(a)(1)(D), which permits the tax-free transfer of assets to a subsidiary by making the result dependent on subsequent distributions qualifying under section 354, 355, or 356, includes all of the safeguards against abuse contained in them. There is a general restriction that the transaction must not be used principally as a device for the distribution of earnings and profits. If a gift or compensation is involved in the transaction, the relevant parts of the law are made to apply; or if money or other property is received and the effect of the transaction is the distribution of a dividend, the fair market value of the money and other property will be taxed as such to the extent of the earnings and profits of the corporation.

A further special safeguard applies when property is transferred by one corporation to another controlled corporation if the liabilities assumed exceed the adjusted basis of the property transferred. In this case, the excess is treated as gain from the exchange of a capital asset, or property other than a capital asset, as the case may be (par. 3309(b)). This is an exception to the general rule that the assumption of liabilities in a tax-free reorganization will give rise to gain only if the purpose is to avoid taxes on the assumption of liabilities and the transaction had no valid business purpose (par. 3309(a)). The special case of liabilities in excess of basis to the transferor corporation was deemed to be so extreme that there is a presumption that in one way or another the original investment in the property has been recovered and that the transfer can be taxed without impeding ordinary business transactions.

LIQUIDATIONS OF SUBSIDIARIES. The liquidation of a subsidiary into a parent corporation is, in a legal sense, a form of distribution by a corporation, and as such was referred to in the chapter on corporate distributions. But changes in subsidiary-parent relations, in practical terms, are thought of as a form of corporate reorganization. The discussion of the relevant tax law is presented here along with the tax treatment of other transfers of property to and from subsidiaries.

Section 332 and its predecessor, in force since 1935, provide simply that: "No gain or loss shall be recognized on the receipt by a corporation of property distributed in complete liquidation of another corporation" (pars. 3316, 3116(b)). To qualify, the parent company must own, at the time of the adoption of the plan of liquidation, at least 80 per cent of the voting stock and 80 per cent of the nonvoting stock, except nonvoting stock which is limited and preferred as to dividends. This requirement insures that the change is simply one of form and that there will be a continuity of interest in the assets of the liquidated corporation. This 80 per cent minimum must be retained by the parent until the liquidation is completed, that is, the receipt by the parent of the subsidiary's property.

A nontaxable liquidation of subsidiaries occurs if the distribution by the subsidiary in complete liquidation involves a complete cancellation or redemption by it of outstanding stock and the transfer of the property entirely within the taxable year, or if the distribution in liquidation is one of a series of distributions in cancellation or redemption of its outstanding stock and is completed within three years (sec. 332(b)–(c)). The former is more readily adaptable to the situation where the parent considers it advisable to continue operation of the subsidiary's business under the single corporate charter of the parent. The latter is usually contemplated where the business of the subsidiary is terminated and its property is sold in bulk or piecemeal to outside interests. The three-year period was considered long enough to provide for liquidation in orderly fashion without the necessity for a distress sale. However, if the plan of liquidation is not carried out within three years, or the stock ownership requirement is lost during that time, then every distribution to the parent will be considered taxable.

Of course, there may be times when the parent wishes to recognize a deductible loss on the liquidation, or a taxable gain in order to raise the basis of the subsidiary's assets. In that case, the parent corporation must fail to meet the requirements of section 332(b), by owning less than an 80 per cent stock ownership, or by not liquidating within the above time limits. Because of these specific requirements and the ease with which they can be avoided, the nonrecognition of a tax on the liquidation of a subsidiary is in effect an elective provision to the parent corporation.

Minority interests—those not meeting the 80 per cent requirement —are taxed in full when the subsidiary is liquidated. Their position is no different from the recipient of property in other complete liquidations falling under the general principle of section 331.

A further provision in section 332(c) states that in liquidations of subsidiaries which are nontaxable exchanges according to the previously mentioned requirements, the subsidiary will not be taxed on any gain due to its transfer of property which satisfied an indebtedness it owes to the parent. For instance, if the parent owns bonds issued by the subsidiary at $90 with a face value of $100, and the subsidiary retires these bonds in the course of liquidation by transferring property to the parent having a value of $100 and a basis of $75, then the $25 gain will not be recognized to the subsidiary. Conversely, no loss will be recognized if the property's basis was more than $100.

Though the statute provides that the subsidiary will recognize neither gain nor loss on discharge of indebtedness to a parent in a liquidation, it is silent on the gain or loss to the parent from discharge of indebtedness of the subsidiary. The regulations provide that the parent will recognize gain or loss (reg. 1.332–7). This position was established in a case in 1949 (*Houston Natural Gas Corp.*, 173 F. 2d 461). Assets acquired in payment of debt are deemed not to be liquidating distributions.

Thus, in the above example, gain would be recognized to the parent to the extent of the $10 discount, and whether this gain would be ordinary income or capital gain would be determined under section 1232 (relating to original issue discount). If there were a loss to the parent on the bond, section 165(g), dealing with worthless securities, would govern, there being a capital loss unless the subsidiary was an affiliated corporation as therein defined. On the other hand, if the debt were not evidenced by a security, the parent would have an ordinary bad debt loss; Section 166(a) and (e).

Section 334(b) sets forth the governing provisions relating to basis when a subsidiary is liquidated. It provides as a general rule that there will be a carryover to the parent of the subsidiary's basis in the assets if the transaction was nontaxable. Thus, as is true in other situations in which gain is not recognized, there is no avoidance of the tax on the property; rather the tax is postponed until a taxable transaction occurs. Property received by the parent in satisfaction of the indebtedness owed it by the subsidiary also retains the basis it had in the hands of the subsidiary, and gain or loss will be recognized to the parent when it later exchanges or sells the property in a taxable transaction. However, this means that the enterprise may be taxed twice upon only a single gain. For instance, in the example above where the parent had a gain of $10 when the discounted bonds were retired, it might have another gain in the event the basis of the property was below the face value of the bonds when it later sells or otherwise disposes of the property it received from the subsidiary. Since minority interests are taxed upon the subsidiary's liquidation, they will take as their basis the fair market value of the property received.

Reorganizations of Insolvent Corporation

The nonspecialist's surprise at the inclusion of mergers of healthy corporations in the general reorganization concept of the tax law in section 368 is always compounded when he realizes that what most people think of as reorganizations, those arising from bankruptcy or insolvency, are never mentioned. This omission is not significant, however, because the following part of the law deals specifically with reorganizations in receiverships and bankruptcy proceedings (pars. 3314–15, sec. 371–74). The rules stated there are essentially similar to other reorganizations, with provision for nonrecognition of gain or loss and carry-overs of basis to both corporations and investors. But the fact that loss is usually involved in such reorganizations creates its own problems and makes one aspect of the tax law a barrier rather than a help in carrying out necessary business adjustments. The problem is to avoid a reduction of basis when debts are written off.

A basic item in the concept of income is gain derived from forgiveness of indebtedness (par. 1319). Some such provision is necessary to prevent income from being paid in the form of a "loan," with the "debt" later being "forgiven." But forgiveness of debt also applies when a corporation buys in its own bonds at less than face value, thereby improving its net worth. As an alternative to the immediate recognition of income, a taxpayer may reduce the basis of property instead of recognizing income from forgiveness of indebtedness (par. 1319(j)). This option gives a time advantage by throwing the tax impact into later years through reduced depreciation or larger gains on sale, with perhaps even a lower rate of applicable tax. It also is important as a relief provision if the "forgiveness" occurs when there is a shortage of cash.

In cases of insolvency, the very idea of imputation of income from scaling down of debts seems a bit ridiculous, and any requirement for current payment of tax would be incongruous since it would compound the underlying difficulties. But the alternative of writing down the basis of property may also be a barrier to necessary business readjustments, since it means that after bankruptcy or reorganization the successor taxpayer will have less depreciation allowable and hence pay higher taxes than if one had continued to struggle along without going through a necessary adjustment. Provision is therefore made in the law to give relief from this anomaly whether the adjustment comes about through bankruptcy of an individual taxpayer or a corporate reorganization. If a taxpayer has his (its) indebtedness discharged under bankruptcy, no income is realized from a forgiveness of indebtedness, and hence no reduction of basis would have to be made on those few business assets, such as one's "tools of trade" which might be retained (par. 1319(f)). This provision applies to a continuing entity.

Parallel treatment is given to reduction (forgiveness) of indebtedness in an insolvency reorganization where a new corporation comes into existence. Here also no reduction in basis is called for and the successor corporation continues the basis of property which it had in the hands of the predecessor company (par. 3314(c)). In the absence of such a provision, trustees in bankruptcy would be loath to bring a new corporation into existence. Similar special rules apply to railroad reorganizations to secure the same result.

From the standpoint of the holders of stock and securities when a loss is involved, the nonrecognition of gain or loss may be undesirable. Thus, from an investor's standpoint, the "relief" may be a tax penalty. There is no option available to investors if the reorganization itself qualifies under the law. But loss, of course, may be realized by selling investments before the exchange provided for in the reorganization or by selling the new stock.

The regulations require the same continuity of interest and business purpose as in other reorganizations (reg. 1.371–1(a)(3)–(4)). A problem might arise when an equity interest is wiped out and a creditor interest is converted into proprietary interest. The regulations waive any difficulties by noting that creditors may obtain effective command of property of an insolvent corporation in a way which gives them a proprietary interest before the exchange of stock and investments in a reorganization. The regulations are also quite liberal in permitting a variety of sequences of steps in transferring property directly between corporations or through creditor's committees or trustees, so long as the transfer is an integral step in a reorganization plan approved by the court which has jurisdiction.

13

Taxable

Purchases and Sales

of Corporations

In contrast to the numerous sections of the tax law dealing with tax-free reorganizations, including mergers of various sorts, the law makes few specific provisions for taxable purchases and sales of businesses. Most of the tax consequences of such transactions are covered by general provisions dealing with purchases and sales of stock or securities, or of corporate property and corporate liquidations. Two very significant relief provisions were added to the law in 1954 to deal with special problems when most or all of the stock or the property of a corporation is sold in a short time, in other words, with situations when a company is sold as such. But one must start an analysis with a review of the general rules applicable to purchases and sales of all sorts of property.

Consider first how a corporate business may be bought and sold. There are two obvious possibilities. The owners can sell their stock in the corporation or the corporation can sell its assets. And the buyers can buy only what is sold; they can purchase either the stock or the assets. In either case, under general tax rules gain or loss will be realized by the sellers equal to the difference between the tax basis of what is sold and the amount realized, and the purchasers will take the amount paid as their tax basis. Thus, a sale of a company, in contrast to a merger, involves a tax on the seller, if there is a gain, and a new basis to the purchaser. A possible conflict of objectives is immediately apparent. The seller may not want to incur the taxable gain, but the buyer may want the purchase price as the tax basis for depreciation and other charges. Conversely, if losses are involved, the seller may want to realize the loss while the buyer wants to keep the old basis for corporate property.

A more involved conflict of objectives may arise under the general rules of the law in the decision as to whether stock or assets are to be sold and, if the latter, whether the sale of assets is made by the corporation directly or by the stockholders after the corporation is liquidated. Consider a corporation with assets worth $200,000 which have a tax basis of $100,000 and with stockholders whose basis for their stock is only $10,000. A purchaser for $200,000 would want that figure as the basis of the corporate assets, but if stock is purchased, making the taxable gain $190,000, the corporate assets hold their tax basis of $100,000. And if the corporation sells its assets, there is first a taxable gain of $100,000 to the corporation and then another taxable on the liquidation of the corporation, or an additional gain of $165,000, for a total of $265,000, on the assumption that the corporate gain was taxed at 25 per cent. The extra $75,000 taxable gain to the stockholders must be balanced against the extra $100,000 of basis to the purchaser.

The extent of taxable gain and the basis of assets are not likely to dominate the decision on the form of purchase. There are other tax factors, including such items as loss carryovers or pension and stock option rights. And nontax considerations may be dominant. The existence of known liabilities, or fear of contingent liabilities, may make a purchaser refuse to consider stock. Or the sheer inconvenience of being left with a corporate shell may make sellers refuse to consider the sale of anything except stock. Taxable gains and the tax bases of property acquired are the subject of discussion here, but they must always be seen in perspective.

The existence of special taxes on the sale of stock in a collapsible corporation should always be kept in mind. A seller of a corporation may assume that he will receive capital gains treatment only to discover after the event that section 341, previously discussed in Chapter 10, is applicable.

Two special rules were added to the law in 1954 to relieve the buyers and sellers of corporations from the dilemmas and conflicts which arose under the general rules of the tax law. Section 337 permits a corporation to sell its assets without recognition of gain if the sale is made and the corporation is liquidated within a twelve-month period (par. 3116(a)). This means that there need be only one taxable gain recognized in connection with the sale of a corporation, equal to the excess of the value of the proceeds of the sale of assets over the basis of stock to the individual shareholders at the time of liquidation of the corporation. And section 334(b)(2) permits a corporate purchaser of the stock of another corporation to liquidate the acquired corporation into itself and use the purchase price of the stock as the basis of the assets (par.

3316). Together these two relief provisions made it possible for the sale to involve only one recognized capital gain, whether stock or assets are sold, and for the buyer to use the purchase price as the basis for assets, whether stock or assets are purchased. Each of them specifies certain objective tests which must be met, including timing. If the results are not desired, it is easy to fail to qualify. The provisions are in fact, though not by wording, options available to taxpayers.

The two relief sections were adopted after extensive litigation had opened the way for some taxpayers to secure the desired results if they arranged their affairs very carefully and were fortunate enough to avoid a challenge by the Internal Revenue Service or receive a favorable court decision if, after a challenge, litigation seemed worthwhile. The Treasury and Congress agreed in 1954 that the existing uncertainty was not justified and that there should not be a premium for those taxpayers who were especially resourceful or lucky. A brief review of the three leading cases prior to that time will help to explain the logic underlying sections 337 and 334(b)(2) and also give a good example of the interplay of the judiciary and the legislature in the evolution of the tax law.

LITIGATION PRIOR TO ADOPTION OF RELIEF PROVISIONS IN 1954

The recognition of gain at both the corporate and the stockholder level on the sale of assets could be avoided before 1954 if the corporation were liquidated prior to the sale, with the stockholders having a taxable gain equal to the difference between their respective tax bases for the stock and the fair market value of the corporate assets received. The stockholders could then sell the assets to the prospective purchaser with no further gain since the basis of the assets in their hands was the fair market value against which their gains had been calculated. This was a cumbersome procedure if there were more than a very few stockholders, but it was feasible by the use of a trustee to receive and then sell the property on behalf of the stockholders. But there might be uncertainty as to who had actually made the sale, especially if there had been any prior discussions about a sale by corporate officers, as were likely to occur.

In the leading case, a corporation negotiated an oral agreement for sale of its sole asset, an apartment house, and then informed the purchaser that it could not proceed. The corporation was liquidated and three days later the apartment was sold by the stockholders as individuals to the same purchaser under substantially the same terms as those previously reached. The Supreme Court upheld the Tax Court's findings that the sale had actually been made by the corporation, which had never abandoned the sales negotiations, and that the other steps taken were mere formalities designed "to make the transaction appear other than what it was" in order to avoid tax liability. It stated:

> The incidence of taxation depends upon the substance of a transaction. The tax consequences which arise from gains from a sale of property are not finally to be determined solely by the means employed to transfer legal title. Rather, the transaction must be viewed as a whole, and each step, from the commencement of negotiations to the consummation of the sale, is relevant. A sale by one person cannot be transformed for tax purposes into a sale by another by using the latter as a conduit through which to pass title. To permit the true nature of a transaction to be disguised by mere formalisms, which exist solely to alter tax liabilities, would seriously impair the effective administration of the tax policies of Congress (Commissioner v. Court Holding Co., 324 U.S. 331 (1945)).

It said further that the mere fact that the oral agreement with the corporation was unenforceable under state law was unimportant since it was shown from the facts of the entire transaction "that the executed sale was in substance the sale of the corporation."

The Court reconsidered this decision in *United States v. Cumberland Public Service Co.,* 338 U.S. 451 (1950). In a situation paralleling the facts in *Court Holding,* an opposite conclusion was reached. It based this result on the lower court's findings of fact that there was a true liquidation of the corporation, and the sale had been made by the stockholders without intervention of the corporate entity. The tax consequences were made to hinge on the lower court's fact findings of who had really made the sale. The Court said:

> The oddities in tax consequences that emerge from the tax provisions here controlling appear to be inherent in the present tax pattern. For a corporation is taxed if it sells all its physical properties and distributes the cash proceeds as liquidating dividends, yet it is not taxed if that property is distributed in kind and is then sold by the shareholders. In both instances the interest of the shareholders in the business has been transferred to the purchaser. Again, if these stockholders had succeeded in their original effort to sell all their stock, their interest would have been transferred to the purchasers just as effectively. Yet on such a transaction the corporation would have realized no taxable gain.

> Congress having determined that different tax consequences shall flow from different methods by which the shareholders of a closely held

corporation may dispose of corporate property, we accept its mandate. It is for the trial court, upon consideration of an entire transaction, to determine the factual category in which a particular transaction belongs. Here, as in the *Court Holding Co.* case, we accept the ultimate findings of fact of the trial tribunal.

The impact of these two decisions was to permit avoidance of taxation at the corporate level to those who knew some tax law, but to trap the unwary. Informed counsel could arrange many transactions to avoid the corporate tax if they were notified in time to liquidate the corporation and have the negotiations for sale carried on by the stockholders. If the necessary formalities were observed, the parties could thus prevent a gain from arising to the liquidated corporation on a sale of its assets. The situation was quite unsatisfactory, however, since similar cases led to different tax results. Section 337 was adopted in 1954 on the recommendation of the Treasury to make one rule available regardless of the mechanics of the transaction.

On the buyer's side, it also became possible under some circumstances to use the price paid for stock as the basis for the assets of the acquired corporation. This possibility, which probably would be desired by taxpayers in most situations, actually came about through a case which was lost by a taxpayer. As has been true more than once, the efforts of the Internal Revenue Service to collect a tax in a particular set of circumstances had led to a rule which on balance has been of benefit to taxpayers. A corporation, P, had purchased for $110,000 the stock of a second corporation, S, whose assets had a tax basis of $140,000 and had promptly liquidated the second corporation into itself, under the predecessor of section 332(a), which provided, as now, for a tax-free liquidation and a carryover of basis. The $140,000 basis was disallowed, and the basis of the assets to P was limited to $110,000 since "the purchase of [S's] stock and its subsequent liquidation must be considered as one transaction, namely, the purchase of [S's] assets which was [P's] sole intention."

The rule works both ways and when the purchase price is greater than the basis of assets to the selling corporation, as is more likely to be the case, the acquiring corporation can use the purchase price of stock as the basis for assets. In such cases, the courts have taken the view that where the liquidation was part of the overall plan, it will in effect be disregarded, no gain or loss will result to the purchaser, and the purchaser's basis for the assets will be the price paid for the stock. These cases regard the transaction as basically a purchase of assets by the purchaser and hence regard the temporary stock acquisition and the liquidation as unimportant taxwise (*Kimbell-Diamond Milling Co. v. Commissioner*, 14 T.C. 74 (1950), aff'd per curiam, 187 F. 2d 718 (5th Cir. 1951)).

On the seller's side, however, the courts looked to the intent of the selling stockholders (*Dallas Downtown Development Co. v. Commissioner*, 12 T.C. 114 (1949)). Although the purchaser was treated as buying assets, the intent of the sellers to sell stock was upheld. Because of this attitude by the courts, it became possible in some situations to have any of the desired tax consequences achieved by both the vendors and purchasers through careful planning.

In adopting the new provisions of the law in 1954, the report of the Senate Finance Committee stated:

> Your committee intends in section 337 to provide a definite rule which will eliminate the present uncertainties [in the *Court Holding Co.* and *Cumberland Public Service Co.* areas]; [section 334(b)(2)] incorporates into your committee's bill rules effectuating principles derived from *Kimbell-Diamond Milling Co.*

ALTERNATIVES AVAILABLE TO SELLERS AND PURCHASERS

In any analysis of the alternative ways of selling and buying a corporation, it is necessary to keep in mind the various differences which may exist between tax basis and fair market value of the various forms of property involved. The market value of the assets of the selling corporation will presumably be different from their tax bases. In successful businesses, the tax basis will presumably be less than current market value, but even for such companies some assets may have a tax basis higher than market value, and the bulk of the excess may represent good will and not be attributable to any specific assets which influence costs of goods sold as through depreciation, or which might subsequently be sold separately such as land.

Furthermore, the tax basis of the stock to the owners of the corporation will almost certainly differ from the tax basis of the corporate assets to the corporation, and will probably not be the same for all stockholders. Indeed, some stockholders may have unrealized gains while others have unrealized losses. And the corporation may have on balance unrealized losses on recently acquired assets while the stockholders generally have unrealized gains, or the reverse might even be true with the corporation having tax bases of property less than current market value, because of rapid depreciation or a recent fortunate invention or development of a successful product, even though most stockholders had purchased stock at high prices in earlier and still better times.

The interplay of the possible combinations of gains, losses, and subsequent tax bases suggests that no one pattern of sale and purchase will always be preferable. In general, one is inclined to start with the assumption that market values are above tax bases for both stock and corporate assets. In that case, a single realized gain would be desired by the seller, and the buyer would want to use the purchase price as the basis for property acquired. Sections 337 and 334(b)(2) are available to assure this result regardless of whether the actual transaction involves stock or corporate assets. But nonrecognition at the level of the selling corporation may be undesirable for any of several reasons.

The selling corporation may wish to suffer recognized losses on the sale if there are any losses since losses offset the previous taxable gains of that year or can be used as the basis for a tax refund to the corporation or as carryover if the corporation is continued. The corporation may desire to have recognized losses on the sale of high basis assets, and nonrecognition of gain on the sale of low basis of assets. Furthermore, if the corporation is to remain active following the sale of its assets, a sale by the corporation which bypasses section 337 may result in a lesser net tax than the tax to the shareholders following a distribution in liquidation to them.[1] This may be the case where the corporation's basis for the assets is considerably higher than the stockholders' bases for their stock.

As a general rule, the purchasing corporation will favor an outright purchase of assets in order to be certain that their basis will reflect its costs. Usually it is possible to allocate the purchase price among the various assets in an arm's-length transaction which will be recognized for tax purposes. A stock purchase, on the other hand, may be advisable where the assets have a high basis to the selling corporation which can be continued as a subsidiary or liquidated tax-free under section 334(b)(1) and obtained for the parent. The purchaser will seek to avoid the application of section 334(b)(2), which provides that the basis of the assets will be what was paid for the stock. Similarly, if the selling corporation has various tax attributes which the purchaser desires to carry over to itself, it is important to purchase stock rather than assets, and thereby retain the corporate existence of the selling corporation with all its tax characteristics.

---

[1] If the corporation is to remain alive following a sale of assets, it is important to consider the personal holding company tax, which imposes a virtually confiscatory rate of tax on the undistributed income of closely-held companies deriving the major part of their income from stock and security investments. A further consideration is the possibility that the sale of assets will result in ordinary income to the corporation, if it is a collapsible corporation.

In brief, the principal alternatives are:

I. Sale of assets
  A. Effects on sellers
    1. Corporation may sell assets and have recognized gain or loss equal to difference between sale price and its tax basis for its assets, with the corporation continuing in some other business or as a holding company, subject to possible tax as a personal holding company.
    2. Corporation may sell assets and liquidate under section 337 with no recognized gain or loss to the corporation and a single recognized gain or loss to the stockholders equal to the difference between the proceeds of the liquidation against the tax basis of their stock.
    3. Corporation may sell assets with recognized loss, and then liquidate outside of section 337 with stockholders recognizing a second gain or loss depending on values received and tax basis of stock.
    4. Corporation may be liquidated before sale of assets with stockholders having a recognized gain or loss equal to difference between fair market value of property received and basis of stock, and then sell assets at the same fair market value with no further gain or loss, but subject to the uncertainties arising from the *Court Holding Co.* decision.
  B. Effects on purchaser: purchaser, having in all cases bought assets, takes the purchase price as the basis.
II. Sale of stock
  A. Effects on seller: seller, in all cases, has a single recognized gain or loss, equal to difference between price received and tax basis of stock.
  B. Effects on purchaser:
    1. Purchaser, individual or corporate, may continue the corporation as a separate entity, using existing basis for corporate assets.
    2. A corporate purchaser may liquidate the newly acquired subsidiary into itself
      a) Continuing the basis of corporate assets, under section 334(b)(1), or
      b) Applying the purchase price of the stock, under section 334(b)(2).

Since section 337 and 334(b)(2) are important relief provisions, utilized in many situations, they are described here in some detail. The problems of interpretation in these sections indicate the importance of accurate legal advice in transactions which are intended to be brought under them, or in some instances excluded from them. These detailed analyses may be omitted by those who are not concerned with legal refinements.

Section 337

(337) (a) General Rule—If (1) a corporation *adopts a plan of complete liquidation* . . . , and, (2) within the *12-month period* beginning on *the date* of the adoption of such a plan, *all* of the assets of the corporation *are distributed* in complete liquidation, *less* assets retained to *meet claims*, then no gain or loss shall be recognized to such corporation from the *sale or exchange* by it of *property within* such 12-month period. (emphasis supplied)

The italicized words present the key to the section. These words raise, among others, the following issues: When and how does a corporation adopt a plan of liquidation? What is a plan of complete liquidation as distinct from partial liquidation? Can the twelve-month period be extended? What is the date of adoption of a plan of liquidation? Does "all" mean substantially all, or does it mean everything? What type of claims constitutes claims for which assets can be retained? What is a sale or exchange for purposes of this section? What is property? The following discussion will attempt to clarify their meanings and discuss other issues which are relevant.

ADOPTION OF A PLAN. The regulations state the following:

Ordinarily the date of the adoption of a plan of complete liquidation by a corporation is the date of adoption by the shareholders of the resolution authorizing the distribution of all the assets of the corporation (other than those retained to meet claims) in redemption of all its stock. Where the corporation sells substantially all its property . . . prior to the date of adoption by the shareholders of such resolution, then the date of the adoption of the plan of complete liquidation by such corporation is the date of the adoption by the shareholders of such resolution and gain or loss will be recognized with respect to such sales. Where no substantial part of the property . . . has been sold by the corporation prior to the date of adoption by the shareholders of such resolution, the date of the adoption of the plan of complete liquidation by such corporation is the date of adoption by the shareholders of such resolution and no gain or loss will be recognized on sales of such property on or after such date, if all the corporate assets (other than those retained to meet claims) are distributed in liquidation to the shareholders within 12 months after the date of the adoption of such resolution. In all other cases the date of the adoption of the plan of liquidation shall be determined from all the facts and circumstances (reg. 1.337–2(b)).

It was recognized that this section might allow a corporation to elect which assets will be sold at a recognized loss and which at an unrecognized gain. It would all depend on whether they were sold before or after the date on which a plan was adopted. The regulations deal with this elective feature of section 337 by looking primarily to the formal date of adoption of the plan, but warning that in certain cases it will not be controlling. As was seen in the general discussion of corporate liquidations, it is quite possible for a corporation to be in a state of liquidation for tax purposes even though it is not such under state law. In section 337 cases, the Treasury will attempt to block corporations from selling part of their assets for recognized tax losses, and part for nonrecognized gains.

The following example illustrates the preceding discussion. S corporation was formed with $100,000 original capital. It purchased two assets for $50,000 each. The taxable income of S during its first three years of operation was $10,000 per year and each of the assets had an adjusted basis of $35,000 each after three years' depreciation. At that time, one of the assets was sold for $5,000 and the other later sold for $65,000. If only the loss were recognized, it would offset the prior earnings and there would have been no corporate tax on the profits. The Treasury would be likely to argue that both these transactions were under a plan of liquidation adopted at the time of the first sale. In order to combat this argument, taxpayers may seek to have the corporation sell its loss items, then liquidate and have the shareholders themselves sell its gain assets. Naturally, this again raises the problem of *Court Holding Co.* as to who made the sales. Or, there may be a loss sale by the corporation, and a nonrecognition sale made when a plan of liquidation is adopted more than twelve months later. There is little in the statute to prevent at least an attempt by shareholders or corporations to obtain recognized losses and nonrecognized gains, the only barrier being the above-mentioned Treasury regulation and argument that section 337 was not meant to allow this maneuvering.

COMPLETE LIQUIDATION. The regulations appear to be quite clear that partial liquidations are not within the purview of section 337. The twelve-month distribution period must be rigidly adhered to. If any assets are retained beyond the twelve months, the statute is probably inapplicable, even though it might be argued that the assets were held purely for the benefit of stockholders and they should be deemed to have received them constructively. This presents an easy out for those wishing to avoid section 337, but is inherent in any provision which defines specific limitations. Although "all" the assets must be distributed, both tangible and intangible, it is likely that some nominal assets besides those retained to meet claims can be kept in the corporation in order to keep the shell alive. Not all assets of a corporation can be reduced to cash or distributed to shareholders since they represent nonassignable claims, though tax refund claims have been made assignable for purposes of section 337. Or, various unknown claims may arise following the twelve-month period. However, most practitioners probably will seek to have a trustee for the benefit of shareholders to accept and distribute such items.

The major difficulty in the phrase "less assets to meet claims" lies in contingent or unknown claims. The regulations state that "Any assets retained after the expiration of the 12-month period for the payment of claims (including unascertained or contingent liabilities or expenses) must be specifically set apart for that purpose and must be reasonable in amount in relation to the items involved" (reg. sec. 1.337–1). No clear understanding of "reasonable" is given. The uncertainty may concern directors who will be personally liable if later claims should arise and the retained assets are insufficient to meet them. In small corporations, the shareholders and directors usually obtain mutual indemnity agreements to avoid personal liability. In the large corporation, where such agreements are unavailable, the directors may be personally liable without a satisfactory means of obtaining restitution from stockholders. However, it is permissible to judge the amount to be retained at the end of the twelve-month period, when the most accurate estimates can be made. The plan of liquidation can then be amended to conform to that judgment.

An object of this regulation is to block retentions of assets which permit a continuation of the business or investment activities of the corporation, or which postpone shareholder gains on liquidation. If retentions to meet claims were made originally in good faith, nothing in the statute prohibits a later use of the assets for further business activity. The regulations are careful in saying that a retention of cash to meet claims is permissible, but they express no views as to the retention of assets other than cash. Here the Treasury will carefully scrutinize the assets in order that they not be those which can give rise to deductible losses following the twelve-month period. In a sense, it is the converse of the problem previously discussed relating to losses prior to the adoption of a plan.

"SALE OR EXCHANGE OF PROPERTY." The general concept of a sale or exchange, as developed under the capital gains provisions of the Code, are probably also relevant in the application of section 337. The sale or exchange concept will be applied when specific provisions of the Code declare such transactions to be sales or exchanges entitled to capital gain or loss treatment, such as the sale of various options under section 1234. However, the nonrecognition treatment of section 337 extends to all assets whether their sale would produce ordinary income or capital gain, provided a "sale or exchange" has occurred. The Treasury originally held that the receipt of insurance proceeds when a building was destroyed by fire was not a sale or exchange for section 337, but reversed this position in 1964. Thus, a gain under these circumstances need not be recognized by a corporation which is promptly liquidated.

Section 337(b) defines "property" for the purposes of the non-recognition provisions of section 337. It broadly includes all property of the corporation except nonbulk sales of inventory and installment obligations in respect thereof, and installment obligations which were obtained prior to the date of adoption of a plan of complete liquidation. The object of these limitations is to prevent what would otherwise be ordinary income items (inventory) from being sold without the recognition of any income or gain, and distributed in liquidation at capital gains rates. The major exception in the Code relating to inventory is the bulk sale; if substantially all the inventory of a trade or business is sold in a single transaction to one person, then the proceeds of its sales and installment obligations arising therefrom will qualify for nonrecognition at the corporate level (see sec. 337(b)(2)).

The regulations state:

> The term "property" in the case of a corporation which is engaged in two or more distinct businesses shall include the inventory of any one of such trades or businesses if substantially all of the inventory attributable to such trade or business is sold or exchanged to one person in one transaction. If installment obligations are received upon such a sale, such obligations are also included within the meaning of the term "property." (reg. 1.337–3(c))

The term "substantially all" means substantially all of the inventory at the time of sale, and not at the time of adoption of a plan of liquidation or throughout the twelve-month period. Furthermore, the exception for bulk sales is inapplicable if the inventory so sold is replaced by like inventory, or by a new kind of inventory, since this indicates an intent to continue corporate operations rather than one to liquidate the enterprise.

These illustrations are taken from the regulations:

(1) Corporation A operates a grocery store at one location and a hardware store at another. Neither store handles items similar to those handled by the other. Both stores are served by a common warehouse. Pursuant to a plan of liquidation adopted by the corporation, the grocery store and all of its inventory, including that part of its inventory held in the warehouse, are sold to one person in one transaction. Thereafter and within 12 months after the adoption of the plan of liquidation, all of the assets of the corporation are distributed to the shareholders. No gain or loss will be recognized upon the sale of all of the assets attributable to the grocery business, including the inventory items.

(2) Corporation B operates two department stores, one in the downtown business district and the other in a suburban shopping center. Both handle the same items and are served by a common warehouse which contains an amount of inventory items equal to the total of that in both stores. The part of the inventory in the warehouse which is attributable to each store cannot be clearly determined. Pursuant to a plan of liquidation adopted by the corporation, the assets of the suburban store, including the inventory held in the warehouse, are sold to one person in one transaction. Thereafter, and within 12 months after the adoption of the plan of liquidation, all of the assets of the corporation are distributed to the shareholders. No gain or loss will be recognized with respect to the sale of the property other than inventory, but gain or loss will be recognized upon the sale of the inventory.

(3) The facts are the same as in example (2) except that the part of the inventory in the warehouse which is attributable to the suburban store can be clearly determined and both the inventory held in the store and that part of the inventory in the warehouse attributable to such store are sold. No gain or loss will be recognized upon the sale of the inventory (reg. 1.337–3(d)).

The examples raise a number of problems. It should first be understood that it is not necessary for the sale of inventory to be made to those purchasing the other assets qualifying for nonrecognition. Inventory can be sold to A and the other property to B. Furthermore, a complete business need not be sold for section 337 to apply. It is only in relation to inventory that an entire sale of all inventory attributable to a trade or business must be made. Furthermore, it will be noticed, especially in example (1), that there is a close similarity ·to that transaction and the partial liquidation of a business under section 346. An equivalent result might have been achieved by a contraction of the business under section 346, and a subsequent sale of the grocery store assets by the stock-holders. This latter sale would presumably be unimpeded by section 337's restrictions. However, the effect of *Court Holding Co.* would still be important in determining who made the sale, the corporation or the stockholders. An analogous issue would arise in example (1) if, following the sale and liquidation under section 337, the stockholders reincor-porated the hardware business. This would raise the same issues as those previously discussed in the section regarding corporate liquidations: Was there actually a reorganization, and is it imperative that the liquida-tion be other than a mere formal step toward reincorporation?

Section 337 is inapplicable where the shareholders have elected a partially tax-free one-month liquidation under section 333 (see sec. 337(c)(1)(B)). In such cases, reference must be made to *Court Hold-ing Co.* and pre-1954 law. Further limitations are made as to collapsible corporations and where the *Kimbell-Diamond* principle is applicable.

Section 334(b)(2)

Section 334(a) states the general rule giving the parent corporation a carryover of the subsidiary's basis when the subsidiary is completely liquidated, that is, the parent's basis for the assets received from the sub-sidiary will be the same as it was to the subsidiary. Section 334(b)(2) states an exception when at least 80 per cent of the subsidiary's stock was acquired within twelve months by purchase in a taxable transaction. In such a case, the parent, if it adopts a plan to liquidate the subsidiary within two years thereafter, takes as "the basis of the property in [its] hands . . . the adjusted basis of the stock with respect to which the distribution was made." The parent would substitute its cost for the stock as the basis of the property, the result of the *Kimbell-Diamond* principle.

In order to have a substituted basis, the Code's requirements must be closely followed. Foremost among its provisions is that 80 per cent of the stock must be bought within twelve months (see sec. 334(b)(2)(B)). This apparently would block utilization of this section where the pur-chasing corporation already owned 21 per cent of the stock prior to the twelve-month period. It could then never acquire 80 per cent within twelve months, even though it ended up with 100 per cent control. In such instances, the purchaser might still be able to argue that *Kimbell-Diamond* was still alive and that the statute only provided a specific alternative to reach its result.

The liquidation of the subsidiary must be by a plan adopted not more than two years after the 80 per cent purchase. The actual liquidation can take place later, but the plan of liquidation must have been adopted within two years. This interim period can be especially useful where the subsidiary has various carryovers or other tax attributes. The parent cannot take advantage of a substituted basis plus the subsidiary's carryovers. But careful planning may allow these to be utilized fully during the two-year period preceding liquidation, and still have a substituted basis when the liquidation is accomplished. The regulations also provide for various adjustments to be made for transactions during the two-year interim period, such as dividends and other distributions to the parent (reg. 334–1(c)(4)). The effect of several of the adjustments is to penalize a delay in the process of liquidation.

The third requirement of section 334(b)(2) is that the stock be obtained by "purchase," as defined in section 334(b)(2). According to the Code, the stock cannot be acquired in an exchange to which section 351 applies (relating to tax-free organization of a corporation). Otherwise, it would be possible to organize a corporation, allow the property to depreciate, and then liquidate and re-obtain its original basis. For similar reasons the stock cannot be acquired in a tax-free reorganization. For instance, in a B reorganization, where 80 per cent control is obtained in exchange for its voting stock, there theoretically has been no substantial change of interests warranting a change in basis.

As a final limitation, the Code applies the stock attribution rules of section 318(a) in this area. In any situation where these attribution rules are applicable, there will be no "purchase" within the meaning of section 334 (sec. 334(b)(3)(C)). Thus, the stock cannot be acquired from a corporation in which the purchaser has a 50 per cent interest, or from any individuals who control 50 per cent of the purchaser. Although in such cases the attribution rules may perform some service by their restriction, it is probable that they will impede some otherwise legitimate transactions.

Interrelationship of Section 337, 332 and 334(b)(2)

A special problem exists when section 337 is to be applied to the liquidation of a subsidiary under section 332. A brief description of the problem will indicate the sort of intricacies which confront practitioners and those who draft the law in complicated areas.

Under section 337, there is no recognition of gain on a sale of assets at the level of the subsidiary corporation, and section 332 allows the parent corporation to receive the subsidiary corporation's assets tax-free.

Since the proceeds of the sale would have a tax basis to the subsidiary equal to the amount received on the sale, and come into the parent with that same tax basis, the result of applying the general nonrecognition rules of section 337 to a tax-free liquidation of a subsidiary would result in never taxing the gain.

However, section 337(c)(2) makes exceptions for the overlap with section 332 (par. 3116(b)). It provides that the nonrecognition provisions of section 337 shall not apply in the liquidation of subsidiaries when section 332 applies. Thus, if a subsidiary (under the 80 per cent requirements of section 332(b)(1)) sells its property and liquidates, any gains or losses on such sales will be recognized to the subsidiary.

In addition, if the liquidation qualified under section 334(b)(2), as well as under section 337, the Code treats the subsidiary's property as if a substituted basis had already been applied to it, and the gain attributable to any increase in basis due to a higher cost of the stock will not be recognized (sec. 337(c)(2)(B)). That is, gain on a sale of the subsidiary's assets will not be taxed to the extent the parent's cost for stock in the subsidiary can be allocated to those assets.

The regulations provide the following example:

> Corporation A owns more than 80% of the stock of Corporation B, which it purchased [within 12 months] for $10,000. All of the assets of Corporation B, having a total basis of $4,000, are sold for $12,000 [B is liquidated into A]. The portion of the realized gain of $8,000 which is not recognized is $6,000, computed as follows:
>
> | | |
> |---|---:|
> | Basis of stock allocable to property sold | $10,000 |
> | Basis of property sold | 4,000 |
> | | $ 6,000 |

In general, where section 337(c)(2)(B) is applicable and where the gain realized from the sale of property is greater than the excess of the selling price of the property over the basis of the stock allocable to the property sold, the amount of gain to be recognized from such sale is equal to such excess. In the above example, the $2,000 gain representing the excess of the selling price of $12,000 over the basis of the stock allocable to the property sold, $10,000, would be recognized to the liquidating corporation (reg. 1.337-4(b)).

A refinement of the law has provided, since 1958, that if a tax is paid by a corporation which sells its assets and liquidates because it is a subsidiary of another corporation and hence cannot get the benefits of section 337, certain minority shareholders are permitted to get the benefits of the tax-free sale which would be available to them if the liquidating corporation were not a subsidiary. This is achieved by permitting them to treat their proportionate share of the tax paid by the corporation as though it had been paid by themselves individually, after increasing the amount realized by them on the distribution by this same amount.

CARRYOVERS

The statutory provisions of the tax law regarding the carryover of various tax attributes, including the carryover of net operating losses, were adopted in substantially their present form in 1954 in an attempt to give rationality in an area where in the absence of statutory direction the previous litigation had let form triumph over substance and encouraged quite extensive buying and selling of corporate shells for their loss carryovers. The continuity of the same corporate entity which had incurred the loss was the critical fact, and a good deal of ingenuity was devoted to buying up a corporate shell and pumping new funds and business into it rather than proceeding with normal mergers and other reorganizations.

Carryovers are now covered by sections 269, 381, and 382 of the tax law. In general, they allow the carryover to successor corporations of most tax attributes provided certain conditions are met. In most cases, it is now possible for an acquiring corporation to step directly into the tax shoes of its predecessor, or, by carefully avoiding these provisions, to eliminate undesirable carryovers.

Section 381 enumerates nineteen tax attributes which can be carried over (par. 3318). For these to apply, there must have been either a tax-free liquidation where there has been a carryover of a subsidiary's basis to the parent (thus eliminating situations in which the purchase price of stock is used as the basis for assets under section 334(b)(2)) or a reorganization of the A (statutory mergers) and C (stock for assets) types, or one under 368(a)(1)(D) in which one corporation transfers substantially all of its assets to another corporation in exchange for stock and securities of the other corporation and is then liquidated. Mere changes in the form, identity, or place of business also entitle a corporation to the carryovers it previously had. B reorganizations are not included since there has been no change as yet in the corporate identity of the predecessor. This section will apply, however, if the new subsidiary is liquidated following the exchange.

In any of the above situations, the date of the transaction governs the extent of the tax attributes available to the successor corporation. In cases of doubt, the date when substantially all the property has been transferred will govern. Furthermore, the corporation acquiring the assets cannot carry back its net operating losses to prior years of the predecessor corporation. Only carryovers are allowed and not carrybacks.

Although nineteen possible carryovers are mentioned in section 381, unmentioned ones are nevertheless available, since Congress did not attempt to enumerate all possible carryovers in this section. In general, the Code requires the successor corporation to adopt all the accounting techniques and tax methods of the predecessor company once it is determined that the transaction was one of the types encompassed by this section. Thus, where changes are sought in the predecessor's inventory methods, for example, it may be unwise to use the reorganization provisions. Also, a carryover of earnings and profits may be undesirable if it would make an otherwise subsequent tax-free distribution of available funds to stockholders taxable as a dividend.

The most significant of the carryovers is the net operating loss carryover. To an investor anticipating the use of the corporate form for carrying on a business, the acquisition of an existing corporation may have decided tax advantages over the creation of a new corporation. If the corporation has assets with a high basis and low market value, there are in essence built-in losses which may be realized through sale or high deductions for depreciation. Moreover, the corporation's past losses may be carried forward to offset any income which the investor might earn for the succeeding five years. These tax benefits make the acquisition of loss corporations desirable also to existing corporations which have been earning large profits, since it is an effective method of reducing taxes which otherwise would be incurred.

Under section 381, the loss carryover is freely allowed to the acquiring corporation in most reorganizations, although certain apportionments must be made between losses occurring prior to or subsequent to acquisition by a successor corporation. Nevertheless, the full carryover may be used up to the five-year limit imposed by section 172 as long as there are offsetting earnings.

However, although it is not referred to in section 381, section 382 also adopted in 1954 severely limits the use of the net operating loss carryover. Subsection (a) proscribes carryover in certain specified situations where an acquisition is likely to be dominated by tax avoidance motives (par. 3220). The carryover is denied if three conditions are met: (1) one or more of the ten largest shareholders have acquired 50 per cent of the stock of a corporation within two years; (2) the increase in holdings is due to the "purchase" or redemption of stock; and (3) the corporation has not continued to carry on a trade or business substantially the same as that before the change in percentage ownership. In determining the group of ten persons, related taxpayers are considered one person and the attribution rules of section 318 are applied except for minor exceptions. "Purchase" is defined as an acquisition of stock whose basis will be determined in the hands of the purchaser by reference to its cost to him.

Section 382(b) applies to certain types of tax-free reorganizations, the same ones that qualified under section 381(a)(2), and requires that the shareholders of the loss corporation retain a 20 per cent interest in the ownership of the successor corporation (par. 3319). The amount of available carryover is reduced in proportion to the extent to which the share of ownership received is less than 20 per cent. For every percentage point below 20 per cent, there is a 5 per cent reduction in the net operating loss carryover. Various qualifying subsections take into account stock held by the acquirer prior to the reorganization, and stock in a subsidiary where assets are transferred to it in exchange for stock of the parent.

Section 269 may also limit loss carryovers. This section was amended and strengthened in 1954 by the addition of subsection (c), which makes it *prima facie* evidence of tax avoidance when it is shown that the consideration paid was substantially disproportionate to the sum of the adjusted bases of the assets transferred and the tax benefits which became available because of the acquisition. It generally provides that deductions, credits, or other allowances may be disallowed when they are claimed as a result of acquisitions, the principal purpose of which was to evade or avoid taxes by securing such tax benefits (par. 3127). This section was adopted in 1940 primarily to prevent avoidance of excess-profits taxes during World War II, but has become relevant to acquired carryovers as well. Only a review of the extensive litigation under this section can give an appreciation of the sometimes rather subtle distinctions which the courts make in determining whether tax avoidance was "the principal purpose" of an acquisition (Prentice-Hall, *Federal Taxes*, pars. 6825–26).

The carryover of losses for a continuing company is generally accepted as both fair and sound economic policy to prevent excessive tax burdens on corporations engaged in risky and fluctuating businesses. The receipt of new capital, a change of management, some changes in stock ownership, and a shift from unprofitable to profitable lines of activity may be necessary to make a company viable and, considered separately, are not likely to make a continued loss carryover seem unfair. But when a corporate shell with no value except a loss carryover is sold for a minor fraction of the value of the potential tax saving, the continued availability of the loss carryover has been regarded as an abuse by many tax experts, as well as members of the general public. The legislation imposing limitations on loss carryovers attempts to draw a line between valid use and abuse. Inevitably, the distinctions made will seem unreasonable to those who just fail to qualify. It has been proposed as an alternative that loss carryovers be transferable with no restrictions with the expectation that full value would be received by the transferors, thereby encouraging investment in risky ventures and preventing windfall gains to financial manipulators.

TAX FACTORS IN THE ACQUISITION OF CLOSELY CONTROLLED CORPORATIONS

An acquisition of a closely controlled company by a new group may present special problems and opportunities to fit together the needs and desires of the old and new owners. All of the considerations previously discussed regarding the capital structures of new corporations are relevant, as are the general propositions concerning tax-free mergers and taxable acquisitions. One distinctive feature which often exists in the acquisition of a closely controlled company is the existence of superfluous assets which may be used in part payment of the purchase price or distributed in a liquidation of the old company and retained by its former owners. Even assets essential to a continuing business may be distributed in liquidation and leased by the old owners to the new group.

The excess of assets is likely to have developed from the general tendency in closely controlled companies to retain earnings and not subject them to individual tax by distributing them as dividends, subject only to the restraint of the penalty tax on unreasonable accumulation of surplus.

Another frequent aspect of the acquisition of a closely controlled company is the desire by the former owners for a substantial income, at least during the remaining lifetime of a former owner-manager who may have become incapacitated by sickness or age. The third and final distinctive feature is the fact that some or all of the stock may be owned by the estate or recent heirs who have a stepped-up basis for computing capital gains. The sale price, in fact, may determine both the valuation for estate tax purposes and the basis for capital gain. Each of these three facts, if it exists, is an invitation to develop a plan, fully within the intent and spirit of the tax law, which would virtually never be contemplated in the acquisition of a widely owned company.

Consider first the possible existence of excess assets. It is in the very nature of most closely controlled corporations not to distribute earnings beyond the needs of the owners. Though a corporate use of retained earnings may give a lower return than could be secured from an alternative investment by individual stockholders, the individual tax applied to the dividend if earnings are distributed is regarded by the stockholders almost as of capital levy on the transfer of property which they feel they already own indirectly in corporate solution. So long as the penalty tax on unreasonable accumulation of surplus is not applicable, there is a strong tendency to retain earnings by building up generous margins in working capital, acquiring more or less related real estate for use and for expansion, and paying off all indebtedness. Anyone who looks only at net worth without examining the composition of assets in a closely controlled company is likely to have a misconception of the funds actually necessary to operate the firm as a going business or to acquire it. In effect, the company may be paid for to a considerable extent out of its own assets or its unused debt capacity.

The way in which excess assets may be used in partial payment depends on whether the acquisition is to be a taxable sale or a tax-free merger with a new corporate entity which is first created to give the desired capital structure. The preference of the seller for a taxable sale or tax-free merger will depend to a considerable extent on his potential capital gain, which in turn depends on whether the sale is being made by retiring owner-managers, who presumably will have a low basis for their stock, or by an estate or heirs who have a basis close to or equal to the sale price.

Ownership of stock by the estate of a recently deceased owner is the simplest situation with the most obvious solution. The proceeds from sale or the current value of assets received from liquidation of the company will simultaneously determine estate valuation and the basis for capital gains. There will be no capital gains either on sale or liquidation and there is no tax advantage in a tax-free merger. The distribution of part of the corporate assets to the former owner-manager would have had the effect of a dividend, except in the unlikely event that it could qualify as a partial liquidation. The complete liquidation of the company would have created a capital gain and the owner-manager also would have ceased to be one, though this role was presumably his preferred way of life. But his estate can make a complete disposition of the company without any tax consequence and, almost by definition, the executor of the estate does not find the role of owner-manager a desired way of life.

The simple solution is for the executor to liquidate the corporation, sell those assets necessary to continue a going business to a new company formed by the new group, and distribute the other assets directly to the heirs or sell them and distribute the proceeds to the heirs. If the process is completed within the twelve-month period for optional estate evaluation, the only tax liability will be the estate tax. The new group needs to secure only enough funds to buy the necessary assets.

The desire of the sellers for maximum immediate income may enter into the negotiations. If there is a surviving widow or minor children, some of the necessary assets, including plant and patents, may be held by the estate or distributed to the heirs and then leased after liquidation of the old corporation at a relatively liberal rental as part of a package acquisition. The rent would provide a greater income than could be obtained on ordinary investments by the heirs. The fact of the lease reduces the amount of investment needed by the new owners and the rent payments will be a deductible expense. To be sure, some of the assets of the estate or heirs will still be at the risk of the continuing business, but in a secured position.

Any proposed arrangement of this sort, of course, raises ethical and legal problems. An attempt to throw an unreasonable part of a purchase price into a deductible expense would be properly challenged by the Internal Revenue Service, but the genuine and legitimate desires of the sellers for maximum immediate income and of the purchasers to minimize their capital outlay may lead to a mutually desired transaction free from any connivance for tax purposes, but with possible incidental tax advantages.

After this brief review of a possible simple set of facts, the more complicated situations can be presented systematically. If the owner-managers are still living and there is a large potential capital gain, a taxable sale would be unattractive. To be sure, under present law only one capital gains tax need be incurred. This is true whether the corporation first liquidates, with the tax paid on the liquidation and the assets then sold by the former stockholders to the new group, presumably with no gain or loss, or the corporation sells the assets and then liquidates within twelve months under section 337, which exempts the corporation from the tax on its capital gain, with the tax paid only by stockholders on the liquidation of the corporation. But even the one capital gains tax may involve a large reduction in capital. An offer of a tax-free merger from a larger corporation will have to be countered by any new group which hopes to continue the company as an independent entity.

One obvious possibility may be noted though it will usually be rejected. The sale by the existing corporation of its trade name and a few assets, with title to most of the assets kept in the firm and leased to the new company, will permit continuation of the old company until the death of the owner provides a step-up in the basis of his stock. However, the old company would almost inevitably become a personal holding company because of the nature of its income. This would mean, of course, that it would be subject to a penalty tax unless all its income is currently distributed. Since the former owner-manager has presumably lost his previous salary, distributions of income will not necessarily be objectionable, but the double tax burden, first at the corporate level and then at the individual level will be onerous. Since the income at the corporate level would be rent, the extra level of corporate taxation would apply in full, without benefit of the reduced rate on intercorporate dividends. The continuation of a personal holding company for a few years might be acceptable, but the interim double tax on the income would tend to wipe out the savings on the capital gains tax. Break-even points would vary with applicable tax rates, life expectancies, and available returns on alternative investments.

A new corporation formed by the prospective new owners may provide an opportunity for a more attractive tax-free merger than that available from a widely owned company. The range of possibilities is not great, however, because if securities (debt) are received in the exchange, they will be taxed at least as capital gains and possibly as a distribution of earnings and profits, to the extent thereof, in the acquired corporation. But preferred stock may be given in exchange, with no immediate tax consequence. The stock presumptively will be section 306 stock, which would mean that if any stockholder sold part of his stock the proceeds would be taxed as ordinary income to the extent of a pro rata interest in the earnings and profits existing in the old corporation when the stock was issued. But if the sellers are interested in income, a preferred stock with a fairly high dividend will be a much more attractive holding than a low-yield common stock in a widely owned company. The latter company could, of course, also offer a preferred stock in a merger, and sometimes does so, but a small amount of preferred issued only in connection with a merger would clutter the balance sheet and not be acceptable.

The preferred stock held by the former owners would create a nondeductible fixed charge for the new corporation and be objectionable from that standpoint. It should, of course, be callable. And the section 306 penalty would not apply if it and any common stock held by any stockholder were all redeemed at once and, in any case, the 306 taint would lapse with the death of the owners. Again, break-even points may be calculated on the period over which the advantage to the sellers of avoiding the capital gains tax would offset the disadvantage to the new corporation of taking on a nondeductible fixed charge.

It may not even be necessary to set up a new corporation. Preferred stock may be issued as a nontaxable stock dividend to the old owners of a company with the common stock interest reduced to a value such that the new group may buy some or all of it with the funds available to them. This process freezes most of the present value in the preferred stock and permits the new group to secure whatever proportion of the equity is agreed upon in a highly leveraged common stock. The choice between a recapitalization followed by a sale of some or all of the common stock or the formation of a new company with subsequent tax-free merger would depend upon the extent to which it was desired to create a variety of securities for the new group of investors which might more readily be provided in a completely new corporation.

After the former owners of common stock convert most or all of their interest into preferred stock, they continue to have their capital at the risk of the continuing business. This is the price they must pay to avoid immediate application of the tax on capital gains. Various provisions regarding voting rights on the preferred stock may be given, including an increase in voting rights if preferred dividends are not earned or paid. The opportunity to keep a connection with a family business which is continued as a separate entity may be a favorable factor which offsets the greater risk; in fact, the risk may be regarded as less than that incurred in a tax-free merger with a larger company.

The greatest attraction in the shift from a common to preferred stockholder interest, followed by sale of the new common with high leverage, is in the opportunity to meet the needs for income of the sellers. Within reasonable limits, the dividend rate and capital amount may be combined in various ways to meet the desires of both the old owners and the new group.

Similar changes in capital structure are possible and desirable in anticipation of the death of one generation of owners, with no expectation of sale or merger. Preferred stock created through a tax-free dividend can be used to provide income for a surviving spouse or other heirs who will not be active in the business, with common stock left to the heirs who will continue as managers and secure their income through salaries. The income of the preferred stockholders will be nondeductible dividends, but all corporate income not needed to meet the anticipated needs of the nonactive owners can be left in the corporation if needed for expansion. Conflicts of interests between groups of heirs may thus be resolved. Precisely this sort of situation, involving either continuation of a closely controlled company within the same ownership group, or continuation as a separate entity with sale of some of the equity to a new management group, was discussed in the tax committees of the

Congress when all preferred stock dividends were made tax-free by statute in 1954 and in defining the escape clauses in section 306 when that section was developed in the same year to control abuses through preferred stock bail-outs.

A distinctive feature of a position as owner-manager of a closely controlled company is that one does not have to retire, regardless of the existence or absence of a pension plan. So long as the individuals are not incapacitated to the point of making salaries unreasonable, they can be continued indefinitely. And even if disallowed as deductions, they can be continued so long as minority stockholders do not protest. This possibility becomes an expectation in the minds of many owner-managers. A sale of the company would ordinarily be expected to preclude this possibility of continuing income, though compensation for agreements not to compete are familiar. But if the closely controlled corporation is continued as a separate entity, there is more latitude to offer continuing compensation and also perhaps more justification for having the former heads of the company identified with it publicly and available for advice.

The absence of a good pension plan for executives is sometimes thought of as a disadvantage by men contemplating a move from a large company into a position as part of the owner-manager group of a closely controlled company or, if not, their wives may be concerned about the loss of pension rights. In fact, however, the prospect of deferral of full retirement may more than make up for the absence of a generous formal pension plan from a financial standpoint, and for those who want to continue active executive work, postponement of retirement will offer psychological as well as financial advantages. But the power to postpone retirement can be dangerous because the failure to get out soon enough may preclude employment of a younger more vigorous management group and pull the company down to a point where little more than a salvage operation is possible when retirement or death finally occurs.

14

Special

Tax Provisions

in Extractive Industries

Some of the special tax provisions applicable to oil, gas, and mining companies are widely known by their descriptive names, but their actual economic consequences, which in turn determine whether they are fair, are in many respects uncertain. Attitudes concerning them often are based on assumptions which may not be valid. The principal provisions can be described easily along with certain obvious ways in which they influence specific business and investment decisions, but there is not yet agreement about their full significance, especially for products with competitive international markets. The principal provisions are the depletion allowances and the allowance of current deduction for intangible drilling costs of oil and gas wells and of certain exploration and development expenses for mines.

INTANGIBLE DRILLING COSTS AND EXPLORATION EXPENDITURES

Intangible drilling costs, which can most simply be thought of as the costs of the hole in the ground, may be either capitalized and recovered through depletion or deducted as a current expense (par. 2103(b)(2)). If depletion is taken on the basis of cost, the advantage of current deductibility is simply one of timing, assuming that there is at all times enough income against which to make the deduction. The fact of the current deduction reduces the capital investment recoverable through depletion or depreciation. But if percentage depletion, to be described shortly, is used, the advantage of immediate deduction is much more important because it in no way reduces the amount of depletion subsequently allowable.

The deduction for intangible drilling costs may be taken against any and all income of a taxpayer. Individuals with large income, even income from salaries and professional fees, by deducting their share of the intangible drilling costs of partnerships and joint ventures can very substantially reduce the net cost of their investments in oil and gas activities. The intangible drilling costs typically constitute about 65 to 70 per cent of the total cost of an oil well venture. A deduction of 70 per cent of cost, against a 70 per cent marginal tax rate, reduces the net after-tax cost of the outlay by about half. And, it should be emphasized, the fact of the deduction in no way reduces the depletion allowance under the percentage method. However, the deduction of intangible drilling expenses for a new well on a property must be taken into account in determining the net income from that property, which in turn will have a bearing on the depletion deduction allowable under the net income limitation, as will be explained later.

A somewhat different treatment is given for exploration and development expenditures for mines (par. 1840). The former may be treated in either of two ways. They are deductible currently up to $100,000 a year for any one taxpayer and up to a lifetime maximum of $400,000. This allowance is related to a taxpayer, not to any particular venture. It is available to both individuals and corporations. If the corporation is the taxpaying entity, a fresh start can be secured by the use of a new corporation.

Under an option effective in 1966, an unlimited deduction may be taken for exploration expenses to discover any deposit of ore or other mineral (except oil or gas) in the United States, subject to a recapture as ordinary income when production commences or when the property is sold. The recapture may take the form of either foregoing depletion until the recapture is completed or taking the amount into income and capitalizing it subject to subsequent cost depletion. The decision on which option to elect will depend on the scale of the expenditures, the confidence with which one expects an eventual recovery, and the discount factor applied to a postponement of taxes.

Development expenses on properties known to contain a mineral deposit in commercially marketable quantities also can be deducted currently or captalized and recovered through depletion. The current deduction does not reduce the percentage depletion allowance except insofar as it may modify the net income limitation. The current deductibility of tangible drilling costs and exploration and development expenditures is a major factor in inducing participation by high-bracket individuals in oil and mining ventures. The fact that the character of expenses of a partnership can be passed through to the individual members is an inducement to conduct ventures as syndicates or partnerships. The fact that losses can be divided differently than profits is a further attraction for the use of partnerships.

DEPLETION

Continued production from any oil or gas well or mine will eventually exhaust the deposit. Physical consumption of a natural resource deposit is analogous to and even more certain than the wearing out or obsolescence of a building or piece of equipment. The period of time for exhaustion of a huge deposit may be very long, as may be the life of a solid building. (Hereafter, the simple word "well" will be used to avoid constant repetition of the descriptive words "oil" or "gas".)

For anyone who has made an investment in a mine or well, it is as incorrect to assume that proceeds from sales less costs of extraction is a fair measure of income as it is for the owner of a building to ignore the exhaustion of its cost over time. Depreciation is necessary to allocate the costs of depreciable property over its probable useful life. Depletion is necessary to allocate the cost of a mine or well over its probable useful life.

Cost Depletion. If the total amount of a deposit is known, the cost may be allocated to the units of production as they are mined or pumped out. "Cost depletion" is allowed as the basic method and is subject to no more controversy from the standpoint of public policy than depreciation which is also based on cost (par. 2103). When the original estimate of the number of units to be produced changes because of new facts, the remaining cost is spread over the revised estimate of remaining units, just as a change in the expected life of depreciable property leads to a revision in the annual depreciation charge (par. 2103(c)). For depletion, the charge is related to units produced; under most methods of depreciation, the charge is related to time.

The cost of structures and of much of the capital equipment associated with a mine or well is recorded separately and recovered through depreciation, the period for which will be based on the estimated useful life. This, in turn, may be much shorter than physical life if the life of the mine or well is expected to be brief and the equipment cannot be removed (par. 2103(b)).

PERCENTAGE DEPLETION. Percentage depletion, at specified rates ranging from 5 to 27½ per cent of gross income or 50 per cent of net income from the property, whichever is smaller, is authorized as an alternative to cost depletion (par. 2104). In most cases of a successful discovery or drilling in a proven field, percentage depletion will be many times as large as cost depletion; percentage depletion can be continued indefinitely regardless of cost. When, however, proven properties are purchased, cost depletion may exceed the percentage allowances.

Percentage depletion was first authorized in 1926 for oil and gas properties, and subsequently extended to other minerals. It was adopted as a substitute for depletion based on "discovery value," which had been established in the Revenue Act of 1918 to encourage exploration and production in World War I. Under that concept, the basis for depletion was the value of the property thirty days after the discovery of a mineral deposit. Though the concept was ingenious, its application led to innumerable controversies over both valuation and the definition of a discovery. By the time a tax return was audited and litigated, it was hard to avoid the use of hindsight and to confine attention to the facts as they could have been seen only thirty days after a discovery. And then what was a discovery? Did one well prove a field? Did a contiguous well constitute a new discovery? And how could it be proven that it was the same vein, if the horizontal shafts were never connected? Percentage depletion was much simpler.

The percentages originally selected were intended to give about the same dollar depletion allowances as those arising from good discoveries. The 27½ per cent figure represented a compromise between the 25 and 30 per cent figures adopted by the two branches of Congress; it does not indicate a precise engineering determination. Percentage depletion, at lower rates, was later adopted for the products of other extractive industries. Over the years, the percentages have been increased on several of the other minerals.

One controversial feature of the percentage depletion allowance involves the question of whether it should be based on the chemical content or the end use. Limestone, for example, is subject to a 15 per cent allowance, but limestone is often used simply as road material in competition with ordinary stone, which gets only a 5 per cent allowance. If the limestone sold for road use gets only a 5 per cent allowance, the owner of the quarry is worse off than the owner selling for building purposes not only in the price but in the tax treatment; but if 15 per cent is allowed regardless of use, the limestone has an unfair tax advantage over competitive minerals for road construction. In general, the Congress has settled on use rather than chemical content (par. 2104(b)(2)(b)(A)).

A second problem involves the "cut-off point" at which mining ceases and processing or manufacturing begins. For many years, the law allowed depletion to be calculated on the price or value of the "first commercially marketable product." If there were no market for clay used for bricks or rock used for cement, did this mean that the depletion could be calculated on the value of the finished brick or the manufactured cement? Several courts ruled that it did, even though the value of the end product was as much as ten times the imputed value of the raw material based on an allocation of costs. This treatment gave a strong inducement to vertical integration and encouraged producers to rely on their captive sources of raw materials, since purchases from independent producers would establish a market value for the raw material before processing. The Treasury contended that the process of fabrication made a new and different product. The Supreme Court finally rejected the liberal interpretation of the "first commercially marketable product," and the Congress established specific cut-off points in section 613(c).

Perhaps the most spectacular example of the significance of the cut-off point applies to the rock from which shale oil can be extracted. The rock has no special value when mined or quarried and crushed; the 5 per cent allowance on its imputed value at that point is a modest one indeed. After being processed in the retort, at a cost several times that of acquiring and crushing the rock, the resultant sludge is somewhat analogous to crude oil. If the depletion were calculated against its imputed value at that stage, and if in addition the 27½ per cent given for oil and gas were applied, the depletion allowance would be increased several fold. It has been claimed that these two changes in tax treatment would make the shale oil industry very close to viable.

The implications of the two limitations on percentage depletion should be understood. For a property with low operating costs, the limitation of 27½ per cent of gross income is the significant constraint; with gross income of 100 and costs of 20, the allowance is 27.5 under the gross income limitation and 40 under the net income limitation. For a property with high operating costs, the reverse is true. With gross of 100 and costs of 80, the limitation to 50 per cent of net gives a maximum allowance of 10, though 27.5 would be allowed under the limitation based on gross. The break-even occurs when operating expenses are 45 per cent of gross; at that level the gross and net income limitations are equal ($27.5 \times 100 = .50 (100-45)$).

On any property with higher operating costs, some of the depletion allowable under the percentage of gross is "wasted." Obviously, from a tax standpoint, it would be desirable to put together into a single property whatever combination of separate properties would make the nearest approach to the break-even point between the gross and net income limitations. For many years, rather arbitrary aggregations of properties were permitted and were made to minimize the "waste" of depletion allowances. New rules were established for mines in 1958 which permit aggregations only on a common-sense basis, that is, of all the properties in a mine, or of two or more mines in an operating unit, but denies aggregations which are illogical except for tax purposes (par. 2106). Rather capricious aggregations were permitted for oil and gas wells until more rational rules were established for tax years beginning in 1964 (par. 2105).

As previously noted, intangible drilling costs of wells or exploration and development expenses of mines, though they may be deducted from any and all income, must be taken into account in calculating the net income from each property to determine the limitation of the percentage depletion deduction to 50 per cent of net income. Large, currently deductible expenses may reduce or even completely wipe out the depletion otherwise allowable against production in the year when the new drilling occurs. A depletion deduction reduced in this way is thought of as lost or wasted. Accordingly, if much new drilling is to be done, a good deal of ingenuity is devoted to arranging the timing to minimize the "waste" of the depletion deduction. Alternatively, there is an inducement to have separate properties for each well to avoid a reduction in the net income from any existing property. But small separate properties may increase the difficulty of aggregations which are desirable to balance high-cost and low-cost production, as already noted.

ECONOMIC INTERESTS IN WELLS AND MINES

The ownership of oil and mining properties may be subdivided in quite involved ways. A property does not simply consist of the sub-soil rights pertaining to a particular land surface. One may own a half-interest in the oil sand at a particular depth and a quarter interest in the sand at another depth under the same surface, and acquire these rights from different prior owners at different times.

The laws concerning the ownership of mineral property, and the contracts for their extraction, are exceedingly complex and seem to the layman to constitute a world unto themselves. There is a great variety of contractual arrangement involving leases, retained interests, minimum royalties, overriding royalties, and various joint ventures which are of interest only to specialists in the area. The essential point is that depletion is allowed to anyone who has an economic interest in the property and to no one else (par. 2101). The regulations distinguish between an economic interest and "a mere economic or pecuniary advantage derived from production" (reg. 1.611–1(b)). The concept of the nature of the property right in oil and gas is not uniform in all the states and, in certain aspects of litigation, even the federal circuit courts have reached different conclusions based on the nature of the property rights which they deemed to prevail in oil and gas.

For several years, for example, a so-called horizontal carved-out interest, consisting of the right to receive the next production up to a certain number of units or a certain dollar value, was regarded as a separate property which could be sold for capital gains. Since the issue arose in only one circuit, it was impossible to get a conflict, which is the normal basis for appeal to the Supreme Court. Finally, the matter was reviewed by the Court and this position rather summarily rejected. To the layman, the horizontal carve-out seemed analogous to the clipping of a bond coupon just prior to its due date.

If the access to mineral property is available without charge, as in a navigable waterway, there is no economic interest. In one instance, it was proposed that if a fee were charged by the government for the right to dredge, this would constitute a basis for claiming the existence of an economic interest, which in turn would permit depletion, including percentage depletion. It was apparent that the revenue from the fee would be much less than the loss in income tax revenue from the artificial depletion deduction, and the proposal was rejected by the Treasury, even by those sympathetic in principle to establishing fees for government services wherever this might be feasible.

In another situation, described by a student in a class discussion, a claim by abutting property owners along a river for payments from a dredging company against which they had no legal claim was happily paid with the apparent hope that it would establish the basis for an "economic interest."

NET EFFECTS OF SPECIAL TAX PROVISIONS

Over the years, the special tax provisions for the extractive industries have been the subject of a great deal of controversy. A lower effective tax rate presumptively gives an unfair advantage to those who can use it, and the combination of current deduction of intangible drilling, exploration, and development expenses with percentage depletion has been quite commonly criticized on that basis. However, as the corporation income tax has increasingly been recognized as a tax cost, rather than a tax burden resting entirely on a company, it has been realized that a lower effective tax rate is more likely to be reflected in the prices of the products than in net profits. Indeed, in a conference of The Brookings Institution on the subject of the effects of the tax provisions for the oil and gas industry in 1962, the principal emphasis was on the extent of their impact on prices rather than on profits.[1]

The concern among economists appears to have shifted from matters of equity to problems regarding the allocation of economic resources. A lower price induces greater consumption and hence greater investment in the extractive industries, the degree of shift depending on the price-elasticity of the products. Many economists are disturbed by misallocations of resources from any non-neutral tax or other policy; an economy in which resources are thus shifted, to the degree of the shifting, is referred to as inefficient. Others feel that "inefficiency" of this sort is a somewhat esoteric matter for either personal or public concern.

Two additional considerations are relevant to an appraisal of the net effects of the special tax treatment of income from extractive industries. Certain of the products, notably gasoline, are subject to high excise taxes which much more than offset any influence of income taxes in the direction of greater investment. Secondly, many of the domestic extractive industries are high-cost producers compared to foreign sources of supply. Indeed, the domestic industries are maintained only through tariffs or more directly through import quotas. For these industries, the effects of a differential tax treatment may be minor compared to other government policies which make them viable.

Finally, some recognition must be given to the tax status of income from production by U.S. companies abroad. The deductibility of intangible drilling costs and percentage depletion are available to all U.S. companies regardless of the location of their activities. Accordingly, there is a strong tax incentive for foreign production of U.S. companies to be carried on through branches rather than through foreign subsidiaries. It is sometimes argued that the special tax provisions should be available only for domestic production, and some of the percentage depletion rates for metals are thus limited. The significance of such a limitation, if applied

[1] Stephen L. McDonald, *Federal Tax Treatment of Income from Oil and Gas*, The Brookings Institution, Washington, D.C., 1963.

generally, can only be appreciated after the discussion of the various tax factors relevant to foreign operations in Chapter 16. In substance, since foreign income taxes are allowed as credits against the U.S. income tax, the tendency of producing countries is to raise their tax at least to the level to absorb the full allowable credits. Thus, any increase in the U.S. effective tax rate would not be likely to increase U.S. tax revenues, though it might increase foreign revenues with adverse effects on the U.S. balance of payments and with a possible tax disadvantage to U.S. companies in comparison with their foreign competitors in world markets.

The analysis of the net effects of the tax provisions for extractive industries is exceedingly complicated and the results are uncertain. Simple arguments in favor of depletion in excess of cost, such as the fact that natural resources are exhaustible or that oil and mining ventures are highly risky, do not seem acceptable. Other assets, such as a popular design of an automobile or a current best-seller, are also exhaustible and many other business activities are subject to high risk. Reiterations of these traditional points, which do not seem tenable, often lead to impatient rejection of the whole idea of differential tax treatment. The much more involved analysis which takes account of the effects of differential tax treatment on prices, the viability of domestic industries, and the status of U.S. companies in world competition deserves much more attention than it has received thus far.

CAPITAL GAINS ON SALES OF TIMBER AND SELECTED MINERALS

Timber is also subject to depletion according to a method appropriate to the lumber industry (par. 2109). Of much more significance, the proceeds of the sales of timber may be treated as capital gains (par. 1615). The intent is to permit capital gains treatment for that part of the income which is attributable to the growth of the timber, in contrast to the income from the cutting and marketing of timber. A land owner always has the option to sell a tract at a price which takes full account of the increase in value of timber through growth, and receive capital gains treatment. The purchaser in turn has his purchase price as his cost, recoverable through depletion. Thus, by a succession of ownerships, capital gains can be secured for the increase in value through growth.

But a succession of ownerships is inconsistent with forest conservation, replanting, and tree farming. The allowance of capital gains treatment for part of the income of a continuing owner is intended to remove the tax penalty against systematic forest management. It is analogous in this respect to the substitution of severance taxes for property taxes in many of the lumber states at the turn of the century, after it was recognized that an annual tax on an increasing value encouraged complete cutting of all marketable timber at one time, perhaps even followed by abandonment of a tract.

The capital gains treatment for coal and iron ore royalties has no comparable economic rationale (par. 1617). The special provision for coal royalties was adopted shortly after World War II; the provision for iron ore royalties, after being rejected in 1954 and on later occasions, was adopted in 1964. Some observers have noted that coal and iron ore are both used in blast furnaces, a fact which suggests a tax discrimination "against" limestone and oxygen.

15

Special
Tax Rules for Particular
Types of Companies

Over the years, various special provisions of the tax law have been developed in response to the distinctive characteristics of particular types of companies. In some instances, the purpose has been to give relief from the application of a general rule which was felt to be unduly harsh in its application, as in the case of the regulated investment companies. In others, the problem has been to prevent tax avoidance which could occur under the general provisions of the law, as would be possible in the absence of special treatment of personal holding companies. In still other situations, there has been an attempt to secure tax neutrality where it would not otherwise exist between companies which are essentially competitive though organized differently and, in the absence of special legislation, would be taxable in quite different ways. Stock and mutual insurance companies and cooperatives which compete with ordinary companies are examples of this third group. Finally, special relief provisions which are avowedly not neutral have been adopted to encourage certain types of business which are deemed to be so important from an economic or social (or political) standpoint that a general policy of tax neutrality should be overridden, as has been done for small business investment companies and for some aspects of farming.

This chapter gives brief explanations of the reasons for the major distinctive provisions of the tax law as it applies to personal holding companies and the unreasonable accumulation of earnings in ordinary corporations, cooperatives, savings and loan associations, and mutual savings banks (along with special provisions for commercial banks to reduce the tax advantage given to mutual financial institutions), insurance com-

260

panies, regulated investment companies and real estate trusts, and small business investment companies. It also brings together in a short section references to the scattered provisions of the law which are intended to give favorable tax treatment to small business.

Personal Holding Companies

The fact that the corporation income tax rate has always been lower than the rates in the higher brackets of the individual income tax makes it cheaper from a tax standpoint for many people to have their income received by a corporation than to receive it personally. This advantage is most pronounced for dividend income since, to minimize penalty taxes on intercorporate transfer of income, no more than 15 per cent of the dividends received by one corporation from another taxable corporation are included in income, giving an effective intercorporate dividend tax of 7.2 per cent with a general corporate tax rate of 48 per cent. To be sure, the income received by a personal holding company is still a step removed from personal ownership, but if one person or one family owns the corporation the funds are available for further investment or business uses about as freely as if they were owned personally. And if one continues to keep the funds in a controlled corporation until death, they can be realized without further income taxation through liquidation because of the step-up in basis at death.

The attraction of transferring investment assets to controlled corporations which then receive and reinvest investment income was sufficiently great even in the middle 1920's when the maximum individual income tax rate was 25 per cent to lead to extensive use of personal holding companies. At that time, the possession of a personal holding company came to be regarded as a status symbol in somewhat the same way as a telephone in an automobile did for a later generation. The tax law consequently was modified to remove any tax advantage from the use of corporations which simply received and reinvested investment income for a single family or a small group. The procedure adopted was simple: the imposition of an additional tax on the corporation on its retained income at a sufficiently high rate to make it preferable for stockholders to receive income directly (pars. 3400–10). The tax law goes beyond neutrality and makes the use of personal holding companies unattractive in an absolute sense. With a 70 per cent penalty tax on undistributed income, there is a clear disadvantage for even the highest-bracket individual to try to use a corporation as a tax shield even on dividend income.

The only issues in establishing the tax penalties have been on the definition of close control and the type of income which would make the penalty tax applicable. Ownership of more than half of the stock by five or fewer families has been selected as the test of close control, with necessary elaboration to prevent indirect control through trusts, partnerships, or options.

The definition of income has involved more problems. In addition to dividends, other forms of investment income including interest and annuities, mineral, oil and gas royalties, copyright royalties, and payments made by a substantial stockholder for the use of corporate property are included in the definition of personal holding company income which, if it exceeds 60 per cent of the adjusted gross income of the corporation, brings the personal holding company tax into operation. The inclusion of payments for the use of corporate property by a substantial stockholder (one owning 25 per cent or more of the corporation's stock) is designed to prevent a person from using his personal income to rent property owned by his corporation, getting a personal deduction in the process and in effect transferring the income from himself where it would be taxed at his highest marginal rate to his corporation where it is taxed at the corporation rate.

Rental income from property leased to outsiders has presented particularly difficult problems of definition. Rental income may arise from an active real estate business which should not be penalized if conducted in corporate form. But the advantages of securing and burying dividend income in a corporation are so great that it would pay to have an investment corporation hold some real estate to receive some rental income if this would legitimatize the receipt and retention of a large amount of dividend income from passive investment in stock. Accordingly, the rules concerning the fraction of income from rent, and indeed the definition of rent, have been tightened at various times by amendments to the law. As the law stood at one time, a rather small part of total assets invested in rental real estate could provide a tax shield for the dividend income from a much larger part of the assets. But in recognition of the fact that a real estate rental business is often carried on through a corporation without any purpose of tax avoidance, rent is not counted as personal holding company income if it equals half of total income. It must, however, be adjusted rent, which means net rental income after deducting interest, taxes and depreciation; investment of a small part of total funds will not produce enough rent to constitute half of a company's total income when rent is thus defined. Furthermore, even when there is sufficient net rent to constitute half of total corporate income, the rent is ignored only if other personal holding income in excess of 10 per cent of the total is distributed as dividends.

Personal holding company income also includes contracts for personal services under specified conditions. This inclusion is intended to prevent a highly paid person from using a corporation which he owns to intercept, as it were, the income which he would receive personally in the ordinary course of events.

The provisions of the law dealing with personal holding companies have been made more strict over the years, as ingenious procedures have been developed to get around their intent. However, operating companies may at times inadvertently fall into this category, as when a closely controlled active business corporation sells all or most of its assets and is continued as a holding company instead of being liquidated; even if it subsequently becomes an active business it may become a personal holding company in the interval during which it holds liquid assets.

Patterns of business may also change in ways that bring an active business into the existing definition of a personal holding company. This was notably the case as the income of music publishers shifted from the sale of sheet music to royalties, after the advent of jukeboxes. In fact, no less business activity was involved in promoting the use of records in jukeboxes, which in turn produce royalty income, than in sales of sheet music. But royalty income was included in the definition of personal holding company income without any qualifications. The Congress and the Treasury were satisfied that the general rule gave a harsh result, and the rather involved rules regarding copyright royalties were worked out to give relief to active music publishing companies without opening the door for a composer to shift his personal income as a composer into sheltered corporate royalty income (par. 3401(d)).

The penalty tax applies only to the extent that the corporation is in fact used to retain personal holding income. Dividends paid up to the middle of the third month after the close of the year, as well as dividends paid currently, are allowed as deductions in computing the income subject to the penalty tax, but without double counting for a series of years. A corporation may even pay a "deficiency dividend" after it has been determined that a tax is due and thereby be relieved of most or all of the tax, though not of interest and penalties, so long as the deficiency was not due to fraud or willful failure to file a return (par. 3407).

As noted above, distribution of income to escape the penalty tax on the corporation does not restore tax neutrality with the situation which would exist if property producing the income were held directly because the corporate tax must be paid first and the individual tax on the remainder when distributed. Direct investment is cheaper from an income tax standpoint for even the highest-bracket investors. However, an older person involved in a personal holding company may consider it preferable to pay the double tax on distributed investment income than to pay a capital gains tax on liquidation if he anticipates that his estate will get a stepped-up basis on his death in a few years. When liquidation is postponed for this reason, a certain impatience may develop among the younger members of a group.

Foreign Personal Holding Companies

After the personal holding company route for tax avoidance was barred by amendments to the tax law, foreign personal holding companies became an attractive alternative to intercept and hold investment income. Since foreign corporations, holding all their assets abroad and doing no business here, were not subject to U.S. jurisdiction in any way, it might have been thought that they would provide an effective alternative to domestic personal holding companies as a device to avoid personal tax on investment income. Any tax advantage from their use was blocked, however, by a new provision in the law which requires U.S. stockholders to include their proportionate share of undistributed income of a foreign personal holding company in their individual taxable incomes (pars. 3412–16). This treatment served as a precedent for the taxation of certain undistributed business income adopted some thirty years later in 1962, discussed in Chapter 16.

The definitions and qualifications of foreign personal holding companies are substantially similar to those applied to domestic personal holding companies. Since the stockholders are taxed currently on the undistributed income, as in a partnership, the basis of their stock is also increased by this amount. The net result of the tax treatment is to make foreign personal holding companies unattractive from a tax standpoint, in comparison with direct individual ownership of investments, to the extent of the tax, if any, imposed on the corporation on its receipt of income. Since such corporations would presumably be set up in countries where income taxes will at most be negligible, the penalty is not great.

Unreasonable Accumulation of Earnings

In addition to the penalty taxes imposed on personal holding companies or their shareholders, a general provision of the law imposes a tax on any corporation which accumulates surplus to an unreasonable extent for the purpose of avoiding income tax of its shareholders (pars. 3422–24). The tax is at the rate of 27½ per cent up to $100,000 and 38½ per cent on the excess above $100,000.

There has been a great deal of litigation in the application of this part of the law. It has typically been applied only to closely controlled corporations. There are interesting possibilities of damage suits against directors by minority stockholders whose personal income taxes would not be large on distributed incomes, if the company is subjected to the penalty tax because of nonpayment of dividends for the benefit of high-bracket controlling stockholders. Furthermore, at one time the tax was asserted against very small accumulations of no more than $10,000 or $15,000 if a corporation had no immediate need for the funds.

The Treasury and Congress agreed on some relaxation in the revision of the Code in 1954 and in later years to make the impact of the penalty tax less harsh. An aggregate accumulation of up to $100,000 was permitted before the tax could be applied regardless of need, and the tax was imposed only on the amount of accumulation during a year which was determined to be unreasonable rather than, as previously, on the entire accumulation of a year whenever some part of it was held excessive. It was also specifically provided that the reasonable needs include the reasonably anticipated needs (section 537).

For many years there was controversy as to whether the use of funds to go into a completely different line of business indicated a reasonable need, and the Treasury was upheld in some cases where it insisted on a strict interpretation of the definite article "the" in the phrase "reasonable needs of the business." In a revision of the regulations following the adoption of the Internal Revenue Code of 1954, section 1.537–3(a) was added; it states that "The business of a corporation is not merely that which it has previously carried on, but includes, in general, any line of business which it may undertake." So long as the funds are needed for an active trade or business, as distinct from passive investment, the tax should not be applied.

It should be emphasized that the tax is imposed only once on the accumulation from a particular year's income; the name of the tax sometimes leads to the erroneous belief that it is imposed in successive years on an existing accumulation of earnings. Each year stands by itself and part or all of the earnings of the year may be taxed, but once taxed, there is no further penalty for continued retention. This treatment recognizes that tax avoidance from nonpayment of a particular dividend can occur only once. The tax does not apply to domestic and foreign personal holding companies since they have special tax rules applicable to them.

The accumulated earnings tax is often criticized as giving tax officials too much authority to assert their opinions over the judgment of responsible business managers, and it doubtless has been used for harassment or its application proposed and then withdrawn in compromise settlements on other issues. But some of the cases involving loans to shareholders and their relatives or to separate business ventures of shareholders reveal such flagrant attempts to withhold earnings to avoid individual income tax on shareholders that most people seem convinced that some provision of this sort is needed to keep the whole tax law from being thoroughly discredited. Other countries have similar problems and some of them have tighter rules, including a general imputation of all undistributed income to shareholders in some closely controlled corporations.

Cooperatives

A cooperative is usually a corporation but with peculiar characteristics, the principal one of which is that its profits do not go to stockholders but are paid instead to members, who are also usually the patrons, or retained for expansion. When retained, the funds are usually allocated to members who receive certificates of beneficial interest for their respective parts of the total.

Cooperatives originally were self-help organizations of small farmers who banded together to market their crops or make joint purchases, and they were made tax-exempt. They had a strong political appeal and were not significant competitive factors in the economy. But they grew larger and become dominant factors in some regions in handling certain agricultural products. They used retained earnings to build processing plants for farm products or factories to make items for sale to their members. As income tax rates became higher, the advantage of being able to accumulate earnings without tax gave cooperatives a tremendous advantage in using earnings to expand at the expense of their tax-paying competitors.

It has become the intent of the Congress that income earned by and through cooperatives should be taxed once when it is earned, either to the cooperative as an entity or to its members. This is done by imposing the corporation tax on cooperatives, but allowing them deductions for distributions to members in the form of allocations of retained earnings in the form of scrip as well as cash (par. 3447). To make scrip qualify as a deduction to the cooperative, the members must agree to include in their current taxable incomes the face value of the allocations or certificates of beneficial interest (sec. 1388). This somewhat roundabout provision of the law was added in 1962 to overcome a situation which had existed for a decade during which the intent of Congress had been thwarted by a series of cases which held that some scrip had no ascertainable market value and hence was not taxable to members though it was deductible by the cooperatives. Nontransferable scrip bearing no interest and with no due date did indeed have no market value, as was evidenced by the fact that many farmers sent it in to the Treasury in preference to paying tax on its face value as was required by Treasury regulations.

The action of the Congress in 1962 in making the deduction to the cooperative conditional upon taxability to the members resolved a major gap through which a large amount of income could pass untaxed. The further requirement that for scrip to qualify as a deductible distribution at least 20 per cent of a patronage dividend of which it is a part must be paid in cash was intended to give the lowest-bracket members enough cash to pay the individual income tax on their scrip, 20 per cent being the bottom individual tax bracket in 1962. Members in higher tax brackets have to find the cash from other sources to pay the additional tax on the face value of qualified scrip. Most cooperatives retain income on a revolving fund basis, redeeming scrip issued in any particular year at some specified future time, with the cycles commonly ranging from eight to fourteen years.

The present tax treatment represents a compromise of opposing views. Some representatives of cooperatives have argued that there should be no tax on members until cash was paid, with cooperatives having the free use of funds in the interval. This position was never advanced generally or even vigorously. Some representatives of companies in industries in which cooperatives were expanding rapidly have argued the other extreme that cooperatives should pay the full corporation tax on all net income, with patronage dividends being nondeductible to cooperatives and taxed to members when received in cash.

Others felt that equity would be best served if a different compromise between the extreme views were applied. Under it cooperatives would be taxed at the corporate rate on any net increase in retained earnings but with all cash payments to members deductible as paid. This would be a tighter rule than the existing one when cooperatives are expanding, that is, when current retentions exceed redemptions of certificates issued previously. To the extent that the average marginal tax rate of the members is less than the corporate tax rate, the tax burden on retained earnings is less under the existing system. Furthermore, and probably more significant, under the existing law the burden of providing the cash to pay the tax is placed on the members and the cooperatives need pay only 20 per cent of current earnings to members.

In addition to retention of some of the profits earned on sales to members of purchased or manufactured products, cooperatives may retain some part of the proceeds from sales of products produced by members and sold through the cooperatives. Additional legislation was adopted in 1966 to provide for taxation of per-unit retain certificates, the common form of indication of the amount of retained funds. Unless the members consent to include in their respective incomes the amounts retained by a cooperative, the retain certificates do not qualify as a distribution.

Savings and Loan Associations and Mutual Savings Banks

The savings and loan associations and mutual savings banks are some-what like cooperatives but operate in a financial field. They, too, retain some of their income, but unlike cooperatives they do not allocate the retained earnings among members or depositors. Retained earnings belong to the entity. On liquidation, they would go to the remaining depositors at that time, but short of liquidation they cannot be taxed to individuals because, to repeat, they are not allocated to anyone and there is no assurance as to who, if anyone, will ever receive them. A tax, if any, must be imposed on the business organization.

Mutual banks and savings associations are taxed as corporations, but for many years prior to 1962 they were allowed to set aside earnings to build up a bad debt reserve of up to 12 per cent of deposits. The bad debt reserves of most savings and loan associations fell far short of the allowable 12 per cent and as their deposits (shares) increased rapidly, the organizations paid no income taxes, retaining tax-free for expansion all funds not paid as interest to depositors. This 12 per cent reserve was much larger than that permitted to all but a very few commercial banks; in fact, it exceeded the combined capital funds plus bad debt reserves of most commercial banks.

The situation under the 12 per cent reserve allowance was criticized as unfair by commercial banks that built up surplus from after-tax income, but it was defended by the savings and loan organizations on the grounds that they needed the funds to protect their depositors and since they were mutual organizations they should not be taxed anyway. (In a few states, stock savings and loan associations are permitted; their status and tax treatment are too specialized to justify explanation here. In brief, they received all the tax advantages of the mutual organizations, with highly leveraged benefits going to the stockholders.) The mutual savings banks with different operating traditions and subject to different regulations than the savings and loan associations often had reserves in excess of the allowable 12 per cent and hence paid some tax.

The existing provisions of the law represented a substantial tightening in 1962 (par. 3433(f)). None of the three optional methods now authorized for calculating a reserve to which earnings may be transferred will permit an indefinite tax-free accumulation of undistributed income. The present rules do not satisfy everyone concerned. Some argue that larger reserves may be needed, in the absence of capital funds, and that taxes should not stand in the way of maximum safety for depositors. Others contend that funds for reserves should come from reduced interest payments on deposits and that the tax law should not depart from neutrality to favor one group of competing financial institutions because of their form of organization and that mutual organizations should have no tax advantages over ordinary banks.

Commercial Banks

Commercial banks have the benefit of two provisions of the tax law specifically limited to them and incidentally may qualify for a third. Banks may build up a reserve for bad debts equal to 2.4 per cent of outstanding loans (par. 3433(d)). This figure, it will be noted, is less than half of the 6 per cent reserve on real property loans for mutual banks under one of the three options available to them. In all other industries, a bad debt reserve must be based on the experience of the individual taxpayer.

The present treatment established by a Treasury ruling in 1965 resolved an intolerable situation which had developed under the previous ruling (rev. rul. 65–92). Banks had been required to fix their bad debt reserves on the basis of their individual experience under the general provision of the law, but were permitted to do so over a long period which could include the depression years of the 1930's. With the passage of time, the events of that period came to be meaningless as an indication of probable future loss, but some banks had a vested interest in being the legal entities which had had large losses under an earlier management group. For the industry as a whole, the allowable reserves were about equal to 2.4 per cent, but with great variations ranging from less than 1 per cent to probably as much as 10 per cent or more. The allowance of a flat percentage reserve for all banks was intended to wipe out the discrimination between banks on a basis which had become meaningless while not cutting back on deductions for the industry as a whole. In fact, the new rule gave relief in an aggregate sense because banks with reserves below the allowed figure were permitted to build up to it gradually while those with reserves above it did not have to bring them down to the level by a transfer to income. As an alternative, a bank may establish a reserve on a six-year moving average.

The second tax rule applicable to banks is their right to deduct in full any net loss from the sale or exchange of securities in any year, while treating any net gain as capital gain (par. 3433(b)). This asymmetrical treatment is comparable to that given to all taxpayers on depreciable and real property used in a trade or business which, it will be recalled, is not included in the definition of capital assets. On such depreciable and real property losses are deductible in full while, under section 1231, net gains are treated as capital gains, subject to the very important limitations of section 1245 and 1250 that some or all of the gains will be taxed as ordinary income, to the extent that they represent a recovery of depreciation previously deducted.

In appraising the effect of the tax treatment of losses and gains on securities owned by banks, one must first realize that the gains and losses arise primarily from changes in money market rates. An increase in rates depresses the prices of outstanding securities regardless of their quality; the longer the period to maturity, the greater the fall in price necessary to give a yield in line with the current market rate of interest. Conversely, a decrease in interest rates leads to increases in the prices of outstanding securities to bring their yields into line with the market rates.

Two other facts must be kept in mind. Traditionally, bankers build up their security portfolios when demands for loans from customers decline, and sell securities to get funds to loan to customers when their demands increase. Reduced customer demands for loans occur when business is slack, which is typically a time of lower interest rates and hence higher prices for securities. Sales of securities to provide funds for loans occur when business is booming and interest rates are high, that is, when the prices of securities are lower. Thus, to the extent that a security portfolio is treated as a repository and source of funds to meet fluctuations in demands for customer's loans, banks are forced to "sell low and buy high," a policy which is hardly acceptable for its own sake. The asymmetrical tax treatment of gains and losses is regarded as a partial offset to the losses which banks incur in their management of funds which are temporarily in excess of customers' needs.

The ordinary loss–capital gain treatment applies, it will be noted, to net losses and gains for a year. This means that a loss taken in a year when there are net gains will only offset a capital gain taxable as the capital gains rate rather than being deductible in full. Thus, a loss taken in a year with net gains is partially "wasted" from a tax standpoint. Similarly, a gain taken in a year of net losses is set against losses, which means that it is, in effect, subject to the full rate of tax. To the extent possible, banks decide early in a year whether it is to be a gain or a loss year insofar as security sales are concerned and, by judicious timing and selections of securities, avoid mixing gains and losses in a single year.

A full appraisal of the significance of the tax treatment of gains and losses on securities sold or exchanged by banks carries one far into the field of monetary policy and federal debt management. The greater availability of funds to meet customers' demands encourages greater response to the changing needs for credit. Thus stated, the result seems desirable. But typically the Federal Reserve authorities tend to tighten credit in booms and ease it in slack times. May the greater availability of funds during booms from the tax treatment of losses on securities operate at cross-purposes with Federal Reserve policy?

In debt management, the Treasury is usually concerned to keep enough of the total federal debt in longer-term issues and the banks are among the principal holders of government securities. Since the longer the term of the security, the greater will be its fluctuation in price, a favorable treatment of losses is urged to make the longer-term securities more acceptable to banks.

If the present tax treatment were to be changed, it could be done by making both gains and losses either ordinary income items or capital items. A discussion of the relative consequences and merits of these two approaches in terms of tax, debt management, and monetary policy provides a useful review of these subjects and indicates the difficulty of reconciling conflicting objectives in even one small field of public policy.

A small special tax rule designed to facilitate debt management is contained in section 1037(a), adopted in 1959, to remove a tax barrier to conversion of the debt into longer-term issues including advance refunding (par. 1403). Under it, the Secretary of the Treasury may permit exchanges of government securities to be made without recognition of gain or loss. Exercise of this authority can be useful when holders of securities are offered exchange rights, whether at or prior to maturity, into longer-term securities. Such exchanges are typical features in offers of new securities. The tax-free exchange, with of course a carry-forward of basis, is available to all holders, but is especially significant for banks because as outstanding securities approach maturity, they tend to move into the hands of banks whose portfolios tend to be concentrated in relatively short-term obligations.

Finally, another provision which contains no specific reference to banks was adopted to prevent what was regarded as an abuse by a few banks. As a general rule, holders of tax-exempt bonds must amortize any premium above par paid for them. If this were not required, bonds could be issued at high interest rates and sold at large premiums which would simply be the counterpart of the exaggeration of nontaxable interest; an artificial deduction could be created by an artificially high tax-exempt interest. But to relieve dealers in securities from the inconvenience of having to amortize premium on bonds which they might hold for very brief periods, the requirement for amortization was waived for dealers on securities which they held for no more than thirty days.

The problem arose because some banks qualified as dealers in tax-exempt bonds, treated most or all of their regular investment holdings of tax-exempt bonds as though they were held in the capacity of dealers, and then developed arrangements to buy and sell particular issues on a thirty-day cycle, with the result that what was in effect a permanent holding escaped the rule requiring amortization. Protests were made to the Treasury and the Congress by banks which did not engage in the practice (referred to at the time as "the daisy-chain"), showing large differences in income taxes paid by banks which had substantially similar income and expense figures in all other respects. As a result of this abuse by a few banks, a further complication was inserted in the law in 1958 requiring amortization of premium by dealers if a loss is claimed and the bonds have a maturity of less than five years (par. 1837(a)). In view of the preference for short maturities in investment portfolios of banks, it was felt that the five-year rule would effectively stop the abuse. All dealers are subject to this additional complication in tax accounting, it having been decided that it was better to establish a general rule which could apply to everyone than to single out one small group whose activities were responsible for the change in the law.

Insurance Companies

The method of taxing life insurance companies has been changed many times during the existence of the income tax. A procedure adopted under one set of circumstances has turned out to yield no revenue when the circumstances changed. This was conspicuously the case in the late 1940's when the tax law was based on industry-wide assumptions regarding both market interest rates and the interest rates assumed to be applied by the companies in actuarial calculations.

Controversy has centered around the breadth of the definition of income. There is the question as to whether it should be confined to net investment income (roughly the amount earned in excess of the amount assumed to be earned when setting premiums) or also include underwriting income (the gain arising from the fact that actual mortality experience is less than that assumed in setting premiums). There is a further question as to whether capital gains and losses should be included in taxable income. For many years only net investment income was included in the tax base. The present law, adopted essentially in its present form in 1959, applies a comprehensive concept of income (par. 3434).

The other major difference of opinion and change in the law has involved the extent to which the taxable income should be based on the status of individual companies or on industry-wide figures. The present law taxes each company on its own requirements and experience.

The details of life insurance company taxation are comprehensible only to a specialist in the field. The text of the applicable sections of the Code (secs. 801–20) occupy more than thirty-six pages in a loose-leaf edition. The point of general significance is that deductions are allowed in computing taxable income of both stock and mutual companies for whatever income is needed to build up reserves against insurance policies, under existing contracts and actuarial assumptions. This allowance, in conjunction with the tax treatment of insurance and annuity policies in the hands of their individual holders, means that investment income can be compounded without tax until insurance and annuity policies mature. In effect, there is no tax barrier to investment and accumulation of income through insurance companies. And for a high-bracket individual investor, the pre-tax return on direct personal investments has to be very high to permit an accumulation of after-tax income equivalent to that available through no-tax accumulations through insurance.

On maturity of a policy, it will be recalled, the accumulated interest may or may not be taxed depending on the type of policy and circumstances of maturity. The excess of receipts over cost of an annuity policy is taxable, on the basis of an assumed recovery of cost over the life expectancy of the annuitant. So too is the excess over cost of a life insurance policy which is cashed in before death. Of course, not all of the interest income is accumulated and paid out on matured policies; some of it, in effect, "pays for" the insurance during the prior period, and this part of the interest is never taxed to anyone.

A series of rules and definitions have been developed for the taxation of other sorts of insurance companies, with the dual objective of imposing a fair share of the total tax burden on them and avoiding any unreasonable discrimination between stock and mutual companies. The problems are so specialized that the provisions of the law are intelligible only to one who understands the accounting and actuarial methods used by the companies.

Regulated Investment Companies

In the absence of special relief, income taxes would make investment companies prohibitively expensive, at least if they held assets other than stock. Application of the full rate of corporate tax against their investment income would reduce it by about half, and what was left, when distributed, would still be subject to tax in the hands of shareholders. Investors would find this extra tax bite, in addition to reduction of income for management fees, quite unacceptable. Since only 15 per cent of dividend income is subject to tax when received by another corporation, a fund invested entirely in stock might be viable, but balanced funds would be impossible.

Because of the recognized economic and social importance of making it possible for small investors to invest in corporate securities with professional management of their funds, the tax law very simply waives the tax on all distributed income of investments trusts and mutual funds which meet certain conditions (par. 3428–31). To qualify, a company must secure at least 90 per cent of its gross income from dividends, interest, and gains from the sale of stock or securities; it must have its assets diversified and not hold more than 10 per cent of the voting stock of any company in which it invests; and it must distribute at least 90 per cent of its taxable income each year. The limitation to a holding of 10 per cent of the voting stock of an issuer is waived for investment companies which qualify as venture capital companies (par. 3430).

In brief, the companies themselves are regarded as conduits through which income passes from the active companies in which investments are made to the stockholders whose pooled funds are managed by the investment company. Net long-term capital gains are segregated and if distributed are so reported by the shareholders and taxed accordingly. In response to pleas from some of the investment trusts that shareholders preferred to leave capital gains with the companies for reinvestment, receiving distributions only of ordinary income, the law was amended in 1956 to permit investment companies electing to do so to pay a 25 per cent capital gains tax on behalf of their stockholders, who in turn report the full amount of the capital gain on their individual tax return, on the basis of information furnished by the investment company, and also show the 25 per cent tax paid by the company as a credit against their own tax liabilities. The paper work involved under this optional treatment in reporting small amounts of capital gain and tax for small investors, including notification to the actual owners of stock held by nominees, seems to many to be excessive for the advantages which it gives. The case, however, was persuasively put by the managements of investment trusts in terms of the problems of stockholders in distinguishing between capital gains and real income and their desire to reinvest the former.

"ONE-SHOT" INVESTMENT COMPANIES: In the early 1960's, someone had the ingenious idea that people with appreciated investments concentrated in one stock could secure tax-free diversification by forming a "one-shot" regulated investment company by simultaneous transfer by all participants of stock in their individual holdings for stock in the investment company under section 351. It will be recalled that this section permits the tax-free transfer of property to a corporation controlled by transferors and is intended to remove the tax barrier to incorporation of a proprietorship or partnership which would exist under the general rule that gain is realized on any exchange of property (par. 1405). It is probable that Congress never intended the regulated investment company provisions and the tax-free incorporation allowance to be combined in this way; at least the two provisions in the law existed together for almost twenty years before anyone thought of using them together.

The key item in the law was the fact that section 351 permits the transfer of "property" with no qualification or exclusion. This is in contrast to section 1031, which gives nonrecognition of gain on exchanges of property held for productive use or investment, but specifically excludes "stocks, bonds, notes" and other securities (par. 1406). The law being as it was, the organizer of the first one-shot investment company applied successfully for a ruling that the transfer would be tax-free and advertised the venture, featuring the Treasury ruling. And others promptly followed.

The subscribers to stock in the investment companies would keep their basis of the stock which they turned in as the basis of the stock in the company, and the investment company in turn took as its basis for the stock in its portfolio the basis which it had in the hands of the individual investors. This follows the standard procedure in tax-free exchanges that no party and no property receives a step-up in basis. These facts regarding basis raised a nice analytical problem as to which investors would benefit most from the formation and operation of the investment company.

The organizers of the companies reserved the right to accept or reject some or all of the stock offered in subscription, with the objective of starting the company with a reasonably balanced portfolio. Inevitably, the subscriptions were in stock which had appreciated greatly because the chance for diversification was significant primarily for the early investors in very successful companies, and the diversification achieved was simply a broader portfolio of such issues. The offer was not attractive for holders of blue chip stocks which had not appreciated greatly. But though all investors would have turned in appreciated stock, the appreciation would have ranged from one or two hundred to many thousand per cent. Therein lay the problem.

The companies proposed to retain realized gain, paying the capital gains tax itself and imputing the gain and the tax to the individual stockholders who presumably would all be in a sufficiently high tax bracket to have the 25 per cent capital gains tax applicable to them with the imputation of gain and of tax being wash items in their own tax returns. But from the standpoint of equity interests in the fund itself, an investor who subscribed stock in which he had 100 per cent appreciation would see his equity interest decreased by the tax payment to a greater extent when stock with a thousand per cent appreciation was sold than if the stock he had turned in had been sold. In a sense, the subscriber with the greatest proportional appreciation in the stocks turned in would gain at the expense of those with less appreciation. Or at least that is the first impression.

If one carries the analysis through to eventual liquidation of the investment company, if that could be expected, one might find a different result. The tax consequences of death also need to be recognized. If an individual kept his greatly appreciated stock until death, his heirs would get a step-up in basis, but once transferred to an investment company, his low basis was frozen in forever on that stock in the hands of the investment company. The fact that stock in the investment company received by his heirs had a higher basis, equal to the book value of the stock in the investment company which in turn includes the appreciation in the portfolio, would not relieve the investment company of the latent tax liability when any of the portfolio stock was sold. In fact, an interesting side issue is the extent to which the latent tax liability on the portfolio should be taken into account in setting the value of stock in the investment company for estate tax purposes. A thorough appraisal of who would gain and by how much and under what circumstances offers an excellent exercise in tax and financial analysis.

A second issue arising from the one-shot investment companies concerns the appropriate policy for the Internal Revenue Service regarding rulings. Favorable rulings were issued at first as a matter of routine. Apparently on reflection at higher levels, it was decided that incorporation of this sort did not come within the intent or even the expectation of the Congress when it adopted section 351. The Commissioner of Internal Revenue announced that he would issue no more favorable rulings, though he did not indicate that additional companies formed without a ruling would be challenged. However, the favorable rulings had been so emphasized in the promotion literature that the organizers of companies felt that they could not proceed successfully without rulings.

It then had to be decided at what point the cut-off in rulings would be made. Would an application which had been processed almost to the point of approval be issued? Would all existing applications be processed? And what should be done for a group which had gone to considerable legal and organizational expense in preparing for a company, but had not yet applied for a ruling because that had been thought of as a simple routine matter on the basis of Internal Revenue policy up to that moment? It was recognized by virtually everyone that the last proposed company to get a ruling would thereby have a competitive advantage and probably receive very large subscriptions on its "last chance" appeal to investors.

A discussion of the merits of the various positions which might have been taken by the Internal Revenue Service always produces vigorous differences of opinion and brings out the difficult role of a tax administrator. In fact, all existing applications and all applications which it could be shown were about to be made were issued. Subsequently, no new one-shot companies were formed for several years when, with the passage of time, the contrast between those with rulings and those without was less conspicuous and another attempt was made to get subscriptions to a one-shot company on the basis of opinion of counsel that the exchange of stock would be nontaxable.

In 1966, the Internal Revenue Service announced that it would challenge the tax-free status of transfers to one-shot investment companies. This led to vigorous protests by those who were in the process of organizing such companies. The Congress amended the law to permit the formation of new companies through June 1967. After that time, if a company is formed without the benefit of an extension of a statutory authority to do so, there will be an opportunity for a court test of the validity of the tax-free transfer of stock to a corporation under section 351.

Real Estate Investment Trusts

A similar conduit or pass-through treatment for the income from real estate investment trusts was authorized by Congress in 1960 (par.

3432). Again, diversification of sources of income and distribution of at least 90 per cent of income are necessary for qualification. The case for special tax treatment was especially strong because they are in fact not corporations and as trusts were not subject to tax until a court decision in the 1930's held that they had so many attributes of a corporation that they should be taxed as such. Since their income was largely in the form of rent, it was taxable at the full corporate rate, without the benefit of the low effective rate applicable to the dividend income of investment companies. With the extra corporate tax, the real estate investment trusts were "worth more dead than alive" and were under pressure to liquidate so that the shareholders could receive income directly and have it taxed only once.

But persuasive though the argument of equity was, it was difficult to draw a line between passive investment in real estate and the active conduct of a business operating a hotel or office building which received its income as rent. The proposed legislation was presented in many versions and was in fact vetoed before an acceptable form was developed. Section 856(d) excludes from the definition of rent any amount received if it is based on the income or profits of the tenant (though rents may be based on a percentage of sales) or if the real estate trust renders any services to the tenants or manages the property other than through an independent contractor. These and other exclusions from the definition of rent greatly restrict the availability of the real estate trust relief provision. But without restrictions, many corporations carrying on active businesses would have switched to a trust form of organization with a windfall gain to their stockholders from the elimination of the full rate of corporate tax merely because the companies sold services paid for by rent rather than commodities or other forms of services.

Ordinary investment trusts invest their funds in corporations which are themselves tax-paying entities; a tax on the investment trusts themselves would be a third level of taxation between the operating companies and the individual stockholders. The real estate investment trusts receive income directly from property which may represent passive investment or active business. The law is intended to give relief to the former, but avoid treatment of the latter which would be more favorable than that available to other forms of business. Any line of demarcation will seem unreasonable to those who just fail to meet the qualifications.

Small Business Investment Corporations

To assist new and small businesses in securing capital funds, the Congress in 1958 authorized the formation of small business investment companies. To increase their attractiveness to individual investors, and their effectiveness after formation, the tax law was amended at the same time to give special tax relief in three ways (par. 3448). Stockholders can treat a loss on sale or exchange of stock in such companies as an ordinary instead of a capital loss. This provision is analogous to the ordinary loss allowable to the original investors in the stock of small operating companies under section 1244, also adopted in 1958. The small business investment companies need pay no tax on dividends received (instead of the regular corporate tax on 15 per cent of dividends received which would otherwise be due), and they can treat a loss from sale, exchange or worthlessness of convertible debentures purchased from small businesses as ordinary instead of capital losses.

SPECIAL PROVISIONS OF THE TAX LAW OF BENEFIT TO SMALL BUSINESS

At various places, reference has been made to particular features of the tax law which directly or indirectly give relief to small business. A listing of the principal ones will serve as a reminder and indicate their extent. They may be conveniently grouped under three headings: formation of a company, operation of a company, and continued independent existence of a company.

Formation of a Company

1. Tax-free transfer of assets to a partnership or new corporation (pars. 2917, 1405, secs. 721, 351).
2. Ordinary loss on sale, exchange or worthlessness of stock held by original investors in small business (par. 1625, sec. 1244).
3. Ordinary loss on sale, exchange or worthlessness of stock in small business investment company (par. 3448, sec. 1242).
4. Ordinary loss on sale, exchange or worthlessness of convertible debentures purchased by small business investment companies (par. 3448, sec. 1243).
5. No tax on dividends received by small business investment company (par. 3448, sec. 243(a)).

Operation of a Company

1. Lower rate of corporate tax on first $25,000 of income (par. 3102, sec. 11).

2. No possibility of penalty tax on accumulation of earnings up to $100,000 (par. 3422, sec. 535).
3. Additional first-year depreciation of 20 per cent of cost of tangible personal property, available annually (par. 2010, sec. 179).
4. Allowance of investment credit in full up to first $25,000 of tax liability (par. 2019, sec. 46).
5. Option of small business corporations to be taxed as partnership (par. 3135–39, secs. 1371–77).

Continued Independent Existence of a Company

1. Tax-free redemption of stock to pay death taxes (par. 1710(b), sec. 303).
2. Extension of time to pay estate tax (sec. 6166(c)).

16

Tax Factors

in Foreign

Business Operations

Two fundamental concepts run through the taxation of income from foreign sources under U.S. tax legislation. This country, in the first place, taxes its citizens and its corporations on a global basis; that is, on their worldwide income as it is earned. The only exception to this general rule is a limited exemption for some income earned abroad by individual citizens who are residents of a foreign country or are physically present in foreign countries for seventeen out of eighteen months. This is a stricter rule than that applied in many other countries, some of which tax citizens resident abroad only on income from the home country or tax their own resident citizens only on income from domestic sources.

Second, the tax law of the United States recognizes the primary right of the foreign country in which income is earned to tax it. But our law permits the foreign income tax paid to the foreign country where the income is earned to be applied in full as a credit against our tax on the same income. This treatment, provided in the Internal Revenue Code without regard to reciprocity by other countries, is a more liberal treatment than that available in many other countries. The purpose and effect of the foreign tax credit is to prevent the combined rate of tax on foreign income from being greater than that in whichever of the countries concerned has the higher tax. If the foreign tax is exactly equivalent to the U.S. tax, the credit for the foreign tax wipes out the liability to the U.S. Treasury. If the foreign tax is lower, a residual U.S. tax will be collected. If the foreign tax is higher, there is, of course, no U.S. tax and no refund from either the United States or the foreign government.

The tax burden is greater than that on U.S. domestic income, but the result comes from the foreign law, not from any provision of the U.S. law.

Since the foreign tax credit is significant for both individuals and corporations, it is considered in general terms in the first section of this chapter. Subsequent sections cover successively the tax treatment of individuals and corporations. Attention is confined to U.S. citizens and resident aliens, who are treated similarly. The tax law with respect to nonresident aliens, that is foreigners living abroad receiving income from U.S. sources, is not covered.

Foreign Tax Credit

The foreign tax credit is available only for foreign income and excess-profits taxes, and taxes in lieu of income taxes (pars. 3701–03). The "in lieu of" clause has been interpreted quite strictly, though there have been many proposals for a broad application even to the point of allowing a credit for any foreign tax which is not required to be passed on to the buyer by the statute enacting it. A really broad interpretation would be an indirect way of wiping out any net revenue from foreign income.

The foreign tax credit is often referred to as preventing double taxation of international income, that is, of income which has its origin or source in one country and its destination or receipt in another. This is true in the sense described above; international income will not be penalized by being taxed more heavily than domestic income in whichever country has the higher rate. But it is not literally true that there is no double taxation. Both countries maintain their right to tax and in fact assert that right. If the country of destination has a higher tax than the country of source, the former will collect a residual tax equal to the difference in burden. Double tax jurisdiction continues to exist under a foreign tax credit, but a penalty burden is avoided.

A literal avoidance of double taxation has also been proposed. It is urged by some that only one country should have the right to tax international income; the other country should renounce its right. Some argue that the exclusive right to taxation should rest with the country of source; as might be expected, this approach is urged by some of the less developed countries which have found it wise or administratively necessary to keep their income tax rates at lower levels than those in the more developed countries from which they import capital. They resent the fact that taxes which they forego on income going abroad goes into the treasuries of the capital-exporting countries through the exercise of the residual right to tax. Also, they argue that the inducements of any special tax concessions which they grant to encourage investment are nullified by the operation of the tax law in the country from which any foreign investment comes; the benefit goes not to the potential investor but to his government. The counterargument of the capital-exporting countries to the proposal to renounce their right to tax foreign income is that this action would encourage capital export by giving a tax advantage to foreign investment whenever the foreign taxes were lower. It would thus violate tax neutrality between foreign and domestic investment in the capital-exporting countries.

The opposite approach is sometimes advocated for adoption among countries with roughly comparable taxes and reciprocal flows of income. Renunciation of taxation by the country of source on income going abroad, with the exclusive right to tax in the country of destination, would be simpler administratively than the present system, and, if income flows are substantially equivalent, would not lead to significant shifts in revenues between countries. This approach is the basis for the concept of fiscal domicile which is used in several countries of Western Europe and has been advocated for more extensive adoption by the O.E.C.D. Fiscal Committee.

Though the foreign tax credit is simple and neat conceptually, it often fails to produce its intended result of limiting the total tax burden to the level of whichever country has the higher rate. Difficulties arise from differing concepts of income, including differences in the timing of realization of income. Our foreign tax credit, quite naturally, is limited to foreign income taxes on foreign income as we define it. But other countries may have different concepts and definitions of the source of income. Virtually all countries, for instance, consider that the act of purchasing commodities for export does not give rise to income. But a few countries hold that the mere act of purchase may create income and impose their income tax on those foreign companies which are so foolish as to make purchases within their borders. Though the tax is imposed under an income tax statute, it is not on foreign source income, as we define it, and hence would not be creditable against the U.S. income tax. The result of the difference in income concepts may produce an aggregate tax burden higher than that in either country considered alone, in spite of the existence of the foreign tax credit.

Another extreme case occurs because a few countries assert that income arises in them for professional services, as for example architect's fees, from the mere fact that payment is made from the country, even though the person or firm rendering the service never entered the country. Since the general rule, followed in the United States, is that the income for services has its source where the services were performed, we would not recognize the foreign tax as applied to foreign source income and hence would not allow it as a credit.

Less extreme situations also produce difficulties. Where commodities are produced in one country and sold in another, some allocation of income is necessary. In the absence of international agreement on the method of allocation, it is unlikely that the methods in the two countries would be identical. If they were not, part of the foreign tax, even if the tax rate were lower, might not be creditable and the total tax burden would be greater than if the income were earned and taxed in one country alone. Thus, if the U.S. concept provided for a 50-50 allocation of income while the foreign country allocated 70 per cent there and only 30 per cent to the United States, a foreign tax at 35 per cent would be greater than the amount we would allow as a credit, and a foreign rate equal to ours would give a foreign tax much greater than the amount creditable here against our tax.

The problem of income allocation exists in allocations among our states within the United States. Even under our federal system of government, we have failed to secure uniformity, though model laws and reciprocal legislation have accomplished a great deal. But for companies operating in a good many states, it is improbable that the sum of allocated income would add up to the total income. The problem of securing uniformity is much greater between separate countries, though substantial progress has been made through tax treaties.

Differences in income may also occur because of such simple reasons as different allowable service lives for depreciation of plant and equipment. If a foreign country with the same tax rate as ours allows faster depreciation than we do on machinery in a foreign branch plant, the foreign taxable income and tax will be less than the taxable income and tax under U.S. standards in the early years of use. We will thus impose a residual tax in early years. Later, as depreciation runs out under the foreign schedule, the foreign taxable income and tax will be greater than the U.S. taxable income and tax, and there will be nothing against which to credit the excess foreign tax. Over the entire life of the depreciable property, the combined taxes will exceed those which would be applicable in either country alone. The difficulties are considerably greater when initial allowances or investment credits are adopted by either country.

In some respects the foregoing problem is one of timing. Liberal carry-forwards and carry-backs of foreign tax credits can give relief for otherwise uncreditable foreign taxes arising from differing concepts between countries as to the time when income is realized. Present provisions were adopted applicable to taxes paid after 1957 for that purpose (par. 3703(b)). Carry-overs, however, also permit an uncreditable foreign tax arising from a tax rate higher than ours in one year to be applied against the U.S. tax in another year when the foreign tax rate is lower than ours, even with identical concepts and allocations of income. It is questionable whether a foreign tax arising from a higher rate than ours should ever be credited against the U.S. tax. An effort was made in preparing legislation for carry-overs of foreign tax credits to limit them to differences arising from timing of the recognition of income and to exclude any unused foreign tax arising from higher statutory rates than ours, but it appeared that the result would be too complicated and the effort was abandoned.

A final issue in the application of the foreign tax credit is the decision as to whether it should be applied country by country or on a composite basis for all foreign income. Prior to 1954, a dual limitation was applied. The credit allowed for foreign taxes was the lesser of that allowed on a per country basis and on an overall basis. This was a strict rule. The effect of the overall limitation meant that if a company already operating abroad commenced operations in another foreign country with the expectation of losses for the first few years, a not infrequent situation, its losses would be applied against the income from other foreign countries, reducing the overall foreign income and with it the amount of foreign tax which could be credited. If the taxes in the countries where operations were profitable were substantially the same as the U.S. taxes on the same income before the loss activity was started, the fact of a loss on the new enterprise, by decreasing the foreign tax credit though not the foreign taxes paid, would actually increase total taxes paid. This perverse result of the overall credit, just the reverse of the usual result within a country where a loss in a new activity reduces taxable income and taxes, led to the repeal of the overall credit in 1954.

It was urged at that time, and subsequently, that each company should have an option to select either the overall or the per country limitation. The latter one, left in the law after 1954, can be restrictive if rates in some countries are higher than in the United States and lower in others, or if allocations of income have produced uncreditable taxes in some countries. Also, it was argued that since many companies consider all of their foreign operations as a single division, a single overall limitation should be available. The law was amended effective in 1961 to give taxpayers a one-time option to select the overall limitation in preference to the per country limitation (par. 3703(a)). If exercised, this option may be revised only with the consent of the Internal Revenue Service.

A final point should be made about the effect of the foreign tax credit on the attitudes of foreign governments concerning their own tax policies. Our tax credit in effect holds an umbrella over foreign tax rates on U.S. business up to the level of the U.S. rate. So long as an additional foreign tax is creditable against the United States tax, it does not impose an additional burden on the taxpayer; the revenue comes not from the U.S. taxpayer but from the U.S. Treasury, which is even more likely to be regarded as fair game abroad than it is at home.

This aspect of our tax credit has not gone unnoticed, nor is the recognition of the situation purely an academic one. Representatives of U.S. companies and industries abroad have requested that proposed new foreign governmental charges on them be imposed in the form of new creditable income taxes; they have even requested, unsuccessfully, that U.S. embassies support them in these requests. Members of foreign governments are fully aware of the opportunities for painless revenue from tax increases directed against U.S. companies so long as any margin remains between the tax in the foreign country and the U.S. rate.

Thus the foreign tax credit extends an invitation to foreign countries with substantial U.S. business interests to raise their tax rates to our level, perhaps even on a discriminatory basis which would apply only to the income of U.S. concerns. This is a wholly perverse influence and must be regarded as a major defect of the foreign tax credit. In 1966, an amendment to the Code, section 901(c), gave the President authority to deny credit for taxes paid to countries which did not allow reciprocal credits.

The foreign tax credit is necessary to prevent discriminatory tax burdens against international income so long as we assert our right, as the country of destination, to tax it. The dilemma could only be resolved by a waiver by us of our right to tax business income from foreign sources. Such action, as a matter of principle, is not appealing. But on pragmatic grounds, to avoid the perverse effects, the complications, and the imperfections of the present system, it is appealing.

The attraction of this policy of waiving our right to tax foreign business income is strengthened by the increasing reliance in other countries on turnover and value-added taxes as a principal source of revenue from business. With the foreign tax credit limited to foreign income taxes, the system fails increasingly to assure that international income will not be subject to higher total tax burdens than income earned in either country alone. High income taxes here and noncreditable turnover or value-added taxes abroad of a sort which we do not impose here can and do give higher total tax burdens on income earned abroad by U.S. business than on income earned abroad by citizens or corporations of the foreign countries or on income earned here by our own citizens. It is questionable whether we can afford to impose this tax penalty, which is an additional tax cost, on U.S. business operating in the increasingly competitive world markets.

Taxation of U.S. Citizens on Foreign Income

Consistent with the basic concept of taxation on global income, U.S. citizens regardless of where they live are taxed on their income from all sources, foreign and domestic, with minor exceptions for income earned abroad as described below. Investment income and capital gains from foreign sources are taxable as fully and as promptly as income from domestic investments and domestic capital gains. This rule in our tax law is as comprehensive as it is concise (par. 1300). Once stated, the fact should not need further explanation or elaboration.

The exclusion of earned income from sources outside the United States is limited both in dollar amount and on the basis of residence or physical presence (par. 3720). U.S. citizens who are bona fide residents of any foreign country for any uninterrupted period which includes an entire year may exclude from their income subject to U.S. tax earned income from foreign sources up to $20,000 per year. After one has been abroad for three consecutive years, the limit is raised to $25,000 a year. Prior to 1963, there was no limit on the amount of earned income which could be excluded by citizens resident abroad. The question of residence is determined by all the facts and circumstances in a particular case. The location of one's family and one's household possessions, explicit and implicit expectations on future employment, and other indications of intent are all relevant. It is easy to establish a bona fide foreign residence if one cuts ties thoroughly but perfunctory attempts are likely to be treated as shams.

An exclusion of $20,000 a year is permitted for income earned from foreign sources by a U.S. citizen who is physically present in a foreign country or countries for seventeen out of eighteen months. Prior to 1953 there was no limit to the amount of income which could be excluded under this rule. This test does not require the establishment of a residence abroad; those qualifying under it in fact usually move around or otherwise avoid establishment of a residence abroad to assure that if possible the earned income will not become subject to any foreign tax jurisdiction. The reference to presence in a foreign country or countries is interpreted strictly. Presence outside of the United States on a ship on the high seas is not presence in a foreign country, as at least one very promient individual discovered after his return from what he mistakenly believed to have been a precisely calculated qualifying sojourn abroad.

The tendency in this country is to restrict tax exemption of income earned abroad, as indicated by the amendments regarding both citizens resident abroad and citizens present in foreign countries. For citizens who are bona fide residents of foreign countries which impose comparable taxes, the assertion of the U.S. tax is frequently resented and is regarded as being more of a harassment than a revenue measure. But the opportunity to establish foreign residence, or to wander abroad for seventeen months while writing a book, making a movie or even continuing a syndicated column led to a good deal of resentment by U.S. citizens who stayed at home and paid full taxes. The unlimited seventeen months provision, originally adopted to facilitate employment abroad of personnel for technical assistance, became a principal reason for making moving pictures abroad. The individual advantages to well-known stars were publicized in the newspapers and tended to bring into disrepute the whole idea of exemption for income earned abroad. Further restrictions in the law appear much more likely than any reversal of policy in the direction of liberalization.

The exclusion of some earned income from foreign sources creates administrative problems in verifying both the nature and the geographic source of the income. The fact of exclusion of earned income gives a strong inducement to withdraw profits of closely controlled foreign corporations in the form of alleged salaries to their U.S. owner-managers resident abroad. Since the foreign corporations are not themselves subject to audit by the Internal Revenue Service, the possibility of abuse is greater than that in domestic corporations, where both the temptation and the chance for success are less. There is also a problem of verifying the geographic source of income of, for example, a professional man resident abroad who flies into a U.S. city for a day or two several times a year in connection with his professional activities. To provide some basis for audit, the law since 1958 has required the filing of a report, form 2555, to support the exclusion of foreign source income.

When foreign individual income tax rates are higher than those in the United States, as is often the case at levels of income earned by U.S. executives, job assignment abroad may drastically reduce net income.

This presents a very real problem in companies with foreign branches and subsidiaries. In some Asian countries where tax rates become very high at what are modest income levels by U.S. standards, it might be necessary to pay a branch manager more than the head of the company at home to prevent a foreign assignment for a subordinate employee from leading to a drastic reduction in net income.

A situation which makes it extremely expensive to maintain the few U.S. executives or specialists who may be needed in a foreign activity discourages investment of foreign capital and economic development. But relief must come from the foreign country. One possible approach is to provide by treaty for reciprocal exemption of foreigners of various categories from taxation on earned income for limited periods. These provisions can be useful for specialized technical people; unfortunately some countries refuse to include in such provisions executives who are necessary to run the establishment in which technical people may be employed, and the periods allowed are usually rather brief.

The United Kingdom taxes resident foreigners only on earned income remitted to them in the United Kingdom. This permits the receipt and taxation in the United Kingdom of only that part of the salary necessary for local living expenses; the rest may be paid into a bank account abroad, even in the home country, and accumulated there free of United Kingdom tax. Though hard to defend on principle, this policy seems wise on pragmatic grounds and has doubtless been of real significance in making London an appealing place for European regional offices. Countries which especially need foreign investment should consider adopting such a provision, if their individual income tax rates are prohibitively high. However, confiscatory income tax rates seem incompatible with economic development in any case and a general rate reform seems even more appropriate than selective relief for foreigners.

Tax treaties often provide reciprocal tax exemption for limited periods for students, professors, artists, and professional people generally, in addition to technical personnel as noted previously (par. 3725). These sections of treaties, referred to as a good-will item, are designed to remove the annoyance of becoming involved with the local tax jurisdiction during a brief stay as much as for any real tax saving. If the country of nationality taxes income on a global basis, as we do, and also grants a credit for foreign taxes paid, as we do, a tax paid abroad for income earned during a brief stay is likely to be fully creditable with no net burden from the foreign tax. But even if there is no real burden, the mere fact of having to compute and pay the tax and obtain a tax clearance before leaving the country can create a good deal of ill will. Treaty provisions of this sort are usually regarded favorably; exemption from the national income tax of the lecture fee of a noted foreign scientist, the salary of a visiting professor, the vacation earnings of a student or the concert fee of a musician is not resented, though sentiments may be different if the person involved is a prizefighter with tremendous earnings in a single night. The tendency is for countries to extend good-will exemptions of this sort reciprocally to citizens of the other country who are present for limited periods.

In the absence of sensible restraint in tax laws and tax administration, executives traveling abroad may be subjected to interminable tax annoyance and additional tax burdens. Does the presence of the president of a company for one day at the office of a foreign subsidiary, during the course of a brief foreign trip, mean that he has earned one day's salary while there, and if so should 1/365 of his annual salary be deemed to be earned in that country and taxed there, or should it be 1/313 on the assumption of a 6-day week, or 1/261 for a 5-day week? And if the foreign country does impose its tax on a day's income, would we recognize it as creditable against our tax? The United States has been one of the worst offenders in requiring income tax clearances for departing foreigners, even those here for very brief periods. Our law was liberalized in 1958 to permit more administrative discretion. The problem is an international one which is increasingly important as international movement of business and professional people becomes more frequent and rapid. The Western European countries have gone a long way in solving it by moving toward the adoption of individual taxation on the basis of fiscal domicile alone.

Taxation of Business Income from Foreign Sources

Until 1963, the basic principle by which the United States taxed foreign business income was simple. U.S. corporations, like U.S. citizens, were taxed on their global income, and there were no special exclusions for "earned" as distinct from all other income. U.S. corporations operating abroad directly were spoken of as having foreign branches; the branch income was included with that of the head office. Problems arose in the allocation of income between U.S. and foreign sources, but these were important only in determining the extent of foreign income tax due and the extent to which the foreign tax could be credited against the U.S. tax.

The law was equally simple with reference to subsidiaries incorporated abroad of U.S. parent companies. The foreign subsidiaries were not taxable here, unless they carried on business here or in some other way had income from U.S. sources. Taxable income arose only as the profits of the foreign subsidiaries were brought into the United States by the parent companies. At that point it was taxable, with a credit for the foreign tax paid on the dividends and on the income of the subsidiary from which the dividends were paid to the parent.[1]

The law was changed in 1962 to make U.S. parent corporations taxable currently on certain undistributed income of some of their foreign subsidiaries. The Administration had recommended in 1961 that U.S. parent companies should be taxed currently on all undistributed income of all foreign subsidiaries, but the Congress wisely rejected this extreme proposal and through a succession of changes confined the application of the new approach to what are generally, though by no means entirely, tax-haven situations. Foreign subsidiaries which operate primarily in the countries in which they are organized still are taxed as they were previously, under the principle that the domestic parent corporation is taxed only as income is distributed to it, a principle generally applied throughout the world. The conditions for current taxation of undistributed income are described later (par. 3723).

Another change in the law, also adopted in 1962, provides that a U.S. parent corporation must treat the gain on the sale or redemption of stock in a controlled foreign corporation as a dividend, rather than a capital gain, to the extent that the gain is attributable to earnings and profits of the foreign corporation accumulated in years after 1962, but only while the stock was held and the corporation was controlled (par. 3723(b)). This provision applies to U.S. corporations owning at least 10 per cent of the total voting stock in a foreign corporation in which at least 50 per cent of the voting stock is owned by U.S. shareholders. This is a more strict rule than the usual capital gains treatment, since dividends from foreign corporations are subject to the full rate of taxation without the benefit of the 85 or 100 per cent credits for dividends from most domestic corporations (par. 3108). The foreign tax credit may, however, be applied against the gains which are treated as dividends.

[1] The foreign income taxes which can be credited include both income taxes on the dividends distributed by the foreign subsidiaries (whether imposed on the subsidiary itself or on the recipient) and on the income of the foreign subsidiary from which the dividends are paid. A U.S. corporation need own only 10 per cent of the voting stock of a foreign corporation to be entitled to a credit for a pro rata part of the income taxes paid by the foreign corporation from which it receives dividends. Furthermore, a foreign corporation (a subsidiary based on the test of 10 per cent ownership) is itself deemed to have paid a pro rata part of the income taxes of any other foreign corporation in which it owns at least 50 per cent of the voting stock (par. 3705).

*Tax Consequences of Conducting Foreign Operations
through Branches or Foreign Subsidiaries*

The relative tax merits of operating abroad through branches or foreign subsidiaries may be noted, on the assumption that the activities are such that new tax-haven rules will not apply.

In many respects the factors to be considered in a decision regarding the relative advantages of operating abroad through branches or foreign subsidiaries are similar to those which are relevant to the decision to carry on a domestic business through a partnership or a corporation. When income is to be retained by the business entity, a foreign corporation is more attractive than a branch, if the foreign tax rate is lower than the domestic rate, always on the assumption that the income of the foreign subsidiary will not be imputed to the U.S. parent for taxation at the U.S. rates under the tax-haven rules. The plans for distribution are relevant in the same way as are plans for distribution in setting up a domestic business. If the domestic business entity is to retain income, a corporation is preferable to a partnership from the start, if the corporate rate is lower than the individual rate, though this conclusion is qualified by the later tax when profits are distributed. It is with reference to the later tax that the analogy between branch or foreign subsidiary and partnership or corporation is not complete.

There is a major difference in the tax treatment of the eventual distribution or realization of income from a foreign subsidiary and the income of a domestic corporation. The payment to stockholders from a domestic corporation is taxed as ordinary income if the business continues or as a capital gain if it is liquidated. By contrast, income from a foreign subsidiary is taxed as regular income but with a full credit against the U.S. tax for the foreign tax already paid on the accumulated income. Thus, though the U.S. tax rate is eventually applied on income from foreign subsidiaries, this tax is no greater than would have been due if the operation had been carried on by a branch. There is no second or penalty tax paid as the price for having the full U.S. rates postponed until distribution. This permits faster accumulation and expansion abroad with no later tax penalty.

Since 1963, the tax law has required dividends from foreign subsidiaries to be "grossed up," in calculating the taxable U.S. income and the foreign tax credit (par. 3705(b)(1)). A "gross-up" means that instead of reporting the net dividend received, a pre-tax income from which the dividend is paid must be included in the income of the parent company. Thus, if the foreign tax rate is 30 per cent, a dividend of 70 would represent pre-tax income of 100, which is the amount that must be included in the income of the parent. A U.S. tax of 48 per cent on the 100, with a credit for the foreign tax of 30, leaves a net U.S. tax of 18. Under this procedure, the combined foreign and U.S. tax always adds up to the U.S. rate.

Under the prior procedure, which is still allowed on dividends from subsidiaries in the underdeveloped countries, only the net dividend received was included in the tax base, and the foreign tax attributable to the dividend was allowed as a credit (par. 3705(b)(2)). Thus with a foreign tax of 30 per cent, a dividend of 70 would be paid from a pre-tax income of 100, with a U.S. tax of 33.6 ($70 \times .48$); against this the foreign tax credit would be 21 ($70 \times .30$). The net U.S. tax would thus be 12.6 ($33.6 - 21$), and the combined foreign and U.S. tax equal to 42.6 (30 foreign tax + 12.6 net U.S. tax). Under this rule, the combined tax would be equal to the U.S. rate only if the foreign tax rate were equal to the U.S. rate or if there were no foreign tax. At any positive rate of foreign tax less than the U.S. rate, the combined rate would be less than the U.S. rate, with a minimum combined rate of slightly over 42 per cent when the foreign rate was just half the U.S. rate or 24 per cent.[2]

If it is expected that foreign activities will involve a loss at the beginning, a branch operation will permit the loss to be applied directly and currently against all other income. If a foreign subsidiary is used, there is no way to apply the loss against the income of the parent company since consolidated returns with foreign subsidiaries are not permitted. Here again the analogy is a close one with the choice between partnership or corporation in a domestic activity; with early losses in prospect in a domestic activity, a partnership will permit the losses to be applied against other income of those who finance the venture.

Oil and mining companies typically choose to operate abroad through branches of U.S. corporations to get the benefit of percentage depletion. If operations are carried on by a foreign corporation, the profits, when repatriated, are treated as ordinary dividends with no allowance for percentage depletion. Immediate taxation of foreign income with a branch operation, after the percentage depletion deduction, is usually preferable to postponement of taxation at the U.S. rate since the U.S. rate finally applied will be the full rate without the benefit of percentage depletion.

[2] The Treasury recommended the general repeal of this method of computation, with its capricious result. The Congress made the change only with reference to dividends from subsidiaries in developed countries, apparently because it was considered undesirable to raise the effective tax rate on income from investments in the less developed countries at the very time when private investment in those was being encouraged as a matter of national policy.

A special provision is made for U.S. corporations carrying on their business in the Western Hemisphere but outside of the United States (par. 3110(b)). To qualify as Western Hemisphere Trade Corporations, all of the business except incidental purchases must be done in North, Central or South America or the West Indies and at least 95 per cent of gross income must be from sources outside the United States and at least 90 per cent of gross income must be from the active conduct of a trade or business. There has been a good deal of controversy over the meaning of "incidental" purchases as well as the national source of income from exports. The latter point has been fairly well settled by a literal application of the rule that income arises when title passes, an objective test which has led to a good deal of ingenuity in arranging transactions to throw income into the desired jurisdiction. A qualifying corporation receives a special deduction which in effect gives it an effective tax rate 14 percentage points lower than the regular U.S. corporate rate, or 34 per cent instead of 48 per cent. With the opportunity to secure this lower rate, U.S. corporations often prefer to carry on their foreign operations in this hemisphere through Western Hemisphere Trade Corporations which must, of course, be incorporated in the United States. Income from a foreign subsidiary, even though perhaps taxed at a lower rate as earned, would be subject to the full U.S. tax rate when repatriated. Western Hemisphere Trade Corporations are used both for regular operations abroad and also as sales subsidiaries for U.S. manufacturers to handle their exports to this hemisphere.

Tax factors are frequently minor in an actual decision on the form of organization to use in foreign operations. There may not even be a choice, as occurs if the foreign country requires local operations to be carried on by a company incorporated under its jurisdiction. Or if the policy of the parent company is to have joint ventures with local capital, a foreign subsidiary may be preferable. There may be other less conclusive reasons for selecting a particular form. Frequently, a parent company will prefer local subsidiaries to minimize the risk that the parent company and its world-wide operation will become entangled in the jurisdictions of the separate countries. Taxation may play a part here, if for example the allocation rules for income in the various jurisdictions were such as to make more of the total income taxable locally than would be recognized under our standard, with the likelihood of a foreign tax larger than the amount creditable. But there are other reasons to prefer to have only the assets of a local subsidiary become subject to a foreign national jurisdiction which may be controlling, including liability for social security benefits or taxes or severance pay.

Pricing and Cost Allocations Between Related Companies

Whenever there is a difference in effective tax rates, as between a domestic parent and a foreign subsidiary, or between a parent and a Western Hemisphere Trade Corporation, there is a temptation to throw income into the entity subject to the lower tax rate. The Internal Revenue Service has to be on guard against artificial pricing on transactions between related companies. Abuses have been considerable; some companies, for example, have attempted to sell manufactured products to their export subsidiaries at no more than direct factory cost even though sales to customers abroad were at prices comparable to domestic prices. Income may also be shifted by the imposition of service charges, fees or commissions by the company in the jurisdiction with the lower tax rates which, if allowed as deductions to the U.S. company taxable at our full rate, will have the effect of shifting income.

The Treasury makes use of the general provision of the law which authorizes it to make such allocations of income between related companies as are necessary to reflect clearly the income of both companies (par. 3124). Though this power is a necessary one to prevent real abuse, it can be applied too strictly without recognition of the business reasons, apart from taxation, which are significant in transactions between related companies. A practice of pricing at arm's length and other conditions of sale similar to those applied to independent third parties is the only sure defense against the application of section 482. But frequently there are no transactions with third parties at the particular stage of production or distribution at which transactions take place with subsidiaries. In such cases, prices and other terms should be established which can be defended as reasonable.

Though there is a need for some control of allocation of income by the Treasury to prevent abuse, there is a danger that a perfectionist approach may be unrealistic and cause harassment of taxpayers with little gain in revenue. Indeed, the administrative burdens may become so onerous that foreign activities will be curtailed, with adverse affects on both tax revenue and the balance of payments. Regulations issued in April 1968, by applying a rather strict benefit test in allocating costs of services, appeared to many to reach for an unreasonable degree of refinement. One pair of examples dealt with the deductibility of the cost of the analysis by a parent company's financial staff of the subsidiary. If the subsidiary does not have personnel qualified to make such an analysis, the cost to the parent is allocable to the subsidiary; if there is a qualified staff in the subsidiary, the cost to the parent is not allocable. How is the competence of the foreign staff to be determined?

Other examples deal with the cost of research and the cost of domestic advertising by an airline which mentions foreign hotels operated by a related company. In the latter case, some part of the advertising expense is allocable to the foreign hotels, which means, of course, that it is not deductible by the domestic company. This degree of refinement opens a vast field for controversy between taxpayers and revenue agents in the United States. Furthermore, since other countries do not make such elaborate distinctions, it is also highly probable that many costs disallowed as deductions here would not be accepted as deductible expenses by foreign tax officials in determining the taxable income of U.S. subsidiaries abroad. Double taxation may drastically reduce the net income from foreign operations or even turn a before-tax profit into a net loss.

Detailed rules on transfer prices for products bought and sold between domestic parent and foreign subsidiary corporations were also included in the April 1968 regulations. In the opinions of many, these also adopted an approach which would require a greater allocation of income to the U.S. corporation at the expense of its foreign subsidiary than would be acceptable to foreign governments under existing standards. Though some recognition is given to competitive conditions and the business realities involved in pricing, recurring references to full cost and normal mark-ups and margins suggest that pricing based on incremental costs is inherently suspect. The management of a small or medium-sized company reading the regulations might well be discouraged from embarking on international business by the extent of doubt and uncertainty which they would expect to find in subsequent tax audits. The problems of income allocation under section 482 promise to become increasingly difficult for companies carrying on international business.

Further problems in transactions between related companies may arise under section 367 which excludes foreign corporations from the general authorization under section 351 and 361 for tax-free transfers of property in exchange for stock or securities in a controlled corporation. Section 367 provides that where the transfer of property is to a controlled foreign corporation, any gain will be taxable currently unless a ruling is obtained from the Treasury prior to the transfer that the exchange is not in pursuance of a plan having as one of its principal purposes the avoidance of Federal income tax. The regulations under this section give no examples. There has been a tendency to apply the provision strictly; where in fact there are substantial tax savings, those savings are likely to be regarded as a presumed principal purpose, with a refusal to give a favorable ruling, even if there are other business reasons for the exchange of property for stock. The problem arises in connection with the establishment of a foreign subsidiary to take over a business previously conducted directly by a foreign branch.

Section 367 also applies, subject to the same requirement for a prior ruling, in connection with the liquidation of a foreign subsidiary. Section 332 permits tax-free liquidation of subsidiaries in which the parent owns at least 80 per cent of the stock, with use of substitute basis of property to prevent any step-up of basis. The fact that section 367 makes section 332 inapplicable to foreign subsidiaries, in the absence of the ruling that the liquidation does not have as one of its principal purposes the avoidance of income tax, means that a rearrangement of foreign subsidiaries may not be possible without incurring a current U.S. tax. If, for example, it is desired to transfer assets from one foreign subsidiary to another with a consequent saving in taxes, and a liquidation is involved, it may not be possible to get a ruling under section 367. In practice, favorable rulings can usually be secured if the parent company will include in its income an amount which will give a U.S. tax comparable to the taxes avoided or saved by the prior use of the foreign subsidiary.

Capital Structures of Foreign Subsidiaries: Effects of U.S. and Foreign Tax Laws

It may be desirable to set up a foreign subsidiary with a small amount of equity capital and a large amount of debt. There are both tax and nontax advantages in such capital structures. To the extent that funds can be borrowed locally, or in other foreign countries without a guarantee by the parent company, the dollar investment at risk may be minimized. Even if a guarantee is necessary, the amount of dollars needed to start the venture can be minimized. Foreign borrowing by foreign subsidiaries was greatly stimulated by the successive U.S. programs for improvement by corporations of their contributions to the U.S. balance of payments which was started in 1965.

From a tax standpoint, earnings used directly to repay debts will not have to be distributed to and taxed to the parent company. Even if the debt is held by the parent company itself, a repayment of that debt by the subsidiary will be treated as such, rather than as taxable dividend, unless the capital structure is so extreme that the debt status of securities is denied under the broad rule applicable to "thin corporations." Generally, it appears that the application of the concept to "thin corporations" is less strictly applied to foreign subsidaries than to domestic corporations with individual stockholders.

But the foreign tax law or other laws may contain provisions which make a thin capital structure undesirable for a foreign subsidiary. Some foreign corporate income tax rates vary with the rate of return on invested capital, making the tax an excess-profits tax on an invested capital base. Or the privilege of withdrawing profits under currency controls may be related to invested capital. There may even be differential taxes on the dividends paid, related to capital. Finally the tax treatment of dividends and interest paid may be different in the foreign country, either by statute or under treaty provisions.

All of the foregoing considerations and others must be reviewed before a decision is made on the capital structure of a foreign subsidiary. The correct decision is at least as important as that regarding a domestic corporation, and the factors to be taken into account are more numerous, because they involve two or more jurisdictions.

Tax Havens: Foreign Base Companies

Until 1963, it was possible to use foreign subsidiary holding companies or foreign sales companies to receive and accumulate income in countries with low income tax rates or with no income tax at all (par. 3723). A foreign holding company could be established between the U.S. parent corporation and the foreign operating subsidiaries. Dividends from the operating companies in other countries would be paid to the holding company which, of course, would be set up in a country which had no income tax, as in Bermuda, Panama, and Lichtenstein, or at least a low rate of tax on foreign income, as in Switzerland. Any residual U.S. tax on distribution of profits from the operating company, if its tax was at a lower rate than the U.S. rate, could thus be further postponed so long as income was retained by the holding company. Accumulated income of the holding company could be invested in other foreign subsidiaries without imposition of the U.S. tax which would have been due if the income had passed through the parent corporation.

The holding company was especially effective if it could withdraw income from the operating companies in a form that would be deductible by them in computing their own taxable income, as in interest, fees or service charges. In fact it was not even necessary to have the intermediate company own stock in the operating subsidiaries; a foreign service or management company in a low-tax jurisdiction could be used to collect income from operating subsidiaries in other foreign countries, hopefully through charges that would be deductible to the operating companies.

A sales subsidiary could be used to buy products from a manufacturing company, either the parent company in the United States or a manufacturing subsidiary in another foreign country, and sell them in still another foreign country or countries, perhaps to and through another subsidiary of the parent company there. To the extent that the intercompany prices could be set to throw the profits into the tax-haven sales intermediary, they would be drained away from the countries of production and sales and taxed at a low rate. Accumulated profits could then be used for new investment abroad or for any other use of the aggregate business as long as they were not distributed to the U.S. parent corporation.

Though many foreign holding companies and regional sales or service corporations had business purposes quite apart from tax savings, the dominant reason for the formation of most of them was probably the tax advantages which they offered. To correct the abuses which were felt to exist, and to create tax neutrality between income from foreign and domestic sources, the Administration in 1961 recommended that all U.S. parent companies be taxed currently on all undistributed income of all foreign subsidiaries. The adverse balance of payments was given as another reason for a change in the law; an increase in taxes on foreign income, through the current application of any U.S. residual tax to the undistributed income of foreign subsidiaries, would reduce the net outflow of capital in direct foreign investment.

The protests against the extreme proposal of the Administration were as vehement as they were numerous. A full volume of testimony, almost entirely adverse, was published by the House Ways and Means Committtee, and the testimony on this subject filled several small volumes in the Hearings of the Senate Finance Committee. Perhaps the most fundamental objection was to the claim that neutrality in U.S. taxation of domestic and foreign investment was an acceptable policy.

It was argued, against the Treasury position, that neutrality between U.S. business operating abroad and its local competitors was needed if U.S. business was to be able to hold its own. It was further noted that U.S. business seldom goes abroad simply to seek lower tax rates and to produce abroad what would otherwise be produced here for export. Rather, as foreign markets, management, technology, and capital do develop, production abroad is going to take place anyway. Only by participating in foreign production can U.S. business and the U.S. balance of payments share in the rapid economic expansion abroad. In view of the heavy reliance on other forms of business taxation, noted previously, the full imposition of the U.S. income tax on top of the full foreign taxes would place U.S. business at a competitive tax disadvantage abroad.

Emphasis was also placed on the long-run importance of income from our foreign investments in our balance of payments, with statements that it was not possible to turn direct corporate investment on and off. A failure to make additional outlays as needed could mean that a new opportunity was irretrievably lost to a foreign competitor or that the value of an existing plant, and the subsequent income from it, would wither away.

As finally enacted in 1962, taxation of U.S. parent corporations for the undistributed income of the controlled foreign corporations was limited to "foreign base company income" (par. 3723(a)). This income was, in turn, defined as consisting of personal holding company income, sales income, and services income. The attempt was to tax only on the basis of passive income of a tax-haven company, that is, one which received income from related companies in still other foreign countries.

Foreign base holding company income includes dividends, interest, royalties, rents, and gains, as in domestic personal holding companies, but excludes these categories of income arising in the conduct of an active business, for example, interest received by a bank, or rents from ships or aircraft. It also excludes income received from sources within the country in which the base company is organized.

Foreign base company sales income is confined to purchases from a related company (or sales on its behalf) or sales to a related company (or purchases on its behalf) when the base company conducts its actual operations in countries other than the one in which it is organized. The inclusion of sales income was surprising to many, since section 482 permits allocation of income if a U.S. producer or purchaser is involved, and in other cases the U.S. balance of payments and the U.S. tax revenues would appear to benefit in the long run from the use of tax-haven sales companies. If, for example, sales from a manufacturing subsidiary in one European country are made through a tax-haven sales subsidiary in a second European country to customers in a third European country, the problem would appear to be one of allocation of income between the three European countries. If the use of the intermediary gives a net tax saving, there is that much more net income for additional U.S. investment abroad and profit for eventual repatriation, and that much less foreign tax to be applied as a credit against the U.S. tax. If other countries do not prevent their large international companies from using foreign sales subsidiaries to secure tax advantages at the expense of other countries, it would appear that unilateral action by us, in the absence of some general agreement on the subject, would place U.S. companies at a tax disadvantage in world competition. If sales intermediaries are not used because of our legislation, the additional immediate revenue will go to the countries of production and the countries of sales, not to the United States.

Three general relief provisions are given. If the base company income is less than 30 per cent of total gross income, it may be ignored. The tax on undistributed income does not apply if a foreign corporation has at least 80 per cent of its assets and gets at least 80 per cent of its income from less-developed countries. (But if base company income is more than 70 per cent of gross income, all income is deemed to be base company income.) This permits an operating foreign subsidiary to have some base company income without running into the complexities and penalties of the law. Also, if there is not a substantial reduction in taxes through the use of the base company, the provision is inapplicable. In general if the income and similar taxes actually paid are 90 per cent of those which would have been paid in the absence of the base company, it will be assumed that there is no substantial tax saving. The final escape clause comes from a provision that if income of the foreign base company is distributed to the U.S. parent corporation, on a sliding percentage scale related to the tax rate in the country where the base company is incorporated, there will be no penalty tax. The last provision is also intended to give exemption when there is no substantial tax saving.

Index